Praise for *Designing with Data*

"A clear, approachable and common sense guide to mastering data-driven design—a skill set that is becoming mandatory for the 21st century designer. This book is an invaluable contribution to our profession."

—KHOI VINH, PRINCIPAL DESIGNER, ADOBE, AND DESIGN WRITER, SUBTRACTION.COM

"King, Churchill, and Tan have produced a magnificently accessible introduction to designing modern software products with data. The authors sail through concepts in statistics that aren't weighed down in math, and instead are grounded in real-life examples from top companies like Netflix and Airbnb. Building on a deceivingly simple model of designer/user behavior, this book will make a designer able to wield key concepts that are now being integrated in the tech industry from the social sciences and modern data science."

—JOHN MAEDA, GLOBAL HEAD, COMPUTATIONAL DESIGN AND INCLUSION, AUTOMATTIC

"A/B testing is becoming an essential component of digital product development, and it's vital for designers to embrace it as a tool of their trade. This book provides the perfect introduction to it and gives practical advice for how to apply, execute, and analyze A/B testing successfully."

—MARTIN CHARLIER, PRODUCT MANAGER, UNMADE, AND COAUTHOR OF *DESIGNING CONNECTED PRODUCTS*

"As an elegant, informed blend of concrete case studies and rigorous knowledge about data analysis, this book not only will help design practitioners familiarize themselves with A/B testing, but will also provide an approach to integrating data and analytical methods into the overall design and development process."

—NALINI P. KOTAMRAJU, HEAD OF USER RESEARCH & ANALYTICS, SALESFORCE

数据驱动设计（影印版）

Designing with Data

Rochelle King, Elizabeth F. Churchill,
Caitlin Tan 著

Beijing • Boston • Farnham • Sebastopol • Tokyo O'REILLY®

O'Reilly Media, Inc.授权东南大学出版社出版

南京 东南大学出版社

图书在版编目(CIP)数据

数据驱动设计:英文/(美)罗谢尔·金(Rochelle King),(美)伊丽莎白·F·丘吉尔(Elizabeth F. Churchill),(美)凯特琳·谭(Caitlin Tan)著. —影印本. —南京:东南大学出版社,2017.10

书名原文:Designing with Data

ISBN 978-7-5641-7355-5

Ⅰ.①数… Ⅱ.①罗… ②伊… ③凯… Ⅲ.①数据管理—英文 Ⅳ.①F279.23

中国版本图书馆 CIP 数据核字(2017)192546 号

图字:10-2014-154 号

数据驱动设计(影印版)

出版发行:东南大学出版社
地　　址:南京四牌楼 2 号　　邮编:210096
出 版 人:江建中
网　　址:http://www.seupress.com
电子邮件:press@seupress.com
印　　刷:常州市武进第三印刷有限公司
开　　本:787 毫米×980 毫米　16 开本
印　　张:23.25
字　　数:402 千字
版　　次:2017 年 10 月第 1 版
印　　次:2017 年 10 月第 1 次印刷
书　　号:ISBN 978-7-5641-7355-5
定　　价:92.00 元

本社图书若有印装质量问题,请直接与营销部联系。电话(传真):025-83791830

[*contents*]

[*Foreword*]

This book offers a simple but exciting promise for anyone involved with the design of internet products:

If you compare what you think should happen (in theory) to what actually happens (in reality), you can better understand how your work changes user behavior.

This book is your training camp to getting started using data—design's often overlooked but essential companion—to improve your work. You can augment this approach with your existing design practices to amplify the impact of each design: from identifying the problem you are solving, to designing for experimentation, to learning from the data.

What's unique about this training camp are the field guides at hand: not only your authors sharing experiences from the world's leading data-driven organizations, but also the contributions from many practitioners offering you the advantage of their standard practices, case studies, and hard-fought lessons from designing with data every single day.

COLIN MCFARLAND,
HEAD OF EXPERIMENTATION AT SKYSCANNER

[*Preface*]

Design and Data: A Perfect Synergy

THE MYTH OF THE "genius designer," someone whose instincts and intuition lead to great design decisions, is a popular one. This seductive myth can lead some to conclude that design is never grounded in data, that design is never an empirical discipline, and that design practice stands in opposition to data and data sciences.

We understand where this myth comes from. On the surface, data science and design practice are not obviously compatible. Design philosophy and practice emphasizes empathy with users, and the creation and crafting of artful user experiences in the form of effective products. For some designers (and for many outside the design world who valorize design as "inspired genius"), design is a nonlinear, exploratory journey. It is a fundamentally human, fluid, and creative process, unlike the procedures and rigors of "science." Design is emotional. Design cannot be articulated as a set of procedures or steps to be followed. Design cannot be rationalized and constrained. For some, incorporating data into the design process is a cause for concern.

Some concerns we have heard expressed include:

- Data undermines and undervalues the designer's intuition and experience
- Data stifles creativity and removes the "art" from the design process
- Data dehumanizes the design process, reducing human experience and design evaluation to "just numbers"

- Data overemphasizes minutiae and optimization of small variations in the design
- Data enslaves you—believing in data as way to evaluate designs takes the power away from design as a practice

On the other side, proponents of design through experimentation and data science value measurement. Some see data as rational, and numbers as irrefutable. Data science reveals the truth—data science is a proceduralized, scientific endeavor where rigor leads to irrefutable results and therefore to certainty. Data science is a trustworthy and precise craft. This view is reinforced by the increasing fascination with measures and metrics for business, commonly referred to today as "big data." An extreme view is that large-scale experiments can be run to gather data from millions of users to answer all design questions and that such analytics can, therefore, replace design. Under this view, font types, colors, and sizes, and questions such as "Should we have a blue or a red dialogue box?", "Do people engage more with a list or a carousel?", or "Does a wizard help with new user onboarding flow?" fall under the purview of data science and not design practice. This could be characterized as "Let the crowd speak with their clicks, and what emerges will necessarily be the best design."

We deliberately present these extreme positions to illustrate a point. We believe that the extreme views we just outlined draw a false dichotomy between data and design. In reality, data sciences and design practices are working toward the same goal: understanding users and crafting elegant experiences for them. Design is and always has been informed by data. The "data" may be an accumulated set of experiences and informally gathered observations that provide the basis for design genius and "craft knowledge." The data may also be derived from more systematic studies of users' activities and opinions, such as lab-based studies, field observations, and surveys. Design practice has always been about different forms of data. In an ever-changing marketplace and industry where new applications and new behaviors are constantly emerging, data can play a big role in helping us learn and respond in a timely way to shifts in user interests and needs. By harnessing and leveraging the power of data *at scale*—that is, data in high volume, often arriving in streams from millions of users, and which may be of disparate types—new ways to understand people, "users," are emerging. Data at all scales from individuals to millions and hundreds of millions of users—systematically collected, analyzed, communicated, and leveraged—can empower design.

We want to acknowledge that designers' concerns about large-scale data collection have some grain of truth. Personally, we have all experienced some circumstances and work situations where these criticisms held—for example, where data gathered at scale contradicts what we know or believe to be true about the human experience. Personally, we believe that these potential misalignments in belief and data reflections arise precisely because designers have historically not been included in the experimental process, data collection, and analysis that informs design. We believe that design intent and evaluation are often poorly matched to the data capture and analysis because designers with a desire to understand user experience have not been in effective dialogue with data scientists and machine-learning experts. This is a two-way conversation: design can bring deeper meaning to data. By developing an awareness of and an affinity for data, such conversations will benefit both disciplines. Similarly, design practice can be enhanced by data. When managed well, data science in the form of large-scale experiments can demonstrate the worth of creativity in design rather than stifle it.

In sum, we believe designers have to engage in the practice and business of designing experiments and managing the data collection process, by being part of the conversation about what data should be collected, when, and most importantly why.

Our Focus: A/B Testing

In writing this book, our intended audience is people who know nothing about large-scale experimentation. We will focus on A/B testing, the most common form of large-scale experimentation and data collection in the internet industry. A/B testing is a methodology to compare two or more versions of an experience to see which one performs the best relative to some objective measure. Essentially, A/B testing is the scientific method applied online, at scale. A primary advantage of A/B testing is that you can test "in the wild"—that is, in the often-messy context of the real world—by launching different experiences to a subset of your actual users. Through an A/B test, you can causally attribute changes in user behavior to design changes that you make. This is the best way to get a true understanding of how each of your experiences will impact your users if launched.

There are many steps and considerations in crafting an A/B test, and we will spend the majority of this book providing practical thoughts on how to be involved. At a high level, though, engaging with quantitative testing of this kind can help you create:

- A direct feedback loop with your users, elevating the way you understand and think about user behavior, ultimately helping you to hone your instinct about your users over time
- A stronger bond between user needs and how your business measures success, helping to align a cross-functional team
- A rigorous approach that can help to eliminate hierarchy, rank, and politics from the process of decision making, allowing you to focus on your users' needs

Using carefully captured and analyzed data will give you a framework for discussions about user behaviors and needs, product effectiveness (including potential innovations), and business goals.

Some Orienting Principles

In writing this book, we have three orienting principles.

One, that design always advocates for users and is accountable to users. Good design brings with it a responsibility toward reflecting and addressing user needs through well-designed products and experiences.

Two, that design practice therefore needs to be invested in representing users accurately and appropriately. This requires a curiosity, engagement, and drive for understanding and developing new methods to create that understanding of users and user behaviors. Data is an integral part of that process.

Three, that a design perspective is needed to ensure that optimal user experiences are appropriately represented in business goals, measures, and metrics.

From these three orienting principles, we believe that designers are, or should be, fundamentally interested in being disciplined about data and its collection, analysis, and use.

We hope that the audience for this book is familiar with the concepts of iteration and continuous learning and that our readers want to bring that perspective to the design of data gathering and analysis, and to the practice of design itself.

Who Is This Book For?

This book is written for designers and product managers who are involved in launching digital products but who have little to no experience with leveraging data in their approach to product development. You might be part of a small startup with just a few people working on building your product, or you might be part of a team in a larger company and looking to apply data methodology in your group. You should have a basic understanding of design thinking, and likely have been working with partners in product and technology to build your products. You might work as an in-house designer or you may be working in an agency with clients. But fundamentally, you have an interest in understanding how blending data and design can help you solve problems for your product.

Based on our experience, the biggest adjustment for a designer or organization looking to leverage data is that they first need to get a solid understanding of data types and how they work together. Very rarely does doing so require a significant change to the fundamentals of how they design; however, it does require an open mind.

We note that our definition of design as a discipline is broad, and encompasses different roles in the industry. It is therefore worth reviewing who we think will gain most from this book:

If you formally trained in design...

We are writing for people whose formal or informal training is in design, but who are unfamiliar with large-scale online experiments with large groups of users. Perhaps you started your career with a strong art or creative background, as opposed to one based in engineering, or you have only worked at companies that haven't had access to rich data.

If you are a user experience researcher...

We are also writing this book for user researchers who are focused on people's everyday experience. Perhaps you started your career with a social science or anthropology background or are trained in qualitative user research, but you haven't had the opportunity to think about how quantitative data at scale can give you a new tool to study human behavior. If you are empathetic and a humanist, with a desire to truly understand how people feel, but want to expand your methods and get a sense of what the fuss is all about with experimentation at scale—for good or bad—you will get something out of reading this book.

If you are a data scientist...
If you are familiar with analyzing logs, but have never done experimentation at scale, then this book can also be useful to you because it will present you with a different perspective on the user experiences about which you are collecting data. We hope this book will encourage you to get more proactively involved at the start of the conversation on user experience, and actively seek out collaborations with designers who you might not have otherwise thought to work with.

If you are a product manager, developer, or something else...
If you are interested in the blending of design and data, then this book could help you gain insight into how designers are beginning to approach their job by incorporating data. We know that great products are only built when you have product, technology, and design working together hand in hand, so we're of course excited to have as many people from other disciplines engage with this book as well.

Scope

Our aim in this book is to help you understand the basics of designing with data, to help you recognize the value of incorporating data into your workflow, and to help you avoid some common pitfalls. There are many types of data that you might use as a designer. As we said, this book focuses specifically on large-scale experiments and A/B testing. We're doing this specifically because we have found this to be where analytics and design have converged the least, but where we believe there is the most potential for fruitful gains and collaborations.

We aim to offer some perspectives on how to develop solid data practices in your organization. Throughout the book, we'll share our experiences and the experiences of others, suggest ways that your team can change the way you work, and get the most benefit from your data.

We want you to be able to argue your case with confidence about what should be measured, when and how to best illustrate, test, and further your design intention. Ultimately, we would love to make you feel excited and eager to embark on an approach within your company or organization that better leverages data.

About Us

We believe that designers, data scientists, developers, and business leaders need to work together to determine what data to collect, as well as when, why, and how to manage, curate, summarize, and communicate with and through data. We started to write this book because we wanted to encourage designers to influence and change the conversation around measures and metrics that purport to reflect the value of a product or service. We believe data and design need to be seen as two sides of the same coin.

Rochelle and Elizabeth have managed and driven user-centered design and evaluation processes in the internet industry. Caitlin is just beginning her career in this field, and we found that having a fresh perspective in the book was extremely helpful in making our point of view accessible to our readers.

All three of us care deeply about understanding the ways in which people interface with, interact with, and derive value from technology. We feel strongly that carefully gathered and analyzed data can and does help develop that understanding but that we need to broaden the conversation. We hope that by sharing our enthusiasm for integrating different forms of programmatically gathered data into the design process, we can persuade others who have a human-centered approach to design to be more centrally part of the data design process. We believe this will lead to better products and better business.

Although we focus on A/B testing in this book, we understand there are many ways to gather data. For example, surveys, interviews, field studies, diary studies, and lab studies are all excellent ways of collecting meaningful data about the users of a wide variety of products. In our daily work, we leverage data from all of these methodologies and others, from gathering feedback by talking with users in a usability session about how effective, usable, or delightful your product seems to them (or not!), to tracking data instrumented to measure exactly what actions users are doing in a product. We believe that if companies consider only one form of "data" (e.g., "click" or "clickstream" data—literally a record of what a user does at a screen), they will not get a full picture of a user's experience. Therefore, we believe that the definition of data needs to be broad and constantly reviewed, as new methodologies emerge with unique capacities to help us capture a holistic view of our users.

We are excited to write this book because we are passionate about empowering designers to be able to formulate, inform, and evaluate their approach to product design with data.

A WORD FROM ROCHELLE

I remember the first time I started to incorporate data in my design work. It was 2001, I was at a small startup, and someone had mentioned how Amazon was applying A/B testing as a technique to make decisions about user experience. Our startup was always great about reviewing the business metrics on a weekly basis and we were keen to get our hands on as much data as possible. However, with the introduction of A/B testing, we really got our heads around using data in an even more effective and sophisticated way than we had previously. During the next few years, our startup took a very DIY and self-taught approach to determining the ins and outs of being more data driven. We studied and learned as much as we could about what other data-driven companies like Netflix and Amazon were doing and tried to apply those learnings in practice.

Over the years, I've gotten more exposure to companies that excelled in gathering data and information from their users—my company was acquired by Intuit, which had a well-established and widely respected approach toward user research. Later, I joined Netflix, which is one of the most disciplined technology companies at using data to make decisions. Witnessing world-class environments that embrace the use of data has made me appreciate how incredible a tool it can be in helping to transform the way an entire product organization works. I've learned that there are many nuances to combining data and design, and that while there are many benefits, there are also many pitfalls as well. My goal is to help more designers appreciate and take advantage of the benefits while avoiding some of the pitfalls that I, and others, have fallen prey to in the past.

I'm writing this book because I hope that I can share my enthusiasm and passion for working in a data-centric environment with other designers and product managers and that this book can help you elevate the way in which you work with data.

A WORD FROM ELIZABETH

For me, a psychology undergraduate degree seeded my passion for design—the design of carefully crafted studies that help us understand people, their traits and motivations, as well as their experiences and behaviors.

Beyond focusing on individuals, though, this degree also seeded a passion for understanding the ways in which people interact with environments and social settings, and how those environments and social settings mold and shape their behaviors.

And thus began my career-long fascination with the human-centered design of situations and settings, including online situations and settings. I have worked in the area of human–computer interaction (HCI) in the decades since that undergraduate degree, working in academia and in a number of technology companies. HCI as a field of enquiry addresses how to build interactive systems and services that work for people. As a discipline, it draws on various academic areas, including applied psychology, computer science, anthropology, and ergonomics.

My desire to write this book stems from the belief that human-centered design practice and the "data sciences" work best when conducted together. As someone concerned with users and their experiences, I believe these two disciplines should be in a more productive dialogue than has been the case to date.

While data science has become a well-regarded tool for companies, the human-focused art of designing effective studies, posing the right questions (hypotheses), designing the right measures, and conducting exploratory analyses has not been equally emphasized. I have seen many designers whose intuitions are excellent and whose sensitivity to human psychology are evident in the products they create, but who, when it comes time for rollout, shy away from engaging with the design of studies that test what they have created. Over the years, talking to designers and working with them, it has become apparent that some designers would like to be part of the conversation around experimentation and data science, but they don't feel empowered. If that sounds like you, this book is for you—this book is intended to help you push the conversation and deepen the connection between design, experimentation, and data analysis. This book is intended to help you participate in the creation of a design-focused data science, to help you demonstrate, with evidence, what good design is, and how good design can have a positive impact on people and on the world.

A WORD FROM CAITLIN

Like most college students nearing graduation, I struggled with the prospects of how to combine my seemingly disparate interests into a professional career. My undergraduate degree from MIT taught me the value of applying an experimental, quantitative approach to problem solving. It instilled in me a deep confidence in how numerical measurement can uncover surprising and generalizable truths about the world. However, I couldn't shake the feeling that pursuing a strictly "scientific" or "technological" postgrad job would neglect my humanistic desire to understand the complexity of people, which in many ways felt irreducible to measurements.

Now, just under a year since beginning my role as a user researcher, I've come to realize that I drew a false dichotomy between the sciences and the arts. The discipline of design—and more broadly, the fields and industries that design is now applied to—provide a space for the arts and the sciences to come together for one unified goal: understanding people. What has been most exciting for me about this synergy is how data can be applied to create deep empathy for not only the humans behind our products, but also our cross-disciplinary collaborators. We need a humanistic view of products in order to ask the right questions, while leaning on the tools of scientific endeavor help answer those questions. Through the shared language of data, folks from a variety of backgrounds can have effective conversations about their users, to challenge our beliefs and assumptions in service of seeking truth. When applied in this way, data both retains and provides nuance to the complexity of human behavior, and gives us the words and tools to speak about that complexity. And, of equal importance, the practice of designing with data opens the channels for communication and collaboration across disciplines that have been previously siloed, but whose sum is greater than the individual parts.

I hope that this book helps infuse that empathy—for our users and coworkers whose backgrounds may lean toward the art or the science side of design—throughout the practice of building better experiences. And equally, I hope that it demonstrates to young people like myself that pursuing interdisciplinary fields like the intersection of design and data can bring together their interests and skillsets in unique and exciting ways. Doing so will inspire the creativity necessary to apply technology and product development to the human problems and needs of the 21st century.

How This Book Is Organized

We've structured the book into eight chapters and give a brief summary of each one here:

Chapter 1: Introducing a Data Mindset

In this chapter, we hope to motivate you to understand our perspective on how we see working with data—that it is both an exciting time to be working at the intersection of data and design, but also that working with data is truly a creative process. We talk about the kind of data that you have access to as a designer and how different roles in a company interact with data, in addition to covering some of our basic terminology.

Chapter 2: The ABCs of Using Data

In this chapter, we'll give you the necessary foundation around data. We talk in more depth about data types and how you collect them. We introduce the experimental methodology that is necessary to make sure you are using your data to its fullest and define the basic components of A/B testing that you will need for the rest of the book.

Chapter 3: A Framework for Experimentation

Here we'll take the concepts and put them into action. We're going to tell you how we've crafted a framework for experimentation, which you can apply. This is our own take on how to do this, but many folks are doing something similar.

Chapter 4: The Definition Phase (How to Frame Your Experiments)

Starting in Chapter 4, we'll get even more concrete about how to apply the framework we've outlined in Chapter 3 by starting with the importance of grounded question asking. We discuss what a hypothesis is and show how you build just one, and then scale to considering many divergent hypotheses. We also show you how to generate multiple statements and then whittle them down to the ones you should focus on.

Chapter 5: The Execution Phase (How to Put Your Experiments Into Action)
In this chapter, we focus on how to create the experiences that you will ultimately be testing. We again talk about how important it is to go broad and show that the design you craft will ultimately have an impact on the data you collect.

Chapter 6: The Analysis Phase (Getting Answers From Your Experiments)
Here we'll take you through some of the considerations when you launch your A/B test. We'll also discuss how to interpret your results, and make decisions about what to do next after running an A/B test.

Chapter 7: Creating the Right Environment for Data-Aware Design
In this chapter, we focus on building and driving a culture focused on learning at your company, and making data a core part of that learning. We also talk about some of the softer side of culture, including the kinds of people that work well in that environment, making data more accessible to everyone at your company, and the longer-term benefits of using data in the design process.

Chapter 8: Conclusion
In this short chapter, we offer a brief summary of the concepts we introduced in this book, and highlight the need for an ethical stance toward data collection and toward experimentation.

How to Read This Book

If you don't know much about designing with data, we'd suggest that you start by reading the first six chapters in order. If you are familiar with working with data, then we suggest you read Chapter 3 to orient yourself to our framework and then hop around to the chapters that you are most interested in.

No matter how experienced you are with incorporating data into your design process, real-world examples from our friends in the industry are a great way to learn more about how the theories are being applied in reality. We've interviewed some of these folks in the field to hear their thoughts on designing with data. We will share a few of their vignettes to provide texture and complement our own perspective. Of course, such vignettes may not be directly applicable to your particular case—you may have a different user base, product, or constraints. But hopefully they will illustrate how to take the more abstract concepts we introduce throughout this book into practice.

In addition to these real-world examples, we also introduce an illustrative example in some of the early chapters of this book to help explain some of the different concepts we cover. Our illustrative example focuses on running a summer camp. These places in the book will be noted with a small camping icon.

At the end of every chapter, we also include a set of questions to provoke you to think more deeply about what you have read; these come under the section header "Questions to Ask Yourself." These questions are included as a way to spark some conversation either with yourself or within your company, and to help you take the concepts introduced in the chapter and apply them to your own work.

We hope this book will give you what you need to start out on this journey and to build a shared understanding with your peers of your product, based on objective feedback direct from your users.

INTRODUCING OUR "RUNNING A CAMP" METAPHOR

You may notice throughout this book that we like metaphors. Starting in Chapter 2 and continuing throughout the book, we'll be using an illustrative metaphor to help explain some of the concepts and situations that we are describing. We've often found that having a strong metaphor that is abstracted a bit can help to crystallize some of the concepts we are covering in a way that real-world examples from companies can't. It's sometimes easier to see how an illustrative example can apply to your own world rather than trying to take something from another company and then do the translation from an example that might feel very specific to their situation and needs.

So periodically, we are going to ask you to pretend that you are the owner of a summer camp. Every year, you welcome back ~200 kids to your summer camp, where they get to go hiking, play outdoors, and enjoy eating meals together. Because your camp is so large and diverse, feedback you hear from just a few campers may not accurately capture the overall experience of your campers. You've been running this camp for a number of years, and have some dedicated families that return every year, but as you are running a business, you also want to make sure you are continuing to attract new families as well. Because you run your camp on a recurring basis, we thought it made a nice tie-in to why you might care about experimenting with new ways to improve your summer camp experience and therefore your business.

In Chapters 2 through 5 you'll see us refer you back to this summer camp metaphor as we ask you to think about:

- How to define and measure your goals
- How to think about your users (both existing users and new ones)
- How to design experiences you can test and learn from as you try to improve your business

As a quick illustration, you can see how this metaphor might apply to running experiments. If you're trying to improve your camp experience, you'll want to get an understanding of what's working and what's not. You'll want to try some new things out on a smaller scale before you commit to investing in big changes across the camp and as you try to expand your business you'll also want to make sure that any changes you consider will have the results and impact that you're looking for. We'll show you how you can use this metaphor to understand statistical terms like *cohorts* and *segmentation* (Chapter 2), and how it can be used to illustrate considerations when you are defining your goals (Chapter 4), designing your experiences (Chapter 5), and then analyzing your results (Chapter 6). Yes, it might seem a bit goofy, but if you bear with us, we think it will help!

And now let's get going... *Designing with Data*!

O'Reilly Safari

Safari (formerly Safari Books Online) is a membership-based training and reference platform for enterprise, government, educators, and individuals.

Members have access to thousands of books, training videos, Learning Paths, interactive tutorials, and curated playlists from over 250 publishers, including O'Reilly Media, Harvard Business Review, Prentice Hall Professional, Addison-Wesley Professional, Microsoft Press, Sams, Que, Peachpit Press, Adobe, Focal Press, Cisco Press, John Wiley & Sons, Syngress, Morgan Kaufmann, IBM Redbooks, Packt, Adobe Press, FT Press, Apress, Manning, New Riders, McGraw-Hill, Jones & Bartlett, and Course Technology, among others.

For more information, please visit *http://oreilly.com/safari*.

How to Contact Us

Please address comments and questions concerning this book to the publisher:

O'Reilly Media, Inc.
1005 Gravenstein Highway North
Sebastopol, CA 95472
800-998-9938 (in the United States or Canada)
707-829-0515 (international or local)
707-829-0104 (fax)

We have a web page for this book, where we list errata, examples, and any additional information. You can access this page at *http://bit.ly/designing-with-data*.

To comment or ask technical questions about this book, send email to *bookquestions@oreilly.com*.

For more information about our books, courses, conferences, and news, see our website at *http://www.oreilly.com*.

Find us on Facebook: *http://facebook.com/oreilly*

Follow us on Twitter: *http://twitter.com/oreillymedia*

Watch us on YouTube: *http://www.youtube.com/oreillymedia*

Acknowledgments

Writing this book has been a long project that has progressed in fits and starts, and we wouldn't have made it across the finish line without the help and support of so many people to whom we owe so much. We have been blessed with incredible colleagues from whom we've learned throughout our careers and we've been fortunate enough to work at companies that have set the gold standard for doing the type of work that we do. Thank you to our friends and peers for your generosity and insights.

We'd also like to thank the good people at O'Reilly. Mary Treseler initiated this project with Rochelle and never gave up on seeing the book come to life. Angela Rufino patiently stuck with us as our editor, prodding us along the way and providing encouragement and support when we needed it most. This thanks extends to the rest of the O'Reilly team as well: Colleen Lobner, Jasmine Kwityn, and José Marzan, Jr.

We are grateful to the many people who were generous with the time they gave to us in interviews; their reflections and perspectives have been invaluable and the conversations they shared with us have given a three-dimensionality to this book. Thanks go to Arianna McClain, John Ciancutti, Katie Dill, Eric Colson, Dan McKinley, Patty McCord, Jon Wiley, Josh Brewer, Chris Maliwat, David Ayman Shamma, David Draper, Amy Bruckman, Casey Fiesler, and Jeff Hancock. We would also like to thank the folks behind the case studies that served as anchors to Chapters 4 through 6 in our book: Marcus Persson, Julian Kirby, Natasa Soltic, Chris Smith, Alvin Lee, Dantley Davis, Steven Dreyer, Neil Hunt, Matt Marenghi, and Todd Yellin. A special thanks to Ben Dressler and Annina Koskinen for providing a sounding board as we worked through various concepts and themes in this book. We are indebted to our peer reviewers and others whose comments helped us immeasurably in terms of shaping the book: Tim Lynch, Kevin Ho, Khoi Vihn, Martin Charlier, and Sean Power.

We owe special thanks to Colin McFarland, who went above and beyond in terms of his generosity, support, and guidance. His insight was invaluable throughout the process. He read rough drafts, allowed us to try out different concepts and metaphors with him, sat through long Google hangouts to share his comments with us, and poked holes in our manuscript when our language got sloppy.

ROCHELLE

I am grateful to my husband Warren and our two sons, Genta and Tatsuya. They patiently allowed me to spend countless weekend hours at my computer instead of hanging out with them, and I now plan to pay those hours back in full. The constant reminders from my sons that "we don't have quitters in this family" was also helpful on the many, many occasions when I would suffer from writer's block. I'd also like to thank my mom, who worked tirelessly to make so much possible for me and whose support and belief in me has never faltered. Finally, a huge hug to Elizabeth and Caitlin, without whom I am certain this project would not have been completed.

ELIZABETH

First and foremost, I would like to thank my coauthors for sticking with this project. It's been quite a journey. I look forward to conversations and laughter in the future, when no conversation involves discussion of a possible chapter edit. I'd also like to thank my friends and family, whose company I have missed while focusing on this book over the course of many weekends. Finally, I want to thank my colleagues, who have patiently indulged me time and again in random conversations about the art, science, and practice of experimentation in these internet days. Thank you all.

CAITLIN

I'd like to thank my boyfriend Harvey for the endless support and endless cups of home-brewed coffee during many long weekends of writing and editing. I owe you many weekend adventures now that we've wrapped up to make up for all that time! I'm also grateful to my family—Mom, Dad, Darrien, and Auntie Amelia—for being my biggest cheerleaders and advocates, and for always believing I could do more than I thought possible. Thanks to all of my lovely friends, especially Cecile, Michelle, and Zoë, who lent me their best listening ears and accommodated my crazy schedule throughout this whole process. And finally, a huge thanks to Rochelle and Elizabeth. I went into this process proud to be your coauthor, but I'm even more grateful to finish up alongside two exceptional mentors and friends.

ROCHELLE KING
NEW YORK, NY, USA

ELIZABETH F. CHURCHILL
SAN FRANCISCO, CA, USA

CAITLIN TAN
BROOKLYN, NY, USA

[1]

Introducing a Data Mindset

Data as a Trend

DATA. THIS SHORT WORD has captured the imagination of the media. Every day, another news story breaks that preaches the power of "big data," discussing the value of data for business, data for adaptive technology experiences, or data and marketing. It's clear that regardless of the application, data is a very hot topic and the currency of the day.

It might feel like using data is big news now, but the truth is that we've been using data for a long time in the internet business. Data in the form of digital content and activity traces is at the core of internet experiences. For the past 20 years, we've been inventing new digital experiences and re-creating physical world experiences in the digital world. Sharing photos, having conversations, finding love: activities that we perform in our daily lives have all become digital. Being digital means we can log and track these activities with ease. Digital interfaces have made data collection so easy that now our biggest challenge is not access to data, it's avoiding the false belief that data is always good, and recognizing that interpreting the data and deriving meaning from it is itself a challenging task. In other words, the ease of gathering data can lead us to be lazy in our thinking, resulting in erroneous conclusions if the data quality is low or unrepresentative or the data analysis is flawed.

There's more potential here than collecting any and all data, of course. The "digital revolution" and the internet as a platform mean we can also run experiments to collect data that allows us to compare one experience to another. We have the potential to run many experiments, sometimes concurrently with many users at once—a practice that has been called "experimentation at scale."

And that leads us to why the three of us wanted to write this book. We had two key reasons. First, so that more people with a user-centric orientation enter into the conversation about data collection, data quality, and data interpretation. And second, so that those who wish to can apply the information we share here and more effectively leverage data in their design work. We hope that you are able to use the information in this book to your benefit and that this will in turn further the practice of bringing data and design closer together.

Beneath the complex and ever-evolving world of experimental design and statistical analysis, there are some basic principles that are surprisingly powerful and very important to understand. Our aim is to give you a framework for thinking critically and carefully about the design of experiments, and to help you avoid the trap of just being excited about data for data's sake. We want you to be excited about collecting and analyzing the right data, in the right way, with the right framework so you can maximize your understanding of what is important in your context.

When working with data and experimentation, you can't take a "one size fits all" approach to your work. Depending on the nature of the problem you are trying to solve or the stage of problem solving that you happen to be in, you might employ different methods or techniques and take into account different kinds of constraints in the scope of your solution. We think it's important to always be aware of this greater landscape in which you might work and understand how the particular method or approach you are using might have different pros and cons. We like to talk about this as being aware of "where you are" and "what is possible" in the landscape of different design activities you could be engaging in (Figure 1-1).

In this book, we focus on A/B testing because we believe that as a methodology, it has seen the least collaboration between design and data, but that this collaboration between design and data has the most potential for impact in A/B testing. However, A/B testing is just one tool in your data toolkit. It can extend the value of other methods you might already be engaging with, and it's a foundational and versatile method that can be applied successfully to many different design stages and for many different kinds of design problems.

FIGURE 1-1.
Charting the landscape of design activities.

As we stated in the Preface, we expect data scientists, designers, user researchers, and others to be involved in the conversation around trying to understand user behavior. We believe that applying data in the design process is definitively *not* about replacing the things that design processes and designers do well already. It's about helping designers extend the value of those things by offering another way to look at the impact of the design work on users. A/B testing can't answer all questions, but it can answer certain kinds of questions that other methodologies and practices cannot. In fact, we think you'll find that working with A/B testing is actually quite similar to other evaluative design processes. When applied correctly, it is creative, iterative, and empowering. This book will help you get started applying A/B testing in this way.

Three Ways to Think About Data

Before proceeding, we'd like to spell out some differences we have perceived in how data and design have been positioned in the industry. The three terms we want to introduce are *data driven, data informed,* and *data aware.*

The terms *data driven* and *data informed* might already be familiar, but we have coined one additional term—*data aware.* One of the best descriptions that we've ever seen on the difference between *data driven* and *data informed* comes by way of Andrew Chen, a popular blogger who writes about online marketing. In a well-referenced post entitled

"Know the Difference Between Data-Informed and Data-Driven,"[1] he explains that "the difference [...] in my mind, is that you weigh the data as one piece of a messy problem you're solving with thousands of constantly changing variables. While data is concrete, it is often systematically biased. It's also not the right tool, because not everything is an optimization problem. And delegating your decision making to only what you can measure right now often de-prioritizes more important macro aspects of the problem."

Taking this perspective on, here are our guiding definitions of these terms.

Data-driven design implies that the data that is collected determines (in other words, drives) design decisions. In some instances, this is the right way forward. At times, the types of questions a team is asking can be definitively answered by collecting data from experiments. The outcome of their data collection maps directly to a clear best design decision.

You can be data driven if you've done the work of knowing exactly what your problem is, what your goal is, and you have a very precise and unambiguous question that you want to understand. This also assumes that your methodology and measurements are sound, and that the type of question you want to answer is one that data can determine. It relies on a keen understanding of the types of pitfalls that data can bring, and taking steps to remediate those pitfalls (Figure 1-2).

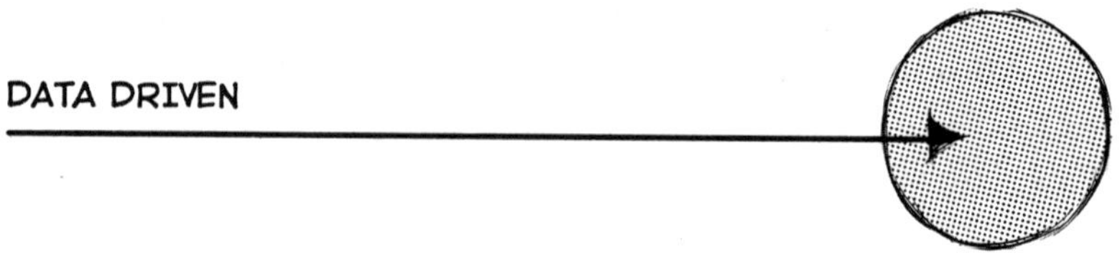

FIGURE 1-2.
Laying out the relationship between "data driven," "data informed," and "data aware"—data-driven answers well-targeted questions, where data alone can help drive decision making.

1 *http://andrewchen.co/2012/05/29/know-the-difference-between-data-informed-and-versus-data-driven/*

In some instances, however, your design decisions may be more nuanced and the data might suggest an answer that is not cut-and-dried. This is what we call *data-informed* design, where a team takes data as only one input into their decision-making process. In this type of design, the output may not be a clear choice but may perhaps result in setting up another iteration or investigation. This is when more research may need to be done, different kinds of data gathered, and/or an informed creative leap taken.

So adopting a data-informed perspective means that you may not be as targeted and directed in what you are trying to understand. Instead, what you're trying to do is inform the way you think about the problem and the problem space. You might answer some questions along the way, but you are informed by data because you're still iterating on what the problem space is within the goals that you have. This is a slightly more creative, expansive, and critically iterative space. You can't be data driven without thinking about your problem space in a data-informed way at some point (Figure 1-3).

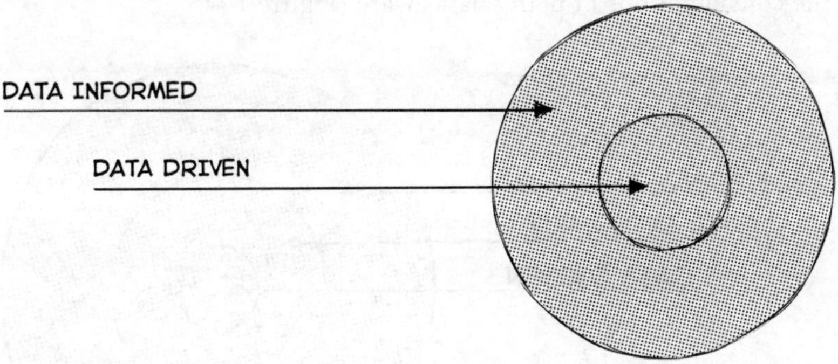

FIGURE 1-3.
Laying out the relationship between "data driven," "data informed," and "data aware"—being data informed allows you to understand how your data-driven decisions fit into a larger design space of what can be addressed.

Finally, we introduce and use the term *data-aware* design to underscore the fact that the design process is a creative one, where design decisions need to be taken not just from data but *back to* data collection practices—that how a system is instrumented, that what data types are being captured and how they are combined, is itself a design problem. In our view, designers and data scientists need to work with developers and business strategists to actively design systems so that the right data types are collected to address the right questions. We believe that designers have an important and unique viewpoint on the design of experimental hypotheses for collecting data to test design assumptions.

In a data-aware mindset, you are aware of the fact that there are many types of data to answer many questions. If you are aware that there are many kinds of problem solving to answer your bigger goals, then you are also aware of all the different kinds of data that may be available to you. You're constantly questioning how you might best approach your goal. This is a more strategic way of thinking about how data can inform what you need. Again, you can't get to the data-informed stage if you haven't properly worked through the considerations of being data aware (Figure 1-4).

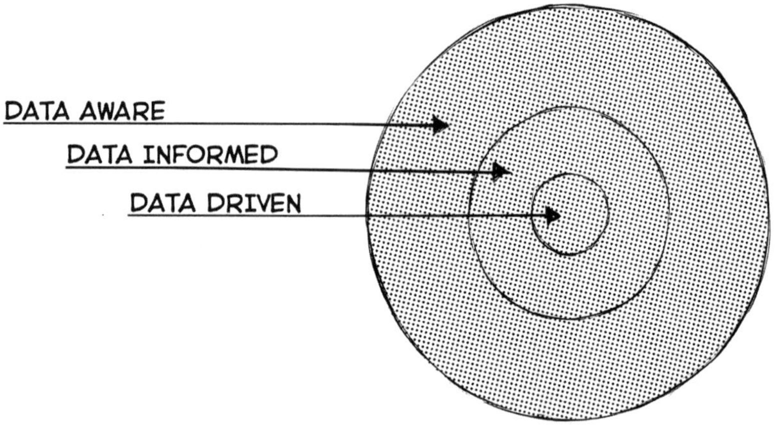

FIGURE 1-4.
Laying out the relationship between "data driven," "data informed," and "data aware"—being data aware means recognizing that there are many related questions and also many related kinds of data that you can draw on to answer and influence a variety of questions.

We think of embarking on a data-driven process like being on a platform about to board a train (Figure 1-5). The train is on the right tracks already (it's reliable, and where it's going is fixed, determined, and repeatable). You have confidence that you're on the right train and that you'll be going in the right direction. There isn't much more problem solving involved. You've already done all the due diligence and work (defining your problem, goals, etc.) to know exactly where you want to go and now your data can answer specific tactical questions. Data is a source of truth. (This is an application of data.)

FIGURE 1-5.

A train on tracks is a good metaphor for data-driven processes: you know the approach you are taking, your approach is reliable, and what you are going to find out is understood, directed, predetermined, and repeatable.

When you're data informed, you're in the railroad station but there are many trains on many tracks that could go many places (Figure 1-6). You're trying to decide which train to get on by thinking about where you want to go. Being data informed is about informing how you think about the problem. This is a creative and highly iterative process by which you learn about your problem space. (This is a discipline and a practice around data.)

FIGURE 1-6.
A train station is a good metaphor for being data informed: you know there are various trains, and they are likely going to different places. You are aware there are options and there are mechanisms for finding out which is the right train for you. There is less certainty and more exploration possible, with many possible destinations at the end.

Finally, when you're data aware, you are thinking more broadly. You understand the landscape of transportation, and are aware of the many opportunities in the transportation space (Figure 1-7). There are many options, many different timeframes, and many different ways of getting somewhere. In fact, there are even many places you could choose to go. You're thinking about many kinds of problems with all kinds of data available to you. You're engaging with many types of data and many methods. (This is a philosophy about data.)

Fundamentally, the difference between data-aware and instinct-driven design comes down to what you rely on to inform your design decisions. With data-aware design, data is a creative production process and is the primary decision-making tool *when and only when* the data itself has been well designed and has been proven to be what we call *fit for purpose*. With instinct- or experience-driven design, decision making is more experimental.

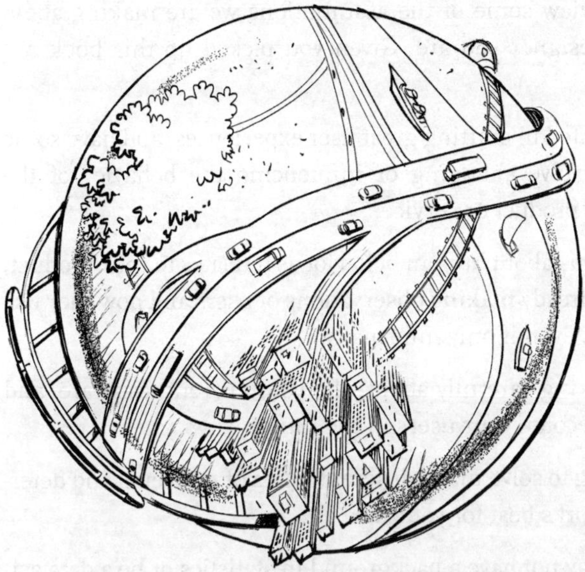

FIGURE 1-7. Mapping, transportation, and navigation are a good way to think about being data aware: trains are just one method of getting around the landscape, and there is a whole world available to explore.

Both paths can lead to great design. Is one way right? Absolutely not. Are these methods mutually exclusive? No. For us, the "right" approach to design will vary depending on the nature of the problem you are trying to solve and how you operate best; it will almost always require a balance between leveraging experience, instinct, and data. You need to have great instinct and experience to be a great designer regardless. Relying on data to help augment your existing skills adds one more great tool to your toolkit.

What Does This Mean for You as a Designer?

User-centered design and data applied to understanding behavior are both focused on establishing effective, rewarding, and replicable user experiences for the intended and current user base of a business or product. We believe that data capture, management, and analysis is the best way to bridge between design, user experience, and business relevance. Based on our previous descriptions, this is why we believe a *data-aware* approach to designing great user experiences is a better description of what we aspire to rather than the more commonly used *data-driven* terminology, as we believe data feeds into a creative design process, and is itself varied and creative, providing many possible ways to approach a problem.

But first, let's review some of the assumptions we are making about which kind of designer you are. Given you picked up this book, we assume that:

- You're interested in crafting great user experiences, and have some goals that involve changing or influencing the behavior of the users of your product or service.
- You are curious about human behavior as it relates to your product, and you are already making observations of users and how they use your product, even if only informally.
- You are thinking carefully about who your current users are, and who might become your users in the future.
- You are trying to solve many different kinds of problems and determine what works best for your users.
- While you may not have a background in statistics or be a data scientist, you are interested in becoming familiar with how you could get involved with the design of experiments to test out your ideas.

We believe that experimental methods and the data they yield can help hone your craft, improve your products, and concretely measure your impact on users and ultimately on the business. In sum, we believe that becoming familiar with the ways in which experiments carried out on the internet with large numbers of users where you can gather large amounts of disparate data types–that is, *experiments at scale*—can help you in your design practice. We believe that great design and smart data practices are key to strategic impact in any business.

Data Can Help to Align Design with Business

In our view, being data aware is also a good foundation for cross-functional collaboration within your business, whether large, medium, or small. It's an excellent way to have impact upon and create alignment between design and business goals, focusing on the critical part of any business: providing the best possible service to your customers and clients, understanding their goals and concerns, and addressing their frustrations. Being user focused and data aware means you and the people you work with should also be *actively* contributing to the creation of meaningful business goals that are focused on the greatest asset of any business: your users.

What this means is that designing the user experience should also involve sketching out what data you will need that will help you understand your designs. *Design the data capture, analysis, and questions as part of your design process.* Be clear about the data that will best help you measure and articulate the effect of your design on your users, and therefore your business. Being smart about data in your decision making has considerable advantages. First, having common success metrics within your company can help designers and the broader product team to align around common goals, understand your target users, and understand the desired behaviors for business growth and maintenance. Data helps you, your team, and your organization make decisions that are based on evidence. Data can help you counteract questionable or poor decisions that may be reflections of the assumptions and beliefs of those in positions of power in the room. In addition, data can help you build empathy with your users; it can give your users a voice at the decision-making table with you as their advocate.

Second, data helps articulate the potential impact of design in service of meeting those goals. Data provides another means for you to defend your design decisions and root them in the needs of your users and your business. It also provides a concrete measure of the value that design brings to your business. Whether or not you believe that you should have to defend the value of your discipline, we find that showing how design has impacted the bottom line can help communicate to and educate stakeholders on why design is so important.

Finally, we believe that leveraging data will also help you become a better designer, as you will get to test your assumptions and hone your instincts with evidence. Your existing design process is likely already based on data—things you've observed about people and the world. As you continue to incorporate data (and more sophisticated forms of data), you'll sharpen your understanding of how people behave, and therefore how to design the best experiences for them.

Notably, the actual data that reflect the users' journey is sometimes not accessible to us. However, it is intuitively obvious that, as you get to know your users better by looking at what they do and how they react to your designed journey for them, you'll become more adept at understanding the different kinds of experiences that engage them and that don't. Data that you capture around your designs will help you reflect on whether your design achieved the goals you set out for it. As a simple example, let's say you are designing a new sign-up flow. You can use data to measure if the design changes you made resulted in more people signing up or if you see them dropping out of sign-up flow at different points; this can also help you understand where your design might be confusing. Using data, you'll get better at understanding which kinds of things will be more or less impactful on them and will therefore show or not show in the resulting metrics. We'll talk more about this in later chapters. After all, one of the core reasons to take a data-aware approach to design is to be able to engage in an ongoing conversation with your customers through the data so that you can create better experiences for them.

ON DATA QUALITY

We want to encourage you to inform your design decisions by specific, objective evidence: data. Using data in your decision making entails that you reflect on the quality of the data, on what data is right for the decision-making setting—that you critically engage with the following:

- Question relevance (Are we asking the right questions?)
- Data appropriateness (Does it answer our questions?)
- Data quality (Is the data reliable? Did we lose something in data collection/curation? Did we bias the data?)

It also requires that we ask:

- Would different data and/or a different analysis be more appropriate? Are we doing what is convenient rather than what is right?

Jon Wiley, Director of Immersive Design at Google, has been working with data as a designer for over 10 years on some of the most popular and most used experiences in the world. At Google, he leads the user experience for all things virtual reality (VR) and augmented reality (AR). We spoke to Jon when he was leading the Search UX team about his experiences with A/B testing at a company known for its world-class use of data in the design and decision-making process.

Here's his take on the topic:

> Design is not art. Design does not exist for design's sake. Design is about problem solving. There is a little bit of backlash sometimes among designers toward metrics and data. Maybe they feel like it's taking some of their creativity away or they don't want to be a slave to the numbers, that sort of thing.
>
> I think designers have a responsibility to know whether or not they've actually solved a problem. Now, there are multiple ways of doing that. You can go out and just talk to users. You can observe them. If you can inject a bit of rigor into it, significant measurements, then you can decide ahead of time what success looks like for a problem and evaluate [the design] against those measures. One of the things that's wonderful about working at Google is that we actually have so many really smart computer scientists and statisticians and an amazing ability to measure.
>
> Let's say I had a design with a blue button and everybody said it was great. Then I had another design that was a green button, and everybody said the same thing. If I go and run an experiment comparing the two, I can say, "Well, you know what. I can tell you, with statistical significance, this blue button is actually better and people will complete this task faster with the blue button."
>
> If you have that level of data, of course, you'll use it. On the other hand, you don't want to be ruled by the numbers. One of the things we discovered is that increasing the number of things that you measure or improving the fidelity of your measurements often actually doesn't result in certainty. It doesn't actually result in something that is crisp as this one is better than that. It just reveals a deeper complexity that there are actually more things involved. Then it really becomes a balance. We still have to have an intuition. We still have to make a judgment about what's important and what isn't.
>
> It's still down to the human behind the actual product. Metrics, data, and A/B testing are tools. They're very important tools. I feel lucky to be able to say, "I know this is solving a user's problem." But these tools are not the sole mechanisms by which we make a judgment.

John Ciancutti from the startup 60dB also has some great thoughts about the relationship between data and design that we also wanted to share here. John has a wealth of knowledge about data-driven product development. He's built his career at some of the industry's leaders in leveraging data, including Netflix, Facebook, and Coursera. Now he's applying his well-honed expertise to his startup, 60dB, which brings personalized audio news and stories directly to a user's phone. John shared some thoughts from his time as Chief Product Officer at Coursera about the challenges of getting started with using data as a designer. He believes that the data and design disciplines have been traditionally siloed in how they're taught and practiced. He shares how education and developing an intuition for data is a key step in getting started designing with data:

> At Coursera, we hired a very promising designer out of school. She had this foreign relationship, an otherness with respect to data and data analysis. It's just not a part of the work that she did in school, or as she was building her portfolio. The tension is natural because it's like, "I don't understand, it's foreign, I'm not good at it." Or, "it's influencing my process, which I don't want. I like the process I have."
>
> There are fundamentals to using data, like understanding the basics of statistics. I don't think it's intuitive that you could go ask a hundred other people about a question and begin to infer about thousands more. That's not intuitive, because you think, "I'm not those people. They don't know me, and I don't know them." Unless you really understand how statistics works and have done the math and seen cases where it's worked, you're not going to trust these random people as a source of truth.
>
> Until data and the rudiments of analysis and data are part of the training of people who are trying to do design, it's hard. As a designer, you are probably more capable than you recognize to raise some great points around data and so forth, but you just don't know how to think about it yet because it's not familiar.

We hope that this book will help you develop a familiarity with some of these key data concepts, and how they can be applied in a design setting.

With a Little Help from Your Friends...

As you start to incorporate the usage of data in your day-to-day work, you'll find that in addition to navigating the data itself, you'll also need to navigate the various important roles around data collection and get to know the people who work with data in different ways in your organization. In some cases, one person may carry out and represent each of the roles we describe—one user researcher, one data scientist, and so on. Or perhaps an entire team is dedicated to one particular role—many companies now have large teams of data scientists whose sole job is to carry out experimental tests and conduct data analysis. Or, in other instances, you will find one person playing multiple roles conducting usability tests, managing large data sets and conducting analyses, and so on. Many startup companies have one person who fulfills multiple roles simply because of their small size. However, while these roles may be fulfilled differently, there are two key functions. One is capturing, managing, summarizing, and analyzing the data to make it interpretable; the second is analyzing and using the data in multiple ways to reveal insights and generate business relevant information. We call those who are involved in managing and capturing data "producers," and those who rely on data to inform their thinking "consumers." A single individual might play both roles.

As you might have guessed, we believe that the practice of integrating design and data should be highly collaborative. You should actively work to leverage the knowledge and skills of people from the other disciplines and backgrounds that we outline here. Having a diverse range of opinions and inputs is always essential to any creative process. And taking a data-aware approach to design doesn't mean that the full burden of gathering and analyzing the data needs to be on your shoulders alone; rather, you (and anyone else you work with) will each bring your own discipline-specific skillsets that can together create stronger and more thoughtful questions, and better approaches to answering those questions.

We've recently noticed that many companies are beginning to build closer organizational relationships between their design team and many of the folks working on and thinking about data—whether that means using open floor plans to allow for more spontaneous collaboration, or shifting around org charts. However, even if your organization hasn't yet started making these kinds of changes, we encourage you to build your own relationships. Your "data friends," as we'll call them, can be invaluable resources for both designers who have never worked with data before and designers who have become experts at using data. We'll devote much of Chapter 7 to discussing these organizational and cultural topics.

DATA PRODUCERS

The people we often find associated with the generative side of data are data analysts, data scientists, user researchers, designers, and marketers. Let's break them out a little.

Data analysts and scientists[2] should be involved throughout the lifecycle of a product. They take the large amounts of data collected from a product and then help to clean, interpret, transform, model, and validate that data. All of this work is done with the intent of helping the business to make better decisions. Data analysts and scientists often bring insight that can help the business predict where it needs to go, but they can also help to analyze the resulting data from a business decision to understand if the business accomplished what it set out to do. Data scientists may also be driving the discussion around defining metrics and measurements for your business and users. Common backgrounds for data analysts and scientists will include statistics, information management, computer science, and business intelligence.

Your friends in analytics know a great deal about your users through rich, generally large-scale data about how your users actually interact with your product. Because they have access to the logging data for your product, they can give you an idea of how past design and product changes have introduced metrics your company measures, and tell you confidently about how many users are currently using different features of your product, and at what frequency. For instance, if you're thinking about removing a particular feature, you might ask your analytics friends about how many users are using that feature, and whether that feature use has historically had any relationship to whether your customers continue to use your product—that is, whether the feature

2 "Data science" is recent. It was in the 1960s that statisticians like John Tukey started to think more about what it was to bring a scientific approach to data analysis. In the 1970s we see these analysts start to recognize that the power they can bring to the data is to fill it with insight and more information. As we jump ahead to today, there is no question that data science is a term that now involves all the work that is done to capture, measure, and interpret the vast amount of data that represents our users on a daily basis. See *Doing Data Science* by Cathy O'Neil and Rachel Schutt (O'Reilly).

has historically *correlated* with usage. Generally, your analytics friends are also responsible for analyzing A/B test results. You'll find that they have great historic knowledge of how various ideas have performed in the past and can provide you with a lot of helpful guidance on structuring A/B tests.

User researchers[3] are complimentary to data analysts and scientists and in some cases will overlap with them in terms of skills and interests—especially as user researchers start to do more of their work on a bigger and bigger scale. Typically, user researchers champion the user by seeking to understand who your users are and what their needs are. They are interested in both attitudinal and behavioral information about your users. They may focus on qualitative information gathering via interviews, surveys, diary studies, and other forms of ethnographic research; however, many user researchers also work with quantitative forms of data as well. Common backgrounds for people involved in user research might include social and behavioral sciences like psychology, cognitive science, sociology, or perhaps anthropology, as well as the backgrounds that many designers have. User researchers and analysts should also be consumers of each other's data. Such sharing allows a broader understanding of user behavior with the product or service to develop; it helps to alleviate myopic and overly focused, feature-specific insights.

If you don't know anything about a particular domain or about your users in general, you could work with your user research friends to understand who your users are, their needs and desires, and the aspects of your experience that are most frustrating to them right now. Because their job involves so much time observing the types of tasks that users struggle with, understanding the contexts in which they live, and asking them about their needs, user researchers have a keenly honed intuition about your users. Because many user researchers are trained in *mixed methodologies*—that is, multiple methods that can be combined to give faceted insights—they can also help you figure out what type of data is most suited to your particular questions.

3 For more information, see "UI, UX: Who Does What? A Designer's Guide to the Tech Industry" (*http://www.fastcodesign.com/3032719/ui-ux-who-does-what-a-designers-guide-to-the-tech-industry*).

Designers, we believe, need to also be concerned with the generation of data. It's not new for designers to seek information about our users or to gather information about our designs as we evaluate them. In some companies that don't have the room for dedicated user researchers or analysts, the designer will have to step into those roles occasionally to get the information that they need to generate their designs. Designers can also play a key role in the generation of data based on what they design and choose to prototype. Designers can reflect on existing business metrics, as well as think about any additional metrics with respect to usability or the user interface. Of course, designers may also be actively involved in understanding the data that comes back from user researchers or analysts on their own design throughout the product development cycle. The key for designers is to interpret these results and understand them within the context of the larger business and product.

Marketers can also be great collaborators in terms of data generation. Too often we find that a weak tie between product and marketing means that a lot of valuable information that could be shared by both teams can get lost. Members of the marketing team seek to understand the target audience and the market size of that audience, and as a result often generate a lot of data around customers. Many people in marketing will have a strong business background.

Marketing is probably the place to check if you want an expert opinion about your users' demographics and target audiences. In Chapter 2, we will talk about the importance of being aware of the differences between your existing users and new users. Your marketing team will be able to help you understand what differences might exist between different types of users and important behavioral patterns based on age, gender, geolocation, culture, language, and other important features. The marketing team is also often responsible for understanding the competitive landscape and helping you understand what other products are in your business space. Having an understanding of how your competitors are faring and how their approach to users might be similar or different from yours can often help to give you ideas for how you might adjust or change your own user experience.

DATA CONSUMERS

On the consumption side of data roles, we find people who are actively taking the insights generated from the data to help them make decisions about how to push the business forward. In this bucket, we typically find business managers, product managers, and, of course, designers.

Business managers and *product managers* look to data to get stronger insights into how the business is performing. Business metrics are monitored and used to provide a health check on how the business is performing. They also look for impacts of business decisions and to see if the changes that are being done in the product are performing as expected. Formulating questions, designing experiments, and analyzing data to address issues that make sense from a design perspective as well as a business perspective can create alignment with business partners, collaborators, and company leadership about the target audience(s) and the desired behaviors for business growth and maintenance. Having a clear picture of what matters to your business will help you to plan and structure your quantitative tests and qualitative engagements.

If you are working with a product manager, they will be a critical partner in helping to set the context for your overarching business goals and the metrics you'll be using to measure your success (or failure) by. You'll be checking in with them periodically throughout the process to help generate ideas, but also to make sure that your designs and the "experiments" that you are conducting are reflective of the things you want to learn from your customers and in alignment with your business goals.

Engineers can be engaged along the way to ensure that as your designs are being built, you are also building in ways to track and capture the data that you are interested in. You want to be sure that the data you gather at the end of the process provides you with a complete picture of how your designs are impacting your users. You'll need to have the tools in place to measure all the different pieces of data you might want to capture about your users, and about how they interact with your product, and this is something you'll partner with engineers on. We'll talk more about some of these considerations in Chapter 6.

The roles we have described here may not have strict boundaries or definitions. In small companies, for example, you will find people who take on several of these roles. However, as you might find yourself playing into either a consumer or producer of data it can be helpful to understand which side of this divide it is that you are fitting into at that specific point in time.

Of course, there could be many other people in your organization who might use data. Our list here is just a starting point, and we encourage you to keep your eye out for other people with whom you could collaborate.

What If You Don't Have Data Friends (Yet)?

We just introduced many roles to you, and how those who fill these roles may work with data. Be thoughtful about who you're already associated with organizationally or perhaps are simply friends with. Also seek to form stronger bonds with those you don't know yet. We encourage you to reach out to those people to understand how they're already working, and learn how your own work might fit alongside or complement what they do. Think about how you may work together to set a data-aware agenda across your organization.

We also recognize that many of you might work in smaller organizations that don't have dedicated user researchers, analysts, or marketing teams just yet. However, this doesn't mean you can't start learning about your user! Many internet companies have started offering affordable services to help you begin building expertise about your users. For instance, UserTesting.com records real users interacting with your site or app, and provides insights about the users you're interested in learning about. Optimizely provides tools that allow you to A/B test your web and mobile experiences. There are also a number of companies, such as Qualtrics and SurveyMonkey, that help you to run surveys and gather other kinds of data from your users. These types of services can supplement your in-house teams with external data experts, helping you get started learning. For a list of some companies that you can utilize, see the "Resources" appendix.

Themes You'll See in This Book

We would like to highlight just a few of the themes that you'll be seeing throughout this book (we may not reflect these in every chapter, but you will see them crop up in at least a few of them):

- First and foremost, working with data is a creative process. Your design background and creativity can help you to enhance experimentation and data practices in your company. Diving into experimentation and data may well also improve your design practice, as you develop your understanding of how the two areas can work in synergy to give your users the best possible experiences.
- You need to understand the problem you're trying to solve, the users you're solving for, and the business you're in. The data you collect, and how you choose to collect it, should be mindful of these factors.

You've already collected many tools in your toolkit that are essential for designing with data:

- Design intuition isn't lost as a consequence of leveraging data, and in fact, is important to shape the questions that data can answer and how to answer them.
- Triangulation between multiple sources of data tells a more complete picture of your users, and helps you reduce the risk of being misled by data.
- You will need to work with others to be successful. You don't need to be an expert in data *in addition* to design. Rather, you should approach this book and designing with data with the goal of understanding how your skillset as a designer can help push the process of collecting data forward. Other folks in your organization will bring complementary skillsets, which combined, can plan and execute the best data strategy.

Summary

We believe you'll find that your training as a designer will give you a lot of advantages when working with data. Designers are often natural facilitators and you'll find that you can be fairly adept at driving participation from many different parts of your organization and from many people with different kinds of skills as a result. Because designers are usually comfortable representing the user and being especially empathetic to user needs, you'll find that incorporating the language of data along the way, and working with others to do so, will amplify your ability to speak on behalf of the user and to understand what ultimately works best for them.

There isn't a "one size fits all" approach to data and design, and understanding the nuances of *data driven* versus *data informed* versus *data aware* can be a powerful tool in design. Depending on the types of problems you are trying to solve, and how far along you are in your design process and product maturity, you may find yourself leveraging data in different ways. We encourage you to always be open minded about the other approaches you could be taking to solve your problem, and how you might use data in different ways if your approach was different.

We are focused on giving you a basic understanding of the relationship between data, business, and design, rather than teaching you how to design or making you an expert statistician or data scientist. Though formal and systematic incorporation of data from large-scale experiments into design is relatively recent, we believe this is the beginning of an exciting and long era to come. We believe that data and design are tools that you use to build great experiences for your users. And, if you are building great experiences for your users, then you have a great foundation for your business. We will feel successful if this book convinces you that understanding the basics of experimental methodologies and the data that you can gather about your users from applying such methods will make your design(s) and therefore your business better, and if you feel that you are not just willing but keen to engage with data in your organization and beyond.

We hope this chapter has given you a foundation for the approach that we would like to encourage as you start to work with data in your design decisions. As a designer, you will play both the role of a producer and a consumer of data at various times. We want you to feel empowered by data and to recognize that by adapting this framework, you're actually engaging in a two-way conversation with your users where both data and design can be a useful tool in that communication.

Questions to Ask Yourself

- What kinds of data does your company use?
- In what ways is your company data driven? Data informed? Data aware?
- Are there large-scale experiments being run in your company already?
- Who is responsible for those experiments?
- Who is currently producing and consuming data in your company?
- Who do you currently work with that can help you on your quest to integrate data into your design process?
- What kind of people might you want to have access to that you currently don't (e.g., data scientists, analysts, etc.)? What external or other resources could you use instead?
- How would you naturally fit in or adjust the way you work with "data friends" or other functions in your company to support the integration of data and design?
- What is the designer's role in producing data? What areas for improvement do you see in the relationship between data and design?
- Are there data "gaps"? How could you close those gaps?
- What kinds of questions would you like to ask about your users? What answers will help you in your work?

[2]

The ABCs of Using Data

In Chapter 1, we argued that crafting experiments to address design decisions is a creative process and that experiments can help you to make defensible design decisions based on your users' needs and feedback. Our goal in writing this book is not merely to evangelize the collection of data from experiments for its own sake. Experimental data provides no value on its own. Rather, we want to show you that using thoughtfully collected data can be a key tool in serving your ultimate design goal: to build the best possible experiences for your users.

No matter what type of company you work for, we expect that one of your biggest challenges will be designing great experiences for all of your users. Your users may be diverse in many ways. Each of them bring their own experiences, competencies, and expectations that will in turn drive their behavior. Going on intuition alone, even the best designers and product teams would struggle to design experiences that meet the needs of all users all the time. Effective use of experimental methods to collect data about your users lets you develop insights about their diversity, their similarities and differences, and how your designs affect them. In effect, your experiments are a way for your users to tell you what they think of your designs. Gathering data from experiments helps you make design decisions that are based first and foremost on your users and providing them the best possible experience.

In this chapter, we will lay the conceptual groundwork that we apply throughout the rest of this book. We'll introduce basic principles of experimentation, and show you how the internet has enabled us to apply those principles to designing products and experiences in a manner that is quick and scalable, a practice called A/B testing. Finally, we'll close by speaking in greater detail about the necessary role of creativity in A/B testing. We hope that by the end of this chapter, you'll feel comfortable with the vocabulary and concepts and ready to dive deep into understanding A/B testing in practice.

The Diversity of Data

So far, we've spoken only in general terms about "data." Before we dive deeply into exploring the topic of experimentation, we want to take a step back and talk in a more nuanced way about data. We believe that most people you ask would agree that the statement "there are 7.125 billion people living in the world" (at least at the time of publication) contains a data point. But what about "green vegetables served at camp dinner never run out"? Is that also a data point? Is that data?

When we say data, what we mean is simply a piece or collection of information that can be gathered or measured and analyzed. Recall that our goal is not merely to discuss data for data's sake, but rather to show you that data is a valuable instrument you can use to learn about your users. If you were trying figure out how to feed a whole program of summer campers, wouldn't knowing that past campers don't eat a lot of green vegetables be a useful piece of information?

We often hear people argue that some types of data are better or more informative than others. Our belief is that there is no one best type of data; rather, the best data is that which helps you to learn the most helpful and relevant information about the question or topic you had in mind. To this end, we're not going to spend a lot of time giving an in-depth look at every type of data or every research method to collect data. Instead, we'll introduce you to some (but not all!) of the different dimensions that data can take. We will then go into much greater depth about these topics in the remainder of the book by focusing on A/B testing, a single method for collecting data.

MANY DIMENSIONS OF DATA

We felt that a discussion about designing with data would be incomplete without a quick overview of the different dimensions of data that one might consider. We give you this introduction primarily to show you that different kinds of data come with different strengths and weaknesses and are useful in different contexts and for different purposes. This forces you to be critical about what the data can and cannot teach you, and whether it's appropriate for the problem you're trying to solve.

This section is structured as a series of questions: the why, when, how, and how much of data collection. These questions help contextualize the series of dimensions we introduce into questions that you might ask yourself as you're thinking about what type of data to collect.

Why are you collecting data?

You first need to determine why you are collecting data. In other words, what are you hoping to capture about your users from this data?

You might be interested in learning about your users' behaviors. Simply put, a behavior is what your user does, or the actions that they take. For instance, say you've just rolled out a new feature in your app. You want to know whether users are discovering it, and what they're using it for. If you're interested in these types of questions, you should consider collecting behavioral data. It's often easy to measure or observe actions—in fact, people who do research with human participants often say that you should trust what a person does, not what they say. However, observing behaviors alone can't always tell you why a user did something or how they feel about it.

You could also be interested in learning about a user's attitudes and expectations. For instance, if you were interested in behaviors, you might ask yourself whether a user clicks a button. If you're measuring attitudes, instead, you might ask what users expected to happen before they clicked the button. You might wonder whether what happened aligned with or contradicted their expectations. Finally, you might be interested in what your users feel. This type of data reflects emotional state; it is "affect" data. You might ask yourself, do your users trust your company and your brand? Are they stressed or satisfied by your new sign-up flow?

Compared to behavioral data, attitudes and emotions can be harder to measure without introducing bias. One common issue when collecting attitudinal data is users often want to give the "right answer," so they'll tell you what they think you want to hear, rather than what they actually believe. This is called the social desirability response or acquiescence bias, and there are many techniques for overcoming this effect.

Despite the difficulties, though, attitude and emotional data is essential to giving users a good experience. Even if every user clicks a new button, if it doesn't do what they're hoping, they'll be disappointed and lose trust in your product and brand.

When is the data collected?

In addition to thinking about what data to collect, you should think about when you're going to collect your data. This breaks down into two categories: longitudinal and snapshot.

First, over what timespan are you going to collect your data? Longitudinal data is collected from the same user over a period of time (which could be days, months, or even years), allowing you to see how users change, adapt, and learn over time. You can answer questions about how previous experiences inform future experiences, giving you context for your analysis of the data you can collect. However, because you must wait until the period of time is over, your data inevitably will take longer to collect.

If longitudinal data could be likened to a video stream, then snapshot data is like a photograph. Maybe instead of seeing how a user's interactions change, you want to observe just one instance of them interacting with your product. This data will be much quicker to collect (you could observe hundreds of participants in the time it would take to follow one person around for two years!), but you will lack the context of seeing how a person's prior behaviors inform their future behaviors, and how their behaviors change over time.

Additionally, you might think about whether to collect data contextually or in isolation. Imagine asking someone to try out your addictive new phone game while riding a busy subway during commuting hours versus asking them to try it out in a quiet, private room in your office. Collecting data in isolation helps you control for factors that might change or interfere with the way users interact with your design. You'll know that if you test the same app with several people, there's nothing about the environment that systematically impacted the experience that they had. However, your app will most likely not be used only in quiet and isolated contexts. Contextual data can give you a flavor of how your design is performing "in the wild," with all of the messy and difficult challenges and distractions that come with being out in the world.

How is the data collected?

Data can be broken down into qualitative and quantitative data to answer different types of questions. Qualitative data uses narrative to answer questions such as "Why?" or "How come?" It can be observed but not measured numerically. In the design process, qualitative data can help build empathy for users, and can inform your understanding of their attitudes, beliefs, values, and needs. Comparatively, quantitative data expresses observations through numbers and measurement. Quantitative data is valuable when trying to answer "How many?" or "How few?" In the design process, you might use quantitative data to measure the impact to certain metrics, such as daily active users (DAU) or user retention rates (the percentage of your users who continue to use your service across two defined periods of time—for example, across two business quarters).

Additionally, you can collect data through self-report or through observation. Self-report data involves asking users to answer questions or tell us something about themselves. Comparatively, watching the user's actions or behaviors rather than asking them to tell us about them yields observation data. As we discussed earlier, self-report data carries the risk of bias because users might tell us what we want to hear, rather than what they actually believe or how they really act. However, certain kinds of data (such as attitudinal or emotional data) cannot be collected through observation.

Finally, depending on whether you want to be able to probe deeper into the data or determine what you're going to be able to learn in advance, you could choose to collect moderated or unmoderated data. When collecting moderated data such as in an interview, a person asks questions or observes. If something is interesting or confusing, they're able to ask follow-up questions about why a user did a particular action. Comparatively, in an unmoderated method such as surveys, if a piece of data is interesting or unclear you're not able to go deeper into what was meant or intended. Moderated data requires having the resources for a person to observe or interview; however, you're able to learn more and can clarify confusion in how you ask your questions. Comparatively, unmoderated research requires a greater upfront investment (writing survey questions must be done with great care and expertise to avoid introducing systematic bias or confusing your user, as nothing can be clarified!), but because nobody needs to sit through each research session or activity, it's easier to collect data at scale with unmoderated methods. Additionally, unmoderated methods ensure that every research participant gets the exact same research experience; they are not subject to nuances in human behavior (such as researchers asking questions using different wording, or in slightly different order).

How much data to collect?

Finally, there remains the question of how much data to collect. This is actually quite a challenging subject that we will only touch on briefly in this book, and the answer depends a lot on the other decisions you made regarding what kind of data to collect, and what your goals are.

Imagine there's a rug at work near your desk. One day, you see someone trip on a bump in the rug. Would you really wait until 10 or 100 more people tripped on that same bump before fixing it? Probably not. This is similar to how many people consider software bugs—if you observe it happen with a few software/hardware configurations you don't know how many people will face it but you have an indication that it is a problem, and one you probably should fix. This same principle applies to usability issues in design. Research with few participants (often called "small sample research") is perfect for identifying these types of problems, because you don't need to quantify exactly how many people in the population will share that confusion to know it's a problem with your design; for instance, Figure 2-1 shows that you can identify more than 85% of usability issues with only five participants. If you spend time with fewer people, you can also collect richer and deeper data in the same period of time. However, for certain types of small sample research, you can't guarantee that the findings will generalize to everyone in your population. You also can't quantify with a high degree of accuracy how many users in the population are likely to experience a problem, or feel the same way as your participants. This means research with just a few people isn't good for making decisions where you have to be confident about the frequency of a problem, for instance.

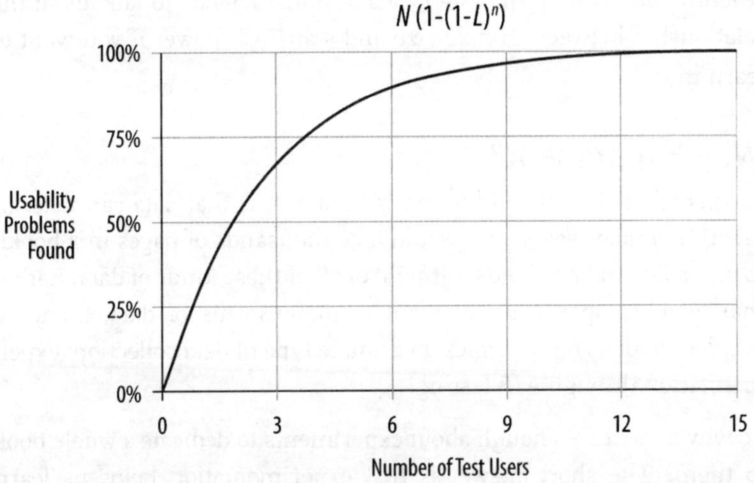

FIGURE 2-1.
As you usability test with more users, the amount of new information you gain from each subsequent user declines. Most people (including NNG, the makers of this graph) are proponents of stopping at five selected users, allowing you to find more than 85% of usability problems very inexpensively.[1]

Comparatively, data collected from many participants (often called "large sample research") can give you more precise quantity and frequency information: how many people feel a certain way, what percentage of users will take this action, and so on. In an ideal world where you had unlimited resources, you might find it better to always collect more data rather than less. This would ensure that you learned everything possible. However, you may not have the time to do this kind of research. Generally, the larger your sample, the more sure you can be that your findings will generalize to the population (so long as the sample is representative, which we will discuss later). There are statistical methods you can use to determine how many users you need to collect data from to reach a certain degree of confidence in your findings. We won't be getting into the details of this here, but we recommend

1 Nielson Norman Group (NNG). Note that this statistic depends on some assumptions, including the homogeneity of your sample and the base rate of the usability issues in the population. The number of users needed to detect 85% of problems may vary. It is worth reading the source research to understand the assumptions made in this figure.

reaching out to your analyst or data scientist friends to talk about the relationship between sample size and statistical power if you want to learn more.

Why Experiment?

We just shared with you the many dimensions that data can take. In practice, it takes years (and would take thousands of pages in a book!) to give a fair and nuanced treatment of all of those kinds of data. Rather than giving superficial treatment to many forms of data, then, we decided to focus our energies on a single type of data collection: experimentation through A/B testing.

So why do we care enough about experiments to dedicate a whole book to them? The short answer is that experimentation helps us learn about causality in a way that is grounded in evidence, that is not anecdotal, and that may be statistically significant. Thus, we can develop informed opinions about what will happen if we released that design, feature, or product in the wild. We realize that that's a bit of a mouthful, so we'll spend a little bit of time now breaking down that statement into its parts.

LEARNING ABOUT CAUSALITY

We'll start with the most obviously important benefit of an experiment. You might have heard the old adage that "correlation does not imply causation"; just because two or more things are correlated, meaning they have some kind of mutual relationship or connection between them, does not mean one thing causes a change in the other(s). In fact, as human beings, we make associations about how one thing affects another all the time in our everyday life.

In our camping example, let's say we were trying to learn more about which advertising causes more campers to sign up. We might conclude that the successful sales of a magazine containing a camp advertisement caused increased enrollment at camp (Figure 2-2).

The problem with assuming that the increased magazine sales caused the enrollment to go up is that we aren't omniscient in an uncontrolled setting: there's always factors we might not be observing perfectly that could provide alternative explanations to our observations. We can't rule these out, so we can't conclude that we're observing a causal relationship.

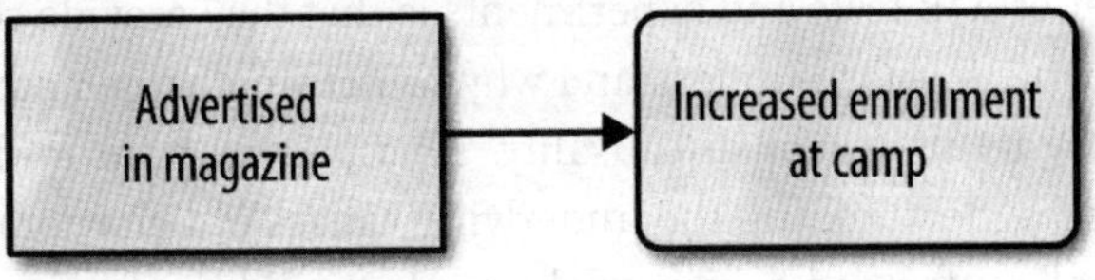

FIGURE 2-2.
If a magazine containing a camp advertisement sold well, and the enrollments at camp went up, we might assume the advertisement for camp caused increased enrollments at camp.

In our example, the fact that the magazine sales containing our advertisement have increased may indeed have caused increased enrollment; however, other causal relationships are also possible. We can show this easily and intuitively by adding another variable. For example, what if we consider the performance of the economy?

In fact, it could be the case that an improvement to the overall health of the economy led to both the successful magazine sales and increased enrollment at your camp, as economic health could lead to more disposable income in families for spending on both magazines and summer camps (Figure 2-3).

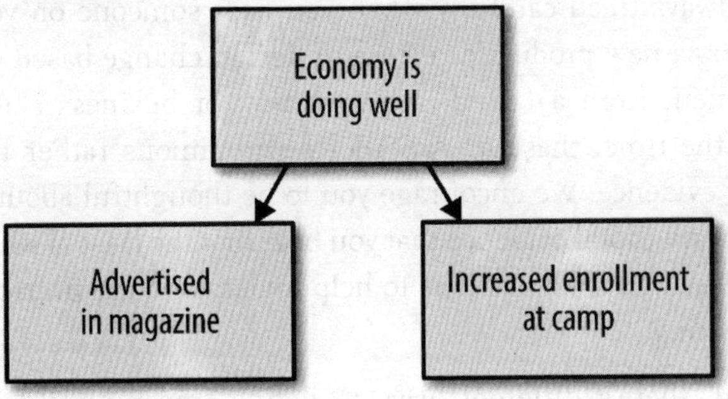

FIGURE 2-3.
However, it's also possible that the improving health of the economy caused both increased magazine sales and increased enrollments at camp. Which is right? We don't know without an experiment.

The power of A/B tests and experiments is that they provide controlled environments for us to understand why something happened; in other words, they let us establish causality. This is important to designers because by understanding the underlying causes of behavioral effects, we can make informed decisions about what will happen if we make a product or design change. This also lets us understand with accuracy and confidence how our decisions cause changes in our user's behavior. Furthermore, we can protect ourselves against the very human tendency to see patterns in data and behaviors that confirm what we already think (what psychologists call "confirmation bias"), and mitigate the risks of investing time and company resources on assumptions that aren't proven.

STATISTICALLY SIGNIFICANT, NOT ANECDOTAL

Learning about causality is unique to experimentation as a methodology, which we believe is already a strong reason to be excited about this book, and about A/B testing in general. But we still want to speak to some of the other strengths of experiments.

Generally speaking, whichever methodology you use to collect data, your goal should be to find meaningful evidence that you can trust to inform the design and product decisions that you're making. You should always tread carefully when you hear someone on your team suggesting a new product direction or design change based on a one-off comment from a friend, acquaintance, or business stakeholder: most of the time, these are anecdotes or opinions rather than true pieces of evidence. We encourage you to be thoughtful about the limitations of anecdotal evidence that you hear (not the least of which is the risk of bias), and ask questions to help understand the impact of what you're hearing.

That said, there's different ways to define "meaningful." Rigorous qualitative methodologies are undoubtedly meaningful sources of evidence, and are essential in making good product decisions. One way to ensure that your data is meaningful is by designing good research—for instance, by asking well-thought-out questions that are not biased, bias inducing, or leading. User researchers, for instance, are trained experts in doing this type of work.

Another way to identify data that *might* be meaningful is using statistical methods. These methods only apply to quantitative measures, but because experiments and A/B tests are quantitative methods, they can be judged against measures of *statistical significance.* Statistical significance helps quantify the likelihood that your data reflects a finding that's true in the world rather than the result of random chance. Depending on the type of data you're collecting, there are different measures you can use to calculate statistical significance such as *p-values.* A *p*-value measures the probability of the occurrence of a given event given a certain set of circumstances. Thus, a *p*-value helps quantify the probability of seeing differences observed in the data of your experiment simply by chance. We won't go into the details about how to calculate *p*-values here, but we encourage you to reach out to your data science or analytics friends or check out the resources at the end of the chapter if you're curious about learning more. We'll also note here that the limited statistics we discuss in this text come from a school of thought called "frequentist" statistics, which are most commonly applied to online experiments.

You'll note that we said statistical methods can help you determine data that *might* be meaningful, rather than data that is definitively meaningful. To weigh in on this, we spoke with Arianna McClain. Arianna is Director of Insights at DoorDash, and was most recently a Design Researcher and Design and Data Specialist at global design company IDEO. At IDEO, Arianna has worked to bring the user closer to the design process by leveraging different kinds of data across a range of projects. She was also on the founding team of Stanford d.school's course "Designing with Data." We believe Arianna has a great perspective on the intersection between these two fields, and how to make data more accessible for designers without much training yet.

When thinking about statistical significance and its relationship to whether something is meaningful, Arianna says:

> Statistical significance doesn't tell me whether something is "right or wrong" and it doesn't determine the actions I should take. Instead, statistical significance simply suggests to me that something interesting is going on.
>
> When I notice that a correlation or model is not close to being statistically significant, I view it as a cue to quickly move on. However, if it is close to statistical significance, it simply tells me, "Hey, you should pay attention to this." It makes me dig a little deeper and ask additional questions.
>
> For example, take randomized clinical drug trials. A pharmaceutical company does not decide to approve a drug simply because the data shows it achieves its intended effect with statistical significance. They take into account the drug's clinical impact, side effects, and cost as well. There are many examples in medicine that show that something has a statistically significant effect, but it isn't meaningful. For example, a weight loss trial may show that a new drug significantly decreases weight compared to a lifestyle intervention with $p < .0001$. However, the patients may have serious side effects and only lose one or two pounds more, which doesn't make taking the drug clinically meaningful or worth taking for the patient.

A small *p*-value alone doesn't mean that something is meaningful; rather, like Arianna, we believe that it indicates that you should pay attention to that result and think about it in the context of how you collected your data, how that change would affect your business, and what other sources of data are telling you.

We caution you against following significance without being thoughtful about what it actually indicates. That said, one of the primary strengths of experimentation is that so long as your test is designed well (more on that in the coming chapters), you'll have a signal that you observed a true effect rather than something random—something that you should pay attention to and think about as you're making design decisions.

INFORMED OPINIONS ABOUT WHAT WILL HAPPEN IN THE WILD

As we have noted, A/B tests are great for identifying statistically significant results, allowing you to form beliefs that you observed a true effect rather than something that happened by chance. Aside from it being very exciting and satisfying to see your work pay off with a statistically significant result, why should you care about significance in experimentation?

When a team decides to invest in building and launching a product and design, they want to make informed bets about how real users would react to the product—for example, in the case of an ecommerce site, would users click that button, navigate successfully through the new flow, and complete the checkout process? For all of their strengths, one primary limitation of research with a small number of participants is that the goal of it is rarely to be representative of the full user base. Rather, many other methodologies help you uncover compelling insights that help you build a better understanding about the type of issues some of your users might encounter, or the needs of specific groups of users.

Recall our dimensions of data introduced previously. Well-designed and well-executed experiments can help fill in that gap by providing product teams meaningful insights that generalize to how a feature or product will perform in the wild. A/B testing is an observation-based, behavioral method that collects large-scale data in the user's context. This means that as long as we do a good job designing our test, we can be fairly confident that the results we see in an A/B test are likely to be mirrored if we rolled out the product to more users. By using A/B tests, then, teams can "glimpse into the future" to see how their product is likely to perform, allowing them to measure and quantify the impact of design changes.

This ability to make data-aware choices about what will happen is extremely valuable. Your company can save time and resources by investing further in projects that perform well, while redesigning, rethinking, or pivoting away from ideas that perform poorly or don't elicit the intended user behavior. In addition to these business advantages, A/B testing allows designers to quantify the value of their work on the user experience or their company's bottom line. This is important because it helps designers articulate why investing in and prioritizing good design is important to their stakeholders and their business. We believe that understanding and speaking the language of data-aware methodologies like A/B testing empowers designers to argue that investing in good design is measurably, not just philosophically, critical to a business's success.

Basics of Experimentation

Throughout this chapter, we've been speaking about experiments and extolling the value of experimentation. We hope that the previous section has illustrated for you why experiments are an essential tool to have in your toolkit during the design process. Now that we've gotten you excited to learn more, we need to step back and teach you the basics of what an experiment is. These concepts and vocabulary may be familiar to you, especially if you studied the scientific method in school. Whether this is your first time learning about experiments or just a refresher course, we hope that by the end of the section you'll be ready to learn how to apply this terminology to an A/B test.

LANGUAGE AND CONCEPTS

In the words of Colin McFarland,[2] "an experiment is a means of gathering information to compare an idea against reality." In some sense, you've probably been running experiments your whole life: maybe last time you cooked brownies, you substituted whole eggs for egg whites. You tracked how quickly your family and friends ate the brownies, and compared it to the rate of consumption last time you made the brownies using whole eggs. This scenario seems basic (and probably resembles things you've actually done), but it contains the basic building blocks of every experiment: a change, an observation, and a control (Figure 2-4).

---

2 *Experiment!: Website conversion rate optimization with A/B and multivariate testing* (New Riders).

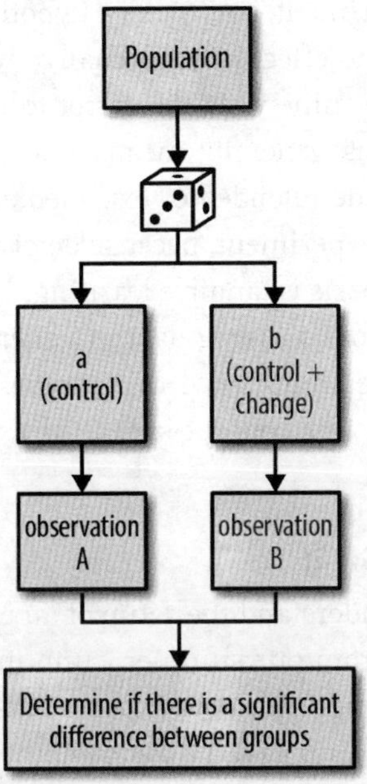

FIGURE 2-4.
The basic building blocks of an experiment are a change, an observation, and a control. At the end of the experiment, the measured difference between your control group (a) and your test condition (b) helps establish the effect of the change you made.

In an experiment, you make some change (using egg whites), and measure that change against a control (using whole eggs, the default recipe), to observe whether the change has had an impact on rate of consumption. The intuition here is that you are comparing two or more things that are almost the same: an experimental group and a control group. The only difference between these groups is the change that you deliberately made; in other words, your experimental group is basically your control group + some change. Therefore, if you observe a significant difference between these groups in a well-designed and well-controlled experiment, you can conclude that that difference was most likely caused by the change that you made (rather than just the result of random variation), because that was the only difference between the two groups. This is how experiments establish causality.

In designing an experiment, you make a hypothesis, or a testable prediction, about what the effect of your change will be. Based on what you observe, you determine whether or not to reject your hypothesis. Rejecting a hypothesis generally means that you assume that your change did not have the intended or expected effect. This is the most important part of an experiment, because determining whether or not you reject your hypothesis is tangible learning. The goal of every experiment (just like the goal of using data in general) should be to learn something. Given the importance of hypotheses, we'll give a more in-depth treatment to this concept later in the chapter, and in subsequent chapters as well.

RACE TO THE CAMPSITE!

Now that you understand the setup of an experiment, we'll use a basic example from our summer camp metaphor to help introduce more granular language about experiments. Imagine that as part of your summer camp, you have a hike to another campsite deep in the woods. This is a bonding activity for your entire camp and a great source of exercise. You're realizing that as you expand the fun activities and offerings at your camp, you need to shorten the time it takes for kids to do this hike, so that you have time for other activities in your summer camp programming. You decide to treat this hike as a bit of an experiment, by varying some factors while controlling for others, to learn about what equipment makes kids faster at the hike. This way, you can invest in equipment for the whole camp that is effective, instead of spending money on equipment that isn't useful for your campers.

An experiment is run on a *sample* of subjects selected from a *population*. A sample is a subset of a population. Generally speaking, your goal in sampling from a population is to capture a group that is representative of the whole (or at least the whole you intend to apply your learnings to), without needing to collect data from every person. For instance, imagine that you wanted to learn about camper satisfaction after you finished a year of camp. You could stand by the exit and speak to every single camper, but of course, that would be extremely time consuming and impractical. You could also ask your favorite five campers for their opinions, but they would be a biased sample, as your favorite campers are probably more likely than the average camper to really enjoy summer camp (why else would they be your favorites?).

Let's assume that campers are assigned to a cabin based on their age; that is, all campers in a cabin are similar in age. We can also assume that there are eight campers per cabin, and we're trying to build four groups for our hike. We could sample campers by assigning two campers from each cabin to each of the four groups, resulting in groups that have a range of camper ages. So long as there's no systematic bias in the two campers who are assigned to each group from each cabin, all groups should be representative of the whole camp.

Now, let's say that your experiment is to vary the different type of equipment that each group gets:

GROUP	EQUIPMENT RECEIVED
1	Map (control group)
2	Map, compass
3	Map, GPS
4	Map, protein bars

When people talk about experimental design like this, they often call these changes *variables*. We talked about control groups earlier. You can also control for certain variables: in this case, because every group (including your control group) received a map, this is a controlled variable. By controlling for this variable, you're designing an experiment that will not reveal any effects of having a map on the child's speed. This probably makes sense—you're likely giving them maps anyway, and maps are cheap to print off or photocopy.

When people speak about variables, you'll most often hear them talk about independent variables and dependent variables. In fact, we've already taught this concept to you—introducing this language just formalizes the intuitions that we've already shared. The *independent variable* is the variable that you change in order to observe a change in the *dependent variable*. Therefore, in this example, the equipment received is the independent variable, and the time it takes for the kids to get to the campsite is the dependent variable.

We told you before that these cause-and-effect relationships can be inferred from experiments only when the experiment is well designed and well controlled. In practice, designing experiments that meet those criteria can be quite challenging. *Confounds* are issues in your experiment that might lead to confusion about what caused the difference in the dependent variable you observed. Generally, confounds are the result of unplanned differences between the control group and experimental group(s) of which you were not aware.

For example, in the experiment about racing to the campsite just described, you assume that randomly assigning campers from cabins to the groups would be enough to make each group the same. However, what if every camper in Group 3 had proper hiking boots, while most of the campers in the other groups were wearing ordinary sneakers? Failing to control for footwear might have substantial effects on the speed the campers could climb. If you didn't account for this difference in groups, it would confound your experimental results: you wouldn't know whether Group 3 was faster due to their GPS system, or their hiking boots.

As you can see, experiments are an effective way to identify causal relationships between an independent variable you change and a dependent variable you observe, so long as you are careful to control for all confounding variables. In practice, designing effective experiments needs to be a collaborative effort where you work collaboratively with other people on your team to account for all possible confounds, thereby designing the best shot at learning what you aim to learn.

We hope that you're excited to learn about how to apply experiments to your design problems. But first, we'll share how the internet has facilitated experimentation that is both fast and scalable. It is these two factors that have made A/B testing a practical method and reality for many companies.

EXPERIMENTATION IN THE INTERNET AGE

People have been running experiments formally and informally for a long time. Back in the 1700s, a British ship captain named James Lind ran a naïve experiment after observing that sailors on Mediterranean ships who received citrus as part of their rations had lower rates of scurvy than other sailors. He gave half his crew limes as part of their rations (experimental group: diet + citrus fruit) and the other half just ate the regular diet (control group: diet only). He found that compared to the control group, the experimental group had a significantly lower rate of scurvy, leading him to conclude that citrus fruits like limes prevent scurvy. He wrote:

> The most sudden and visible good effects were perceived from the use of oranges and lemons; one of those who had taken them being at the end of six days fit for duty.... The other was the best recovered of any in his condition; and being now deemed pretty well, was appointed nurse to the rest of the sick.[3]

The digital age has radically changed the speed and scalability of experimentation practices. Not too long ago, the primary way that you shared photos with someone was much more complicated: first, you would have to load your camera with film and then take a series of snapshots. When your film roll was done, you'd take that film to the local store where you would drop it off for processing. A few days or a week later you would need to pick up your developed photos and that would be the first time you'd be able to evaluate how well the photos that you took many days prior actually turned out. Then, maybe when someone was at your house, you'd pull out those photos and narrate what each photo was about. If you were going to really share those photos with someone else, you'd maybe order duplicates and then put them in an envelope to mail to them—and a few days later, your friend would get your photos as well. If you were working at a company like Kodak that had a vested interest in increasing people's use of their film, processing paper, or cameras, and you were asked to collect insights about customer behavior to drive designs that would increase usage, there would be many aspects of customer behavior and parts of the experience that would be hard to accurately measure. You'd also have almost no way to collect insight into your customer's behaviors and actions along the process, and it would be even harder to conduct experiments to compare different product offerings. How would you observe the different rates of photo taking or sharing with different kinds of cameras, or the performance of real user's photos with different kinds of film? It would be extremely challenging to track down that kind of data, especially outside of a customer experience research lab and in real (and therefore imperfect) contexts.

3 *http://www.ncbi.nlm.nih.gov/pmc/articles/PMC1081662/pdf/medhist00113-0029.pdf*

Now let's take the same example of sharing a photo in the digital world. Your user will take out their phone, open the camera app, and take a photo. They may open up Instagram, apply some filters to the photo, and edit it on the spot before adding a caption and then sharing it. They might also choose to share it on different channels, like Twitter, Facebook, or via email. The entire experience of sharing a photo has been collapsed and condensed into one uninterrupted flow on a single screen, one that you can hold in the palm of your hand. And because all of this is digital, data is continuously being collected along the way. You have access to all kinds of information that you wouldn't have had before: location, time spent in each step, which filters were tried but not used, what was written about the photo, and to whom the photo was sent. In addition, you're not limited to observing just one user—you can gather this information from each and every user. You can make changes to your interface, filters, flow, or sharing options and observe—at scale—how real users respond as they take real photos of real moments in their life. And, because the data logging can be made automatic and seamlessly integrated into your experience, you can amass huge amounts of data quickly.

This example illustrates the power of digital interfaces for data collection. Although experimentation has been around a long time, the internet enables us to collect large amounts of data about our users cheaply and quickly. Many internet companies invest in internal tooling to enable anyone in the company to deploy an A/B test and collect results in a matter of days or weeks, helping them make business-critical design decisions in real time, as a fundamental part of their existing product development processes. For instance, Skyscanner has "Dr Jekyll,"[4] LinkedIn has "XCLNT,"[5] and Etsy has "Catapult"[6] for this purpose. Imagine how much more effort it would have taken Kodak to learn enough about their users to make reliable decisions in the pre-internet age. For these reasons, now more than ever is an exciting time to embrace designing with data. A/B tests—or online experiments—are one powerful, versatile way to do that.

---

4 *http://codevoyagers.com/2016/11/03/building-products-for-large-scale-experimentation/*

5 *https://engineering.linkedin.com/ab-testing/introduction-technical-paper-linkedins-ab-testing-platform/*

6 *http://www.slideshare.net/mwalkerinfo/data-daytexas2013*

A/B Testing: Online Experiments

As we have been discussing, A/B tests are essentially online experiments. The concepts—making a change and measuring its effect compared to a control group—are nearly identical. However, over time, A/B testing has adopted a language of its own that is more closely aligned to existing business terms. Here, we'll help map over the general concepts we introduced to A/B testing-specific terminology that you're more likely to hear in your business context. We'll also get a bit more specific with a few additional concepts that are practical and important to understand, such as statistical significance.

SAMPLING YOUR USERS ONLINE

When we kicked off our race to the campsite metaphor, we started out by talking about how you would assign your cabins of campers to groups for the purposes of your test. This is an extremely important area of focus for A/B tests as well. Even small differences in the groups you assign to your experimental and control conditions can compound when your sample sizes are large, resulting in confounded and therefore unreliable experiments. This is why it's crucial that assignment to each group is random. When assigned randomly, there's less chance for one group to have an advantage over the other.

Before we kick off, we want to introduce one new term. So far we've been talking about different conditions: the experimental and control groups, for instance. In A/B testing, these conditions are often referred to as *test cells*. These are conceptually the same as the conditions we've already been speaking about: test cells are the different experiences that users in your sample can be randomly assigned to, which vary systematically in ways you choose.

Now that we've introduced that term, in this section we'll review some important considerations to think about when sampling selected users from your entire population of users. We hope that the terminology and concepts in this section will help you have more meaningful conversations with your team about the right users to experiment on to gather meaningful data about which designs best serve your target audience.

Cohorts and segments

When you're looking to learn more about your users through data, one of the first questions you need to ask is which users to gather data about. Doing research with the right group of users is really important and will play a factor in how you interpret your results. Your user base is probably quite varied. By subdividing your user base into either cohorts or segments, two ways of thinking about how to split your users, you can gain different insights into their behaviors or motivations that you wouldn't have seen if you had just considered them as one large group.

A *cohort* is a group of users who have a shared experience. That experience might be based on time (they all signed up for your product or service at the same time) or it may be that they have another factor that gives them a common experience (e.g., students who graduated in 2015).

For example, perhaps in January you get a lot of visitors to your service who are coming because they got mobile phones for Christmas. These people might be different or have different motivations than the people who might sign up for your product at other times of the year. Applied to our summer camp metaphor, one cohort might be first-time campers in summer 2016. The types of activities you ran that summer, as well as the advertising you focused on prior to that year, will define their baseline and expectations for summer camp.

Alternatively, you can also *segment* your user base into different groups based on more stable characteristics such as demographic factors (e.g., gender, age, country of residence) or you may want to segment them by their behavior (e.g., new user, power user). A summer camp example of a segment might be campers of a certain age, or campers who come from New York City. Where a camper grows up and how old they are both likely affect the types of camp activities they'd be interested in.

We'll talk more in later chapters about the importance of analyzing the success or failure of the experiences you design by looking at how different groups of your users react to them. For now, it's just important to recognize that different groups of users might have different reactions to your product or experience driven by different needs.

For instance, according to former Chief Product Officer John Ciancutti, online learning and course site Coursera has several different segments that they consider when building products: lifelong learners, seasoned professionals, and unseasoned professionals. These different segments have unique needs, approach the product in different ways, and may be more or less likely to pay for Coursera's offerings. He said:

> You've got your lifelong learners. They're looking for entertainment. They skew older. Learning is more interesting than television: they're thinking they want to exercise their brain, learn a new thing. Or they're thinking, "Hey, I'm going to travel to Italy, so I want to learn a little Italian, I want to learn about Roman architecture and history." The lifelong learners want access to the content, but they don't care about completing courses, don't care about credentials. But they want to give you some money because you're giving them value, and that's how their brains work.
>
> Then you have the seasoned professionals. They're engineers, they've already made it. They've got a job, but they want to keep their skills fresh. This is about making them better at their job, if there's some new data analysis technique, or analytic software or new programming language, new technology. They don't care about the credential, or about completion. It's just about sharpening the blade.
>
> Then there is the unseasoned professional. They want to get a job as a data analyst, so they care a ton about credentials, about completion, about getting a "badge." Going to a prestigious university is a badge that you will have forever. You have this badge that says to the world, "What you learned is amazing and you're an amazing person because you got accepted," and all these different things. People want that badge.

As you're thinking about your A/B test, making a decision about which cohorts and segments to test with is essential. Focusing your sampling on a single cohort might help you understand the unique problems and needs that face that particular user group in depth.

For instance, perhaps you decide to focus on a cohort of campers who attended your summer camp for the first time in 2015. This might help you learn meaningful insights about campers who are very similar to that cohort—for instance, they might extend to other middle school–aged campers from similar home backgrounds, as your camp only accepted middle schoolers in 2015, and you advertised primarily to suburban neighborhoods near New York City. However, the data you gather if you do research with this cohort would not necessarily apply to other potential future campers, such as whole families (if you became a family camp), high school–aged campers, or campers from the West Coast or other countries, because those perspectives weren't reflected in your original cohort. As you can see, then, the sample(s) you focus on in any given A/B test will determine the population(s) to which your insights will apply; you should confine insights and generalizations to the groups of which your sample is representative.

Demographic information

When defining segments, you sometimes want to segment users based on more stable characteristics, such as demographics. The following questions might help you to determine what kind of information you might be asking yourself and how you might go about gathering it:

- What demographic information can I gather on my users? (Consider what you already know about your users based on questions that you ask during the sign-up process or think about reports that you can purchase about audiences that you might want to target but don't currently serve.)
- How do factors like location, age, gender, race, disability, and income change their needs relative to the experience I'm trying to craft?
- What behaviors and habits have your users established? How does time of day or location affect those behaviors?
- What devices do they use?
- What are their values and expectations that might affect their reception to your product?
- How comfortable/experienced are they with respect to technology, devices, and the internet in general? What is their attitude toward using new technology or experiences?

For example, online accommodations rental service Airbnb answered some of these questions by sending some of its top experience researchers directly to their population in question: Japanese superhosts. The company was curious about why the number of home listings in Tokyo was so low relative to the urban city's large population. The team did ethnographic research with some of Tokyo's Airbnb hosts to understand what demographic these hosts occupied, what their values were, and what made them different than people in Tokyo who didn't host. Airbnb's researchers found that although the hosts in Tokyo seemed very different at face value, all of them were "outliers" in the sense that they had a positive defining experience with outsiders. Unlike many Tokyo residents, these super-hosts were willing to share with outsiders and bring foreigners to Japan, making them ideal early adopters of Airbnb in Tokyo.[7]

As you're trying to learn more about your users, not all of these questions will be relevant, but hopefully you can see how getting some of this information and data will shape the way you design for your customers. It's also rare that your experience won't need to adapt and change as your user base evolves and grows over time. For this reason, it's also important to remember that gathering data and understanding your users is an ongoing effort.

New users versus existing users

For most products and design decisions, you're probably already thinking beyond your existing users toward the acquisition of new users. Data can help you learn more about both your existing users and prospective future users, and determining whether you want to sample from new or existing users is an important consideration in A/B testing.

Existing users are people who have prior experience with your product or service. Because of this, they come into the experience with a preconceived notion about how your service or product works. This learned behavior can influence how they think, what they expect, and how they experience new features that you introduce to your product or service, which is an important consideration when testing new designs in front of existing users. Compared to existing users, new users do not have experience with your product. If you're trying to grow your business, you might be more interested in learning about new users because they aren't predisposed to your current experience.

7 *https://www.nytimes.com/2015/02/22/magazine/meet-the-unlikely-airbnb-hosts-of-japan.html?_r=0*

To illustrate the difference between new and existing users, imagine that you're going to make some changes to the layout of your camp during the off-season, by moving the outhouse closer to the dining hall. The previous layout of your summer camp is shown in Figure 2-5.

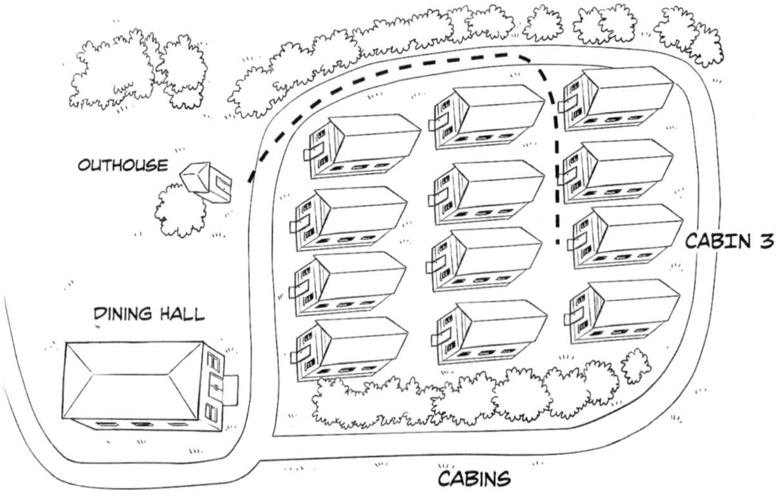

FIGURE 2-5.
The old layout of your summer camp. Old campers have an established habit of walking out to the street and then to the outhouse.

After you move the outhouse, you observe that returning campers from cabin 3 take a much longer path to get to the outhouse, while new campers in cabin 3 take a more direct path. This makes sense; they are basing their navigation on their past experiences. Returning campers need to overcome the learned behavior about how to get to the old outhouse location by using the road; they have engrained habits that lead them to walk that direction whenever they need to use the toilet. By contrast, new campers lack these old habits about where the outhouse used to be, and therefore can walk to the new location more directly through the other cabins. Figure 2-6 demonstrates the differences between returning and new campers.

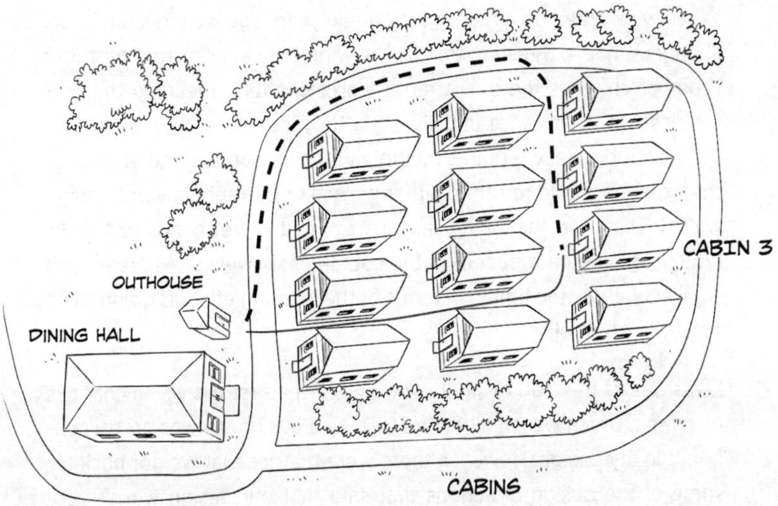

FIGURE 2-6.
Routes taken by old versus new campers on their way to the outhouse. Old campers have learned habits that affect the routes they take, even after the outhouse has moved. New campers don't have these existing habits and therefore take a more direct route.

Thus, it's important to be careful about whether your test is with new or existing users, as these learned habits and behaviors about how your product used to be in the past could cause bias in your A/B test.

Jon Wiley from Google shared his experiences around taking into consideration whether your experiment has a "learning effect" when thinking about how long to let them run. When you make a change to your experience, users may need time to overcome any habits or learned behavior that they've established with your original design. Jon said:

> We run our own experiments for longer periods of time particularly for anything that is a visual change, anything that they'd notice. The reason that we do that is because of learning effects. We know that there are a lot of things that happen when you get hit with a new interface or a new design.

> When we worked on a redesign a couple years ago we did a big visual change. What A/B testing told us time and time again is that for these types of changes there is often a learning effect, meaning that our metrics will go haywire initially, then they'll start to stabilize. That's because it basically requires multiple times for someone to encounter the experience and return to either normal or better behavior for what we're looking for. The timing can vary by what we're changing. A really big change might impact over the course of six weeks. Whereas for a smaller change, the timing in terms of the learning effect is going to be much, much smaller.
>
> I was one of the lead designers on one of the first big visual changes to search, which we launched in 2010. As a designer, I was pretty confident in my design. However, there were metrics that we got back for some of the design directions that said that our design wasn't very good. I did not believe them. I started poking and prodding a bit, working pretty closely with our analysts and our engineers and really digging into these numbers.
>
> One of the things I did was to ask, because of this learning effect, "Well why don't we look at these numbers for high-frequency users, people who use Google search a lot, who enter a lot of queries and do a lot of searches? What would the numbers look like for that group?" We discovered that the numbers were actually very different for that group. They were a lot better in several of the places that we were concerned about. That was our first clue that maybe there is an effect going on here that had to do with the exposure of these visual design changes. We decided to let the experiments run a little bit longer. As we did that, we discovered that the low-frequency users and the medium-frequency users started to fall in line over a much longer period of time with the high-frequency users.

This is also a great example because it shows how active a role Jon played in both defining and understanding how his design was being measured. When designers become very curious about the effects that they are seeing in the data, it often empowers them to push harder for a better understanding of what is really going on in underlying user behavior that they are trying to affect.

In addition to learned habit effects, you also need to be thoughtful about demographic differences between your existing users and folks who might become your users in the future. For instance, your existing user base might have a different demographic bias than potential new users. If your initial offering had high traction with tech-savvy or younger audiences, then it's likely that any sample of existing users will actually have disproportionately more representation from younger and more tech-savvy folks than the average population. It's good to ask yourself if your original customers are representative of the kinds of people that you want to be your customers one year from now. Will you continue to target tech-savvy people or are you hoping to gain audience share by moving toward a more mainstream, less tech-savvy population?

Similarly, when thinking about new users, what does your future demographic look like? Just as we described earlier, you'll want to make sure that the users who you learn about are representative of those future users when you're using them to think about design.

In this section, we introduced three considerations when you start thinking about who to include in your A/B test samples: what cohorts or segments do you want to represent in your findings, what demographic considerations are relevant, and are you interested in learning about new or existing users? You should revisit these three considerations for every A/B test you run. Taking time to think about your sampling practices upfront ensures that you will be able to collect the right insights about the right audience, which is essential to running effective A/B tests.

METRICS: THE DEPENDENT VARIABLE OF A/B TESTING

Now that we've covered some practical considerations for sampling from your population in an A/B test and taken a quick vocabulary break to introduce the idea of test cells, we're going to revisit what dependent variables look like in an A/B test. Recall that the dependent variable is the variable you observe to see the impact of the change you made. We want to start off this section by getting a bit more specific about how dependent variables generally look in the context of an A/B test.

Broadly, a *measure* is anything you observe, capture, and count. Examples of measures might be the number of users that visit a page on your website or the number of people that successfully complete a process. A *metric* is a predetermined and evaluative benchmark, which has been determined to have some business value. Metrics are sometimes the result of comparing several measures, often as a ratio. Metrics are used because they can tell a compelling story about the health of your business or your designs. Acquisition, retention, and activation rates are all examples of metrics.

Metrics are the dependent variables of A/B testing; that is, the thing you measure to determine the result of your A/B test. For instance, thinking back to our example of racing to the campsite, your metric was time—specifically, time for the campers to go from their start location to the campsite.

In this case, and more generally, metrics allow you to measure and quantify the impact of your designs or product changes, and therefore measure your success or failure at causing some change in your users' behavior. To observe these changes, you often look specifically at your company's key metrics. *Key metrics* are the focus of your business and the main metrics you would like to see improve and the determining factor on whether or not your design is a success. Key metrics should be based on what drives the success of your business—you can think of it as a way of measuring the customer behavior that correlates to your success. Generally you want to increase some metric that is essential to your business (such as customer retention or conversion, which is the percentage of your users who take a desired action), so the metrics determine whether your design is successful or not. However, in developing tests and analyzing results, you should also be thinking about deriving new metrics for the business. This is where data, design principles, and business come together.

A simple example of a metric intimately related to a business's goals comes from Dan McKinley's time at Etsy. Dan McKinley was a Principal Engineer at Etsy and was part of the journey in seeing it grow from a small company of 20 to the success that it is now. His talks about how Etsy leveraged A/B testing have helped to inspire many companies to do the same. He talked to us about how defining a key metric at Etsy was fairly straightforward:

> At Etsy [defining key metrics] is less controversial than it would be at many companies. Etsy is a business selling things, so the metric that we can optimize for is how much money we can make. The other way that we were lucky is that those metrics directly correlate to our users' interests. The point of Etsy is to have other people sell stuff, and we

> make money when all those people sell stuff. When we sell more stuff, our sellers are happy and we are also happy. Those are the things we at Etsy cared about.

A more complicated example comes from the online learning platform Coursera. Coursera is a credential-driven business; in other words, they make money when users pay for credentials (certifications) after completing a course. One of their key metrics might be the number of credentials sold, or the revenue generated from credential purchases. You might be skeptical about this metric, though, and for good reason: because Coursera courses are often 13-week college classes, measuring how a design changes this metric would take far too long to be practical. John Ciancutti walked us through the process of how Coursera derived other metrics they could use to track the impact of their work with more immediacy:

> With Coursera, the business model is to get people to pay for credentials. To buy a credential, it requires that you complete a course. So we wanted people to complete the courses. And courses are divided into modules. So then we found, of course, that the number of modules someone completes correlates with course completion. Then we did even better, and we found two big actionable things that happen even earlier on.
>
> The first one is: Do they get through the first test? Getting through that first test is really important, so then you can even do things like, let's inform the pedagogy and design courses so that you have a test early, because learners get more invested.
>
> Then another is: Do they come back and engage with the course two or three different times on different days? This is again because of that feeling of commitment. If you were quitting smoking and you make it through two days, you're like, "I'm not going to do it on day three even though it's hard. I'm not going to lose all that investment, right?"
>
> These are two ways that you take this overall company goal and you bring it back to something that you can test in just a couple of days. That enables whole teams to iterate more quickly.

When you can't discern any effect on key metrics easily, *proxy metrics* can be used. These metrics measure behavior from your users that give you an indication that they will likely also change the behavior behind their key metric as well. Proxy metrics are easier to measure than your key metric, or a leading indicator that something you have done successfully created the behavior that you wanted to change. To pick good proxy metrics, look for other metrics that are strongly correlated with your key metrics. You can also think about what behaviors might indicate early on that a user is going to engage in the desired behavior.

With some key metrics you'll get the answer right away—for example, if you're measuring revenue, you'll know at the end of their session if they've actually purchased something or not. However, as we just discussed with this example from Coursera, other key metrics might not be so easily measurable. Coursera has intelligently developed several proxy metrics that they found to correlate and predict credential purchases and course completion. Course completion is predicted by module completion, which is in turn predicted by test completion and how often a user engages with a course. So Coursera measures test completion or course engagement as proxies for their key metric, allowing them to cut down the time to measure the impact of a design change dramatically.

As you can see, then, a huge part of designing your A/B test will be making thoughtful decisions about what metrics to measure—that is, what data to track when the test is over. How do you make these kinds of decisions?

For one, the kind of business you're in will influence how you measure the "health" and success of that business. Business health is an extremely complex concept. It includes a myriad of different measures that roll up into a "bottom line" that defines whether the business is viable or not. Such measures include engineering analytics (service delivery and robustness metrics), business analytics and metrics (focused on balancing profit and loss, and assessing the business impact), and analysis of markets and business competitiveness.

Ultimately, whether you are focused on one group of users or on many disparate groups of users, the dynamic quality of the market today means our focus as designers is on what users do; their behavior is key. And, although your job may be focused very specifically on designing the user experience, it is worth always considering how what you do impacts the core signals of your business's health. How what you do intersects with these other metrics and measures depends on three things:

- What kind of business are you?
- What is your revenue model?
- How mature is your business?

Your answers to these questions will determine the kind of data that you will want to collect. As John Ciancutti shares, choosing metrics that tie to your business is essential for making data actionable at your company:

> People care about all of these metrics that seem good, where it intuitively seems like more of something would be better than less of it. More clicks, more this, more that. But if you can't find a way to tie that metric to your business, it's not actionable. Whereas if you can drive retention, or if you can drive course completion at Coursera, you're driving the business.
>
> When I think about a subscription business, it's like people are expressing their value very clearly and directly by saying "I choose to pay for this service another month" versus not. For almost any consumer business, a big resource that people invest in, other than money, is time. So time spent often correlates with the business and the metrics you really care about. Measuring these things can often trump other things, but data doesn't obviate the need for judgments. You're the pilot, but it's really nice to have a compass. If you're trying to get to a particular place, you need a compass, but it's not like the robot's flying the plane.

We won't go into detail about how these different factors affect the metrics you should be thinking about here, but a great starting place is to ask around and find out what metrics your company is already measuring. As John shared, metrics that track time or money are often intimately connected to your business. Many companies will track key metrics even outside of A/B tests. For instance, you might be interested in how many "engaged" users you have. A basic engagement measure is the Active User (AU). The idea is to capture how many people use your product or service on a daily or monthly basis. Business reports often include summaries of Daily Active Users (DAU) and Monthly Active Users (MAU), potentially across many categories if the nature of the business is complex. To Wikipedia, an AU may be someone who contributed to more than one article. According to the *Wall Street Journal*, Twitter considers a user active if they log in once a month. For a social platform, an active visitor is someone who has come back to the platform at least once within 30 days. For an ecommerce platform, a metric like active browsing 2 days out of 7 may be the metric the business considers successful. For a news media outlet, active engagement with stories once a day may be sufficient.

As a designer, you're probably most concerned with giving your users a good customer experience. Good business metrics should always keep the user in mind. For instance, you would expect that your users would not be very engaged if using your product is a terrible experience. We encourage you to question metric(s) which seem inconsistent with a good user experience—stop and assess whether the metric needs to be changed, and if so, consider proposing a metric that is more reflective of the user experience and the long-term, business-positive customer journey. Remember, a successful business should always prioritize giving its customers a great experience.

The point we are trying to make is that deciding what to measure—and knowing that you're measuring it well—can be challenging. Think about how this might apply to your race to the campsite. Originally, we said your metric of interest was time to the campsite. But maybe emphasizing time over all else really isn't the most important metric, because campers will be happy doing less activities at camp but with a more fun and enjoyable pace. A different key metric you could measure is camper happiness. As you can see, there's no objective way to determine whether camper happiness or time to campsite is more important—this is a judgment call that you'll have to make, and the kind of judgment that designers and other folks on a product team have to make every time they run an A/B test.

We wanted to close out this section with a great comment from Arianna McClain about the subjectivity of measurement. Arianna reminds us that, "Measurement design is subjective. Someone decides what to measure, how to measure it, and how to build the model. So all data is subject to human bias." As we just alluded to, the decision about what to measure and how to measure it is subjective; the way we usually phrase it is that behind every quantitative measure is a set of qualitative judgments. Designers have a big role to play in asking thoughtful questions and applying their expertise about users to guiding how a design or experience should be assessed, what matters from a user experience point of view, and how to get meaningful data that informs those questions.

DETECTING A DIFFERENCE IN YOUR GROUPS

When we talked about the basics of experimentation, we told you that in order to determine whether your change had an effect, you observe a difference in the dependent variable. But how do you know whether that difference actually mattered? What if Group 2 beat the other groups to the campsite by 30 seconds—is that enough of a difference to invest money in compasses? These are questions of statistical significance. We don't aim to write a statistical textbook here, though there are many great sources about this topic. Instead, we hope to share the role these statistical concepts should play from a design perspective, in service of helping you understand and have empathy for the work your statistics-minded teammates would be thinking about in an A/B test. We believe that having some language will give you the ability to partake in discussions about significance and power, and empower you to ask good questions when you help design A/B tests to see how your work performs in the wild.

Recall from earlier in the chapter that statistical significance is a way of measuring the probability that the difference you observed was a result of random chance rather than a true difference in your groups. You calculate significance at the end of your test once you have the results, to determine whether the differences you observed were due to random fluctuations in your measures or a meaningful consequence of the change you implemented; you thus engage with determining the likelihood or probability of a causal relationship.

Even though statistical significance is calculated at the end of a test, you'll need to think about whether you can measure a statistically significant result during the design of your A/B test. *Power* is the probability that you can correctly detect a statistically significant result when there is a real difference between your experimental and control groups. When you design an A/B test, you want to make sure that your test is powerful enough to detect a difference in your groups if one does in fact exist. Unlike statistical significance calculations, this is an upfront calculation, before you launch your test. Here's one way to think about the difference: power tells you whether you're capable of observing a difference, while statistical significance tells you if you did see one in the samples that you observed. You can think of an underpowered test as having glasses that are too weak to correct your eyesight: if you don't have a strong enough prescription, you probably won't be able to tell the difference between a cat and a dog, and you'll end up with a blurry and untrustworthy view of the world.

We won't go into too much detail about the difference between these two concepts and exactly how to calculate power here. Instead, we'll walk through a few factors that influence the power your test needs.

How big is the difference you want to measure?

Besides wanting to know whether or not there is a difference between two groups, the next obvious question is, how big is that difference? Effect size is the size of the difference between the control and experimental groups. Unlike statistical significance, which only tells you whether or not there is a difference, effect size helps you quantify how big that difference is. In science, a larger effect is generally taken to be more meaningful than a small effect. This is probably also true for products—you stand to gain more by implementing a design change with a large effect size, because that design change can have a very big impact on your user's experience or your company's key metrics.

In product design, we define the minimum detectable effect (MDE) to be the minimum difference we want to observe between our test condition and control condition in order to call our A/B a success. The MDE often depends on business factors, like how much revenue increase would result from a difference at least that big in your metric. The intuition here is basically that the cost to test and implement that change should be "paid off" in some way, through a meaningfully large difference in some metric that is key to your business's health and success or a sizable improvement to your user experience. You might also choose an MDE based on previous A/B tests you've run—this knowledge of how big an effect you've seen in the past can help benchmark how big of an effect you'd want to see in the future.

The statistical power required for your test depends on the minimum detectable effect you're trying to detect. It's easier to detect bigger differences—imagine if some of the campers could take a cable car up the mountain instead of having to hike. This would lead to an enormous difference in time to campsite compared to the other groups, and you wouldn't need a very powerful test to detect that difference. Comparatively, much smaller MDEs require more powerful tests in order to meaningfully detect a difference.

A big enough sample to power your test

Depending on the minimum detectable effect you want your test to have, you'll determine how powerful your test needs to be. Sample size is one factor that changes the power of your test.

Let's say that one camper tells you they saw a skunk behind the outhouse. You might be inclined to think that they just saw a squirrel or a raccoon but thought it was a skunk. Now, what if you heard from five campers that there was a skunk behind the outhouse? This would probably make you a little bit more inclined to believe it, and you might even have an inkling of worry about a camper encountering the skunk. What if you heard from 50 independent campers that there was a skunk behind the outhouse? By now, your confidence that the skunk is there would likely be so strong that you'd probably temporarily allow campers to use counselor bathrooms, lest they get sprayed on their way to or from the outhouse.

Here is another example. Let's say that each of your four groups for the race to the campsite had only one camper, because everyone else got sick and couldn't go. You might observe a difference between the groups, but you'd probably be skeptical about making purchasing decisions on such a small sample—it's only one child who was faster, how do you know that it wasn't just because she was extra tall or extra athletic? But what if, now, each of the four groups had 40 campers? Assuming that the groups stayed together, if you observed that Group 4 was fastest to the top, you'd probably feel fairly confident basing decisions off of that data because you have more information. All of the differences between the groups would probably level out, and 40 kids beating out 120 other kids would be more compelling than 1 kid beating out 3 kids.

The principle behind this intuition is that when you observe something in a larger sample, you're more inclined to believe it. As a result, a larger sample size is more powerful—observing even a small difference in time or happiness would be compelling if you observe it in many campers, whereas the same small difference with just one or a few campers would not be as convincing.

Significance level

Recall that *p*-values represent the probability that the difference you observed is due to random chance. When we see a *p*-value of .01, for instance, this means that 1% of the time we would observe the difference we saw or an even bigger difference just by random chance, not because of any meaningful difference between the groups. But how small of a *p*-value is small enough? This depends on how confident you want to be. In many social science fields like psychology, any *p*-value less than .05 (5%) is taken to be statistically significant—that is, the observed difference is assumed not to be due to chance. Another way to say this is that 5% of the time, you'll think you're observing a real effect in your data when actually it's just random noise in the data that occurred by chance. In other fields such as physics, only *p*-values less than 0.0000003 are taken to be statistically significant.[8] This is of course impractical for the types of changes we make in product design, even for the largest Internet sites.

Part of designing an A/B test is determining the degree of confidence you will accept ahead of running your test. Are you OK with the result of your tests being wrong 5% of the time? That's the typical range most internet teams set. How about 10% of the time? 20%? Only you and your teammates can decide the type of risk you're willing to take. The main reason to be more generous about your risk taking is that more risk means you require less statistical power. And less power means smaller sample sizes, which in practice probably means shorter and less costly tests because you need less time to get data from less users.

8 *http://www.graphpad.com/www/data-analysis-resource-center/blog/statistical-significance-defined-using-the-five-sigma-standard/*

As you can see, much of designing an A/B test involves making tradeoffs between these different factors that depend on your context. However, the statistics of your test are only one important piece of the puzzle for gathering important learnings about your users. Having a solid hypothesis that expresses what you aim to learn is equally important. This is the topic of our next section.

Your Hypothesis and Why It Matters

So far, we've tried to highlight that the work of a designer isn't only to design; rather, we believe that the most effective designers are engaged across the entire process of designing with data, from designing the data strategy based on thoughtful questions, to understanding the analysis of the data, to recommending what to do in response to the data. At its core, the reason to leverage data in the design process is to learn: to learn something about your business, something about your product, or something about your users.

It is especially important that designers, product managers, and others you might work with (such as user researchers or analysts) all take responsibility for defining the hypothesis statement or statements together. As we have said earlier, a hypothesis is a testable prediction of what you think the result of your experiment will be. When we say testable, what we mean is that the hypothesis can be disproven through the experimental methodologies we outlined earlier. A well-crafted hypothesis should express your beliefs about what the world will be like if you launch your design change. As a designer, you already have a well-honed intuition for how design changes can lead to differences in user experiences and behaviors, which we believe is an essential perspective in crafting worthwhile hypotheses to test with real users.

DEFINING A HYPOTHESIS OR HYPOTHESES

Defining your hypothesis defines what you will learn from your test. It's as if you're putting forth a belief about the world to determine whether it holds up: if it doesn't, you've learned that your belief was wrong. If it does, you'll likely have gained some confidence in that belief. With that in mind, let's dive deeper into what a hypothesis is.

Notice that we defined a testable hypothesis as one that can be disproven. Colloquially, many people will talk about this as whether or not you "proved" your hypothesis. We wanted to highlight that formally speaking, you can never actually "prove" a hypothesis, you can only disprove it. A famous illustration of this comes from the philosopher Karl Popper:

> No matter how numerous; for any conclusion drawn in this way may always turn out to be false: no matter how many instances of white swans we may have observed, this does not justify the conclusion that all swans are white...but it *can* be shown *false* by a single authentic sighting of a black swan.[9]

We find that keeping the formal definition in mind is helpful because it can be a good reminder to us that the beliefs we form about the relationship between user behavior and metrics should not be held so strongly that we become blind to the possibility that they can be disproven. Having this mindset will allow you to maintain a healthy attitude toward experimentation. Sighting a black swan—that is, being disproven—can often be the most valuable kind of learning. We challenge you to embrace these opportunities as a way to correct misconceptions and build sharper design intuitions.

With respect to data and design, your hypothesis should be a clear articulation of how you think your design will affect customer behavior and metrics and why it will have that effect. Said slightly differently, it states what you presume will happen to your metric(s) because of a change that you are going to make to your experience—essentially, it's a prediction about the outcome of an experiment. If you have formulated your hypothesis well, then you will also have a good understanding of what you will learn about your users whether your hypothesis holds or is disproven. Having a strong hypothesis is key to the experimentation process and having a hypothesis that can't be tested is ultimately of no value to you.

Your hypothesis should be a statement, a proposition that you make to describe what you believe will happen given specific circumstances. It often but doesn't follow the form: "If we do *X*, users

9 Karl Popper, *The Logic of Scientific Discovery* (*http://strangebeautiful.com/other-texts/popper-logic-scientific-discovery.pdf*).

will do *Y* because of *Z* which will impact metrics *A*." Returning to our earlier example of the race to the campsite, recall that we assigned the following equipment to our four groups:

GROUP	EQUIPMENT RECEIVED
1	Map (control group)
2	Map, compass
3	Map, GPS
4	Map, protein bars

As you might have noticed, relative to the control group, Groups 2 and 3 both received equipment that have to do with facilitating navigation, while Group 4 received equipment that has to do with food. These assignments might have been made based on the following three hypotheses.

Hypothesis 1

If we give campers equipment that makes it easier to navigate to the campsite, then they will be less likely to get lost and more likely to find an optimal route, which will decrease the time it takes to get to the campsite.

Hypothesis 2

If we give campers additional food during the hike, then they will have more energy and hike faster, which will decrease the time it takes to get to the campsite.

Hypothesis 3

If we give campers additional food during the hike, then they will not be hungry during the hike, which will increase camper happiness.

It's easy to see here how giving campers navigational equipment like a GPS or compass would help test Hypothesis 1, while giving them protein bars would test Hypothesis 2. Simply put, if we observed that there was no difference in the time to the campsite for Group 1 (control) and Group 4 (experimental group, Hypothesis 2) then we could disprove Hypothesis 2—giving campers additional food did not decrease the time it took to get to the campsite. Similarly, if there was no difference between Group 1 and Group 2 or 3 we could disprove Hypothesis 1—navigational equipment did not help to get to the campsite faster. One important note here is that both Group 2 and Group 3 address navigation. These are two possible ways we could test the same Hypothesis 1. In Chapter 5, we'll talk about different ways to "get at" the same hypothesis.

We might also observe that Hypothesis 3 is not disproven—the campers who got food are in fact measurably happier relative to the control group. As you can see, then, what you stand to learn depends not only on the exact experimental setup but also the metric you specify in your hypothesis. This is important, because it illustrates one major reason why defining a clear hypothesis is important: it helps build alignment among you and your team around what you think is important, and the criterion by which you will evaluate your test outcome. A clear hypothesis that involves a specific metric makes it clearer whether a test is a success or failure, paving a clearer path to next steps based on data.

There is always a temptation when embarking on a new project to jump right into exploring different design solutions or to begin to plan how you might execute on your ideas. It is a commonly accepted best practice in the design world that it takes many iterations to find the best design. The same is true for experiments. We don't want to mislead you here into thinking that you should make one hypothesis and then go straight into testing it with an A/B test. In the remaining chapters, we'll deep dive into how going broad is essential to learning the most from your A/B tests. But for now, just remember that choosing what you test is critical, and taking upfront time to focus your efforts on the most meaningful tests will help you learn the most.

That's what A/B testing is at its core: uncovering the most meaningful insights about your users and how they respond to your product and design changes. We believe that if you start by considering why you think a design will have an important or meaningful impact, it will ensure that you and your team can learn from each design in an A/B test. In order to emphasize learning as central to your A/B testing process, we encourage you to clearly articulate what it is you'll learn from each hypothesis you test.

You should aim to have two things when crafting a hypothesis:

- A hypothesis statement that captures the essence of the change you propose to make and what you think the effect will be.
- A clear understanding and a plan that addresses what you would learn by testing that hypothesis.

You should reach a clear agreement on both the hypothesis statement and learning statement with the other folks you're working with (your team and any other stakeholders) before you embark on your design process. This is especially important when your hypothesis is disproven. Working with your team early on to articulate your possible learnings for all outcomes will help ensure that no matter what the data shows, you'll have gained interesting and actionable insights about your users.

KNOW WHAT YOU WANT TO LEARN

In order to keep learning at the center of each hypothesis, you should aim to answer these questions:

- If you fail, what did you learn that you will apply to future designs?
- If you succeed, what did you learn that you will apply to future designs?
- How much work are you willing to put into your testing in order to get this learning?

For example, if the changes that you made to the experience you were testing resulted in metrics that were negatively impacted instead of positively impacted (e.g., you lowered the sign-up rate rather than raised it) what useful information did you learn from your test? Did your customers behave differently than you expected or did they behave as you expected but the result of that behavior was different than what you predicted would happen? We'll cover analyzing your results in Chapter 6, but the point here is that tying your hypothesis back to the lesson you are trying to learn can be really helpful in the long term. Don't run a test, conclude that it failed, and forget about it. Unfortunately, this is a pitfall we see teams fall into all the time. Emphasizing that all experimentation is about learning ensures that negative test results aren't really "failures" at all, because you still gain valuable insights into your users and the impact of your designs, data that will inform and improve your future experiments. Only when you can leverage failed results as well as successes can your company truly be "data aware."

Running Creative A/B Tests

Anyone involved in product or design work would agree that creativity is essential to doing good design work. However, typically there is more pushback on the claim that experimentation is a creative process. Unfortunately, the narrative around A/B testing that we often hear is that it's "just a way to validate your design before shipping" and "it's for crazy and meaningless optimizations, not interesting design problems." If you take nothing else away from this book, we hope that you come away feeling that A/B testing and other data methodologies can be as creative as the design process you already know and love. To help make that point, we'll emphasize two main ways that you can bring creativity into your A/B tests.

DATA TRIANGULATION: STRENGTH IN MIXED METHODS

In the beginning of the chapter, we spoke at length to some of the strengths and limitations of different kinds of data. Recall that A/B testing is an unmoderated quantitative method that involves observing a large sample of user behavior in context. This has many strengths: it helps you gather statistically significant learnings about causality so that you and your team can form a rigorously informed opinion about what will probably happen if you launch your design in the real world.

What we haven't emphasized as much so far is that for all its strengths, A/B testing has several important weaknesses. A/B testing alone cannot tell you why the different test cells performed differently, give you insight into the attitudes or emotions that users feel about the change (beyond those reflected directly in the metric you're measuring), or let you probe deeper into behaviors that might be interesting or confusing. Especially for designers who are used to approaching work from these very perspectives, these sacrifices can feel lofty.

We firmly believe that best way to do A/B testing is to also do things other than A/B testing. Mixing methodologies is the only way to gain a truly complete picture of your users and how your designs affect them. Moreover, using different kinds of data can inspire new approaches or hypotheses to A/B test. Using other forms of data, therefore, is a way to inspire more creative A/B testing.

Data triangulation is using multiple methods to form a holistic picture of your users and your data. It can help further improve your understanding of user behavior by explaining why you found a result to be true among many users in an A/B test, or understanding the magnitude of a finding you saw in a small-sample, moderated research activity like a usability test. Data triangulation also helps you avoid falling into the pitfall of relying too heavily on a single source of data and can spur endless new ideas for future A/B tests or design iterations.

Let's imagine after the race to the campsite that you were surprised to find that Groups 2 and 3 (the compass and GPS groups) were even slower than the control group. This would undoubtedly be a puzzling result—how could having equipment that intuitively seems to make group fasters by helping them take a more direct route actually make them slower? To understand what happened, you decide to interview some of the campers in those two groups to learn about their experience. In those interviews, you might discover that many of the campers complained a lot about mosquitoes. They stopped often during the hike due to bug bites, and were slowed down by swarms of mosquitoes in their face. Just by looking at the results of your experiment you never would have understood such a puzzling result; data triangulation gave you a more complete view of your campers' experience.

What would the outcome of this data triangulation be? One simple idea is that bug spray is a worthwhile investment for your hike in the future—no doubt the mosquitoes not only made the campers slower, but also less happy. In the grand scheme of things, this is a small change to make. But perhaps learning about the mosquito infestation could have larger consequences as well. You worry about sending future campers through the same buggy patch, because mosquitoes can carry dangerous diseases. Perhaps next time, you'll try to find a new campsite instead of just optimizing routes for the existing campsite. This might make the hike more pleasant and faster overall, a creative opportunity you never would have discovered without data triangulation.

Arianna McClain gave us a great real-world example of how different research methods can lead to different insights and outcomes. She shared the following example of a time she was consulting on a healthcare-related project at IDEO:

> On a healthcare project, when we asked people through a survey what was most important in choosing a healthcare provider, people chose "costs and coverage." Had we taken this data at face value, we would have designed a solution that was wrong, like a cost calculator.

> That's because when we spoke to people to hear their stories and looked at the behavioral data from the healthcare site, we saw and heard something very different from what they reported in the survey and told us through their stories. Even before costs, people consistently first clicked on "Things you should know when choosing a provider." And afterwards, they made their final decision by figuring out costs. By merging the insights, we were able to create a more valuable product by designing for that tension.

This example shows how triangulating different methods gave her and her team a stronger understanding about how people make healthcare-related decisions. Had they not used both methods, they would have designed for the wrong thing (for instance, by focusing too much on things you should know, or by focusing too much on cost). Combining methods in this way gave the team a richer understanding of how these decisions are really made.

THE LANDSCAPE OF DESIGN ACTIVITIES

Data triangulation can help you understand why you saw the data that you did, and inform creative approaches to future A/B tests. We want to make another claim about why A/B testing is creative: A/B testing can help you approach many types of problem spaces, giving you the flexibility to try out different ideas and approaches and learn substantially from them. In other words, A/B testing is not only for small optimization problems; it can also help you take a stab at understanding a space you've never designed in before.

In Chapter 1, we showed you an illustration (shown again here in Figure 2-7) to get you in the mindset of thinking about the types of problems you're trying to solve. Design can solve many problems, and from our experience it can be easy to lose track of the landscape of possible design activities you could be engaging in, depending on your goals and type of problem you're trying to solve.

FIGURE 2-7.
Revisiting the space of design activities from Chapter 1.

Previously, we left the space of possible design activities very vague. Now, we're going to take a moment to provide a framework for thinking about how you could understand this space. One of the themes we hope you take away in his book is that using experimental methodologies as a means of gathering data fits seamlessly within the existing design process. Flexible methods like A/B testing can be used for a wide variety of design problems, but in order to do so successfully, you need to be aware of the design activity you're trying to work on. This is another way that creativity makes its way into the process of designing with data: the data can answer many questions, but you need to be the driving force behind asking and solving the right design questions.

You can imagine taking the space of design activities and overlaying it with a grid. One axis represents the scope of the problem you're solving: Is it a global or a local problem? The other indicates how far along you are in solving that problem: Are you close to finished, and just trying to evaluate your work, or are you just beginning to explore the space of possible solutions (Figure 2-8)?

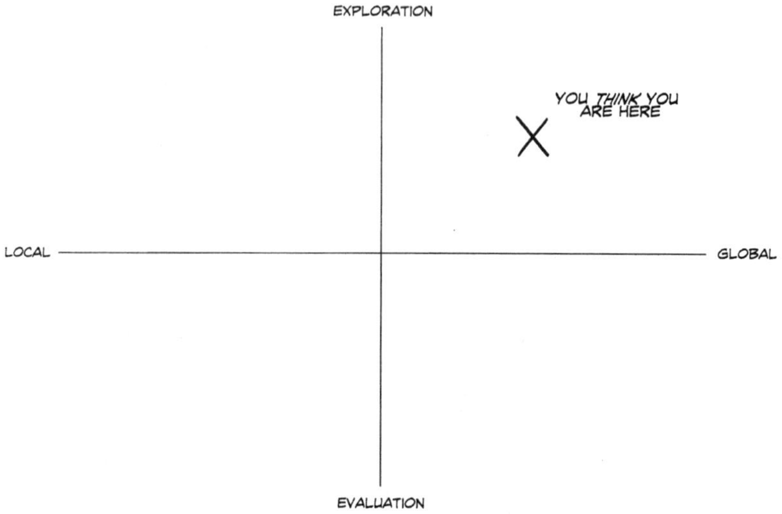

FIGURE 2-8.
We can take the space of possible design activities and make it more concrete, by considering the framework of where we are on the spectrum of scope (is the problem global or local?) and how close we are to finishing (are we just starting explorations, or evaluating our work?)

EXPLORING AND EVALUATING IDEAS

As a designer, you may have already encountered conflicts with your team about how "finished" your design output is. We've often heard designers complain that they agreed to launch a piece of work they deemed "unfinished" thinking that it was a temporary placeholder, only to find that their team thought it was the finished and final product. Thinking about whether your problem is *exploratory* or *evaluatory* can help you address these team-wide decisions on how close you are to finishing the work. As a general rule, you can think of this dimension as conveying how close or far you are to coming up with a solution to launch to your entire user base (not that this is to say the process is purely linear; you might be evaluating a solution only to uncover something that forces you to start exploring other alternatives!). In other words, exploration helps you figure out what to build next, while evaluation helps you measure the causal impact of your work.

When you are at an *exploration* stage, you don't necessarily have a specific solution in mind. Instead, you are seeking directional input on the types of solutions that will or will not work for your users. In the exploratory phase, your attitude will need to be more open minded; you might discover things out about your users that you weren't expecting, which could alter the way you are going to approach your design moving forward. When you're in an exploratory stage, the types of questions you might be asking are "How will my users respond to this change?" or "What happens to the metrics when I do this?" If instead you are at an *evaluation* stage, then you will likely be looking for very specific answers. You'll want to know whether or not your design works in the way you expected and why it performs that way. When you're in the evaluation stage, you might ask yourself "Can my users complete their goals with this design?" or "Did this design improve or maintain my company's key metrics? Did I observe any drops in my metrics?"

If you're designing in the exploration phase, you should feel empowered with the freedom to take risks and try out designs that you're not sure about, knowing that the designs aren't final. We often see the pitfall of designers not getting creative enough here—in an exploratory test, your test cells don't have to be finished pieces of work that you would be proud to ship. You could pursue seemingly crazy, potentially risky, or groundbreaking ideas with the intention to learn from them, rather than ship them. An example that Colin McFarland, Head of Experimentation at the travel site Skyscanner, shared with us involves his team's investigation of a "share" feature. The team tested two different ways to share—one that was a very subtle sidebar button that the team would have felt comfortable shipping, while the other was a prominent pop-up that would have been too extreme for them to ever ship. They found that because neither the subtle nor the extreme treatment led to a difference in their metrics, they abandoned the idea. Had they only tested the subtle sidebar button, the team might have thought that they hadn't gone "big" enough, and they might have run more experiments chasing a dead-end idea.

The result of your A/B test should never be a decision to launch the winning design and move on when you're in the exploration phase; rather, it should be to take the learnings from the test and apply them to future design work, iterations, and more A/B testing. Comparatively, as you move toward evaluation of your designs, you should expect that you're getting closer and closer to a "finished" piece of work that you would be comfortable launching to your users. At this point, you and your team should already be directionally aligned and you might be making smaller tweaks or polishing your work. The output of a successful A/B test might be to start launching the design to more of your user base. We'll talk more about this in Chapter 6.

THINKING GLOBAL AND THINKING LOCAL

A second dimension you want to think about defines the scope of how broad or narrow your design thinking is, and how optimal you want your solution to be. We can classify this decision of scope as looking for global versus local solutions. You can think of this dimension as determining how big of a design change you're willing to make; that is, how much you are willing to optimize.

When designing for a *local* problem, you are focused in on a specific solution, and you're making small changes to just one or two pieces of the experience in order to understand their impact or importance in isolation. In design folklore, these are the types of problems traditionally assumed to use A/B testing—for instance, when varying factors like the placement, color, size, and copy of a button to yield the best click-through rate. Local problems generally involve shorter time scales and are most appropriate when your existing solution is already performing adequately. Your design iterations for a local problem are generally less pronounced, changing only one or a few factors at a time (Figure 2-9).

FIGURE 2-9.

In a local test, you will change just one or a few variables at a time; for instance, centering your button (Test A), or changing the placement from the bottom left to top right (Test B).

By contrast you are solving a *global* problem when you're completely redesigning an existing experience. This might be because your existing solution is performing poorly, because it's outdated, or because you're looking to make many large changes to your experience or product at the same time (for instance, you want to change the entire sign-up flow for your product because user attrition during the existing flow is very high). Your design iterations will likely be quite dissimilar, and it will take more time to land on the best solution when you're changing many factors at once, because you won't be able to separate what part of your change caused a difference. You might be trying to understand whether a given feature matters at all by changing many variables at once (Figure 2-10).

FIGURE 2-10.
Comparatively, in a global problem, you might be comparing two entirely different experiences which don't necessarily resemble each other at all (Test C).

Closely related to the concept of global and local problems is the idea of *global* and *local maxima*. These concepts are borrowed from mathematics, although we find that they apply well to thinking about design and are used for this purpose among many designers. Many people explain global maxima and local maxima using the metaphor of a mountain range. Within that mountain range, each mountaintop is the tallest point in a region; however, only one of the mountains will be the tallest in the entire range. Each mountaintop symbolizes a *local maxima* in design, and there can be many possible local maxima. These are the best solutions within the space you are considering. For instance, perhaps you've done a lot of work to optimize for the color, size, and copy of a "Sign Up" button. It yields the best subscription rate of any of the designs you've tried. For many types of problems, optimizing for that local maxima will be good enough for your purposes. However, you can't be sure that the local maxima you've found is the best overall way to get folks to subscribe to your product. That optimal point—the tallest peak in the entire mountain range—is called the *global maxima*. Identifying a global maxima can be challenging, because unless you explore many divergent solutions it's hard to know whether there's a better point than the one you're currently at. We'll discuss this more in Chapter 5 when we cover how to design for the hypothesis you have in mind. In the case of driving more registrations, you might do global explorations and find that the global maxima involves offering a free trial of your product before asking your users to pay money to subscribe.

Getting back to the question of whether you're tackling a global or a local problem, you might ask yourself which of these two approaches is right for your design problem? Are you thinking too broad (your problem is actually local), or too narrow (your problem is actually global)? The answer depends on many factors. We want to be clear that a global change is not necessarily going to be more impactful to your metrics than a local change—global versus local defines how big a difference is in your experience relative to your control, *not* how big of a difference you'll observe in your metrics. Often, making a global change to your app or experience will require more resources and a much longer timeframe. In those cases, you should be thoughtful about how much "better" the global maxima (that is, the best possible result across the whole of the app experience) is compared to the local maximum (that is, the best possible result on the specific thing you are testing). Does it justify the extra resources, effort, and time? Is solving for this global problem the most important thing for you to be working on right now, or is a local optimization good enough? Does local optimization have the potential to create a large effect on your metrics? These are questions you can't decide on your own. Bringing your team into alignment on these issues at the beginning of the project will help you design solutions that are best suited for the constraints and goals you're currently trying to solve. Bringing other teams in and engaging with business strategists can also be useful because "global" can be confusing—some simple or local experiments can impact the whole product, and can be global. A good example is changing a "call to action design" on every page.

Notably, both of these dimensions can vary together: you can do global evaluations and local explorations. And, as we noted in Figure 2-11, these two dimensions are not binary but rather exist on a spectrum. Our goal in introducing this framework is *not* to encourage you to pin down exactly where you are or introduce more bureaucracy into your design process. Instead, we believe that giving you a framework to think about the type of problem you're trying to solve is essential for two reasons:

- It forces you to take the time to consider the space of other possible design activities you could be working on, and confirm for yourself and with your team that you're focusing your efforts on the right scope and problem.
- Different spaces in the design activity landscape leverage data in different ways, and by being thoughtful about your specific problem space you can be more effective in how you design your A/B test (or other research methodology).

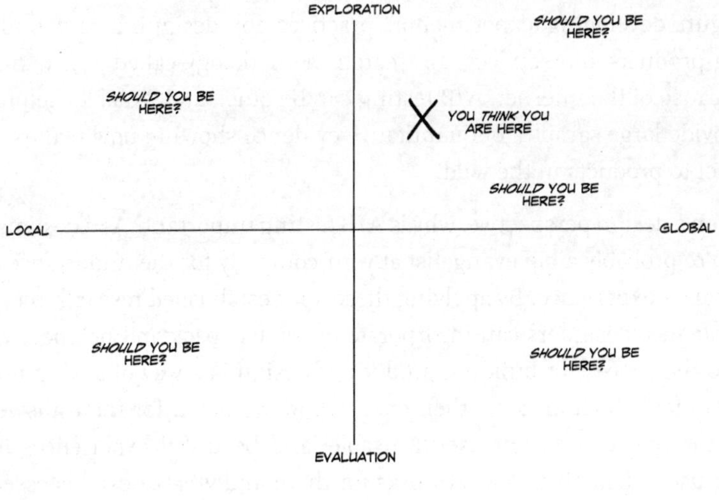

FIGURE 2-11.
This framework helps you think about whether you're approaching the design of your experience and A/B test through the right lens, depending on the scope of your problem, and how close you are to being "finished."

Throughout the book we will return to the framework introduced here to remind you about how designing and executing your A/B test might be different depending on the design activity space you're in. Certain types of design problems will empower more creativity in your A/B testing, giving you the opportunity to pursue design work that may be a little outside your comfort zone in order to maximize learning. In the coming chapters, we will comment specifically on how different spaces in this graph lead to differences in how you build, choose, and design for different hypotheses, and how they might inform the next steps you take.

Summary

Using data to learn something about the world is nothing new. Even if you have never run a formal A/B test, you've undoubtedly used naïve experiments in your daily life by drawing generalizable conclusions from observations about the way the world behaves. These observations and conclusions have helped you think about the world in a different way, inspiring creative solutions for everyday problems, big and small.

As a practice, *experimentation* helps formalize those intuitions by providing trustworthy and generalizable data about causal relationships that exist in the world. In an experiment, you systematically vary some factors of interest while keeping others controlled in order to observe differences in outcomes or responses. Many internet companies have begun developing experimental practices for designing and building products and services, a research methodology called *A/B testing*. Because of the internet, A/B testing can be quick and scalable, helping provide large samples of quantitative evidence showing how real users react to products in the wild.

From a design perspective, why is A/B testing important? As a designer, you're probably a big evangelist at your company for the importance of the user experience. By applying these long-established research methodologies, designers can incorporate users' feedback and perspectives into the process of building product. If design is a way of asking how users feel about an idea, then data is how we listen for their answer. In the quest to design useful, usable, and beautiful experiences for our users, listening to what works for them and what doesn't is essential. Additionally, although you already believe that good design is an important area of investment for your users *and* your business, your counterparts in other areas of the business may not yet share this belief.

Quantifiable data can help communicate how your design work contributes to the health of your business and your user experience, helping you demonstrate to stakeholders why taking time to design is important.

We hope that in this chapter we gave you the necessary foundations to feel empowered to get involved in A/B testing as a designer. The next four chapters will apply the frameworks and concepts we introduced here into a practical how-to guide about designing and running the best A/B test for your design needs. Hopefully you're excited to learn more, and eager to see how designing an A/B test is itself a creative endeavor that will push the limits of your creativity in the future.

Questions to Ask Yourself

- What different kinds of data have you used in the past? What types of data have you not tried, but might apply to your work?
- How many users does your company have? How could you use small sample research to learn more about them? How about large sample research?
- Do you have instances where people have used anecdotes to make design decisions? What may have changed if the design decisions had been addressed with experiments instead?
- Have you come across situations where a correlation was mistaken for causation? How might you have established that causation with confidence?
- Are there other examples of human activities, like photo-taking, that you have studied that have changed significantly since becoming digital? Can you think of the ways in which that change has opened up potential for broader and/or deeper understanding through experimentation?
- Does your company currently run A/B tests? Who "owns" these experiments? What has the role of the designer been in these tests?
- What other methods does your company use to understand its users? Are there opportunities to triangulate those methods with A/B testing data?

- Think of a study you recently conducted or one you would like to conduct. What would your hypotheses be? What would your independent and dependent variable(s) be?
- Can you think of instances where a small change (e.g., a button change) has had a major impact on the way you or your users use an application?
- Can you think of a global change you've made recently, such as in a product redesign? What was the impact to your users and business?

[3]

A Framework for Experimentation

In this chapter, we move from the theoretical to the practical by introducing the framework that we'll be using over the next three chapters to dive into the practical integration of data and design. This framework is our own particular take on how to think about A/B testing. You'll find that many people use similar ways of thinking about A/B testing design and implementation, and we hope that you will find your own ways to adapt our framework to suit your needs. There are three phases that we'll go into more detail on: definition, execution, and analysis. We'll dedicate a chapter to each of these and go into much more detail about applying the concepts in Chapters 4–6.

What is the relationship between data, design, and user experience? We say that there should be no divide between data insight and design insight. We believe designers have a significant role to play in the design of data-gathering activities (what should be captured and why), in the design of data itself (what format should data take, what data types need to be triangulated), and in the presentation and communication of insights and results that derive from the data capture and analysis. We believe that data capture, data validation, data curation and management, and data analysis for insights are central to design practice. We believe that design practice is central to effective data design.

Furthermore, a user experience that is useful, usable, and elegant—and that offers your users a consistent and reliable experience—is a critical foundation for a great business. The best way to assure you are meeting these goals is to gather data, learn from it, and iterate on your designs to enhance the elements that have a positive impact on the user experience while diminishing those that contribute to a negative user experience. A data-aware approach to design enables you to be more systematic and more ambitious about your design and product development process, helps you understand how to determine different user types and their needs and expectations, and effectively relates your design work to your business goals and metrics.

Many of you already have a design process that you are comfortable using on a regular basis. In the upcoming chapters, we want to show you how data can easily fit with and help augment your existing design process. We want to reiterate that experimentation is a *mindset*. It's iterative, just like your existing design process, and encourages you to constantly focus on improvement by questioning your assumptions about your users and your design, which you do by seeking out evidence about how your work performs in the world. Taking an experimentation mindset lets you challenge those assumptions to see which ones hold up, and which ones need to be revised for your further work. We hope that the framework and toolkit we introduce in this and the subsequent chapters helps get you excited about applying this lens and mindset to your future work.

Introducing Our Framework

In the previous chapter, we introduced you to a formal definition of experimentation. If we start to think about what we do as designers as being synonymous with experimentation, we'll find that working with data will require just a few small shifts in mindset from the normal approach. We focus on "experimentation" in this book because we think it's an important construct for designers working with data. However, we hope that our focus on experimentation generalizes to our belief that it is possible to be disciplined in your usage of data without restricting your freedom.

In fact, there is a lot of flexibility introduced when you think broadly about what the goal of an experiment is. Experimentation implies that you are not sure of your outcomes. You could be exploring ideas and evaluating them. Experiments might be big or small. Similarly, the framework that we introduce isn't meant to be a "one size fits all" structure that you must memorize and follow precisely.

Experimentation is an activity that you participate in for the purpose of learning or discovering something. In this book we are mostly focused on cause-and-effect relationships between the experiences you design and the impact they have on your user behavior. Experimentation lets you test an idea about that relationship by seeking evidence that supports or disproves that idea. So like any activity, you can improve at it through practice and by expanding your knowledge.

Although we've chosen to focus on A/B testing here, this experimentation framework and general approach to working with data should be extendable to other methodologies that leverage data as well, not just A/B testing. Working with data is simply a systematic way to be thoughtful about how you are generating and capturing the insights that help you learn more about what works or doesn't work for your customers. We're sure you can imagine how being systematic about data collection could apply to surveys, interviews, diary studies, or other research methodologies as well.

With this in mind, we wanted to introduce you to a slimmed-down version of the experimentation framework that we'll use in the next three chapters. Each of these components may in practice have many substeps but here, our goal is only to highlight the general roadmap of an experiment. At the basis of the framework is the flow shown in Figure 3-1 and described here:

1. First you define a *goal* that you want to achieve; usually this is something that is directly tied to the success of your business. Note that you might also articulate this goal as an ideal user experience that you want to provide. This is because it's often the case that you believe that delivering that ideal experience will ultimately lead to business success.

2. You'll then identify an area of focus for achieving that goal, either by addressing a *problem* that you want to solve for your users or by finding an *opportunity area* to offer your users something that didn't exist before or is a new way of satisfying their needs.

3. After that, you'll create a *hypothesis statement*, which is a structured way of describing the belief about your users and product that you want to test. You may pursue one hypothesis or many concurrently.

4. Next, you'll create your *test* by designing the actual experience that represents your idea. You'll run your test by launching the experience to a subset of your users.

5. Finally, you'll end by getting the reaction to your test from your users and doing analysis on the *results* that you get. You'll take these results and make decisions about what to do next.

Data should be used throughout and at every step of the way in this process. We encourage you to think about what kind of data can be brought into the process to help you along the way (shown in blue in Figure 3-1) and what kind of data might result from the process (shown in orange). As we noted in Chapter 2, it's important to keep in mind that data can come in many forms, be derived from many different activities and sources, and fulfill many different kinds of purposes. You could say that this captures the minimum components of an experiment.

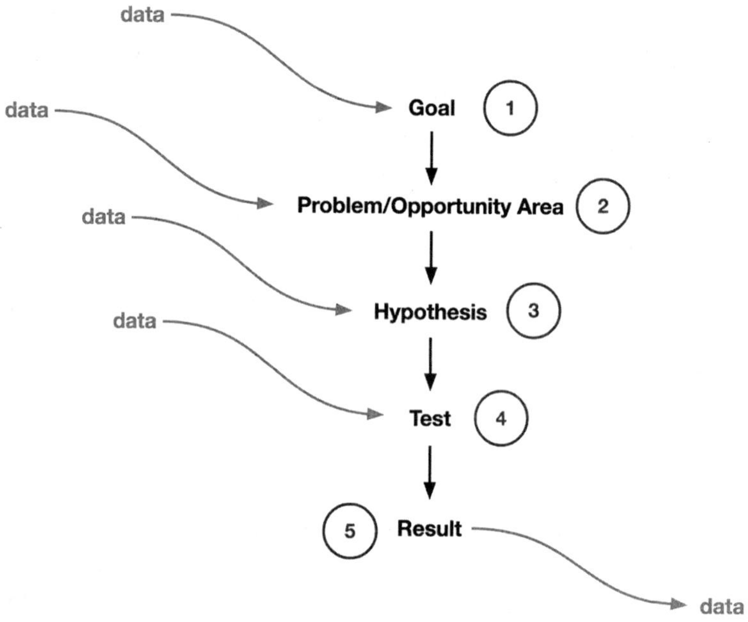

FIGURE 3-1.
Data can flow into all the stages of your experimental design, test launch, and analysis process.

For us, this whole chain of activity is part of the design process. The act of "design" goes beyond defining what your test experience *looks* like; it's also articulating a clear goal, coming up with the structure of your test (as captured by the hypothesis), and then participating in the analysis of your results to make sure you can apply what you've learned to future design work.

WORKING WITH DATA SHOULD FEEL FAMILIAR...

We wanted to show how working with data might be similar to your existing design process. One example of a commonly used design framework is the "double diamond" introduced by the Design Council in the UK in 2005. Fundamentally, the double diamond is about exploring broadly before narrowing down to either the problem definition or the final design that you will be launching to your users. Other design processes are similar: most designers are encouraged to iterate a lot and explore many ideas or solutions to a problem they're designing for. It is this notion of *going broad* and keeping an open mind as you explore which we want to highlight.

In a data aware design process, you should always be thinking about the volume of ideas or potential solutions you are generating, the variation between those ideas or solutions, and how you can learn the most about them. However, unlike the double diamond, which implies that you are narrowing down to a single problem definition or to a single solution at the end of your exploratory process, we want to introduce you to an experimentation framework with the goals of generating and articulating multiple solutions that you can test and learn from along the way. One of the places where working with data truly exercises your creative muscles is in being able to generate multiple divergent perspectives and solutions, to learn from the strengths and weaknesses of these different approaches you might take.

In Figure 3-2 we illustrate what this might look like if you were to take our basic framework (outlined in Figure 3-1) and simply "go broad" with it—identifying multiple problem areas/opportunities, generating multiple hypotheses, and then creating multiple tests for each one. So if you were just focusing on volume and variety, you might get a process that branches out to many possible experiments.

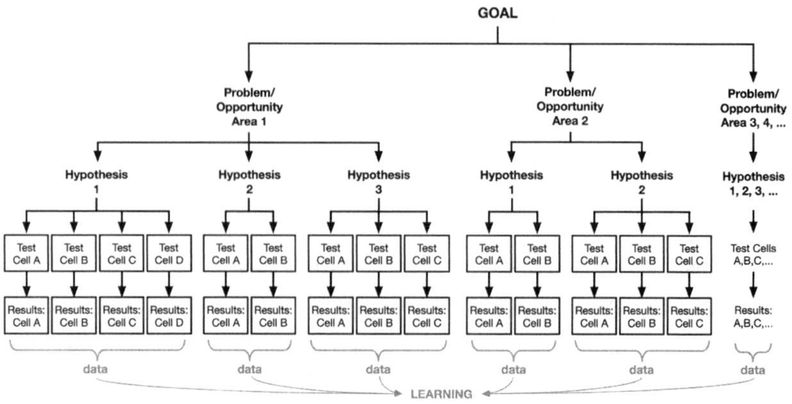

FIGURE 3-2.
Identifying multiple problem areas with multiple hypotheses and multiple tests.

We recognize that it's not always practical to generate and launch every possible solution to your users. It can be challenging to keep track of so many concurrent experiments, which may introduce the risk of bias, for instance, if a user ends up in multiple test cells at the same time. And every experiment comes with the cost of designing and launching a test to your users, which takes time and energy. Data used intelligently throughout your design process can help inspire new experiments, but also slim down and evaluate your ideas into experiments that might be worth pursuing. This ensures that you're running meaningful learning tests rather than relying on A/B testing as a "crutch"—that is, where you to stop thinking carefully and critically about your overarching goal(s) and run tests blindly, just because you can. Unfortunately, this is a pitfall that we have seen some teams fall into.

For example, after you've generated a number of hypotheses, you might be able to gather additional data by using other methodologies to help you prioritize where you want to focus your efforts. You might also find more evidence from the results of prior experiments that also helps you to refine, change, or eliminate some of the ideas you were considering. Therefore, by leveraging data and insights at every step in this process (shown in blue in Figure 3-3) and taking into consideration how and what you are trying to learn, you might find that you're able to eliminate some of the possible paths you were considering earlier in the process (shown in red in Figure 3-3). We'll discuss this in more depth in Chapter 4.

As we pointed out in Chapter 2, you will get different kinds of insights from different sources of data. Every form of data tells a different story, so it's important to collect varying types of data and triangulate what they might mean with each other. While we won't be comprehensive in our coverage of the other kinds of data-gathering methods, it's ultimately important that you find the questions, methods, metrics, measures, and analytic techniques that work best for your context and your needs. We hope that our deep dive into using A/B testing as a way to integrate data in the design process will help to demonstrate how you could employ similar techniques with other forms of data as well.

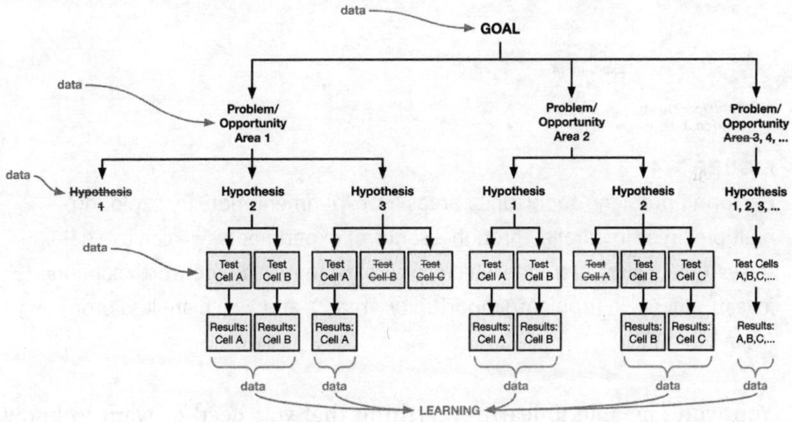

FIGURE 3-3.
Explore your multiple hypotheses and tests, and eliminate less promising paths using data.

Finally, one of the things we want to emphasize is that because we are talking about creating a mindset of continual learning it's also important for you to not just think about each experiment that you are conducting in isolation, but rather to think about the series of experiments you might run to learn about your customers over time. Figure 3-4 illustrates what we mean here.

You might be able to explore multiple problem/opportunity areas at the same time. As you explore each of these, the data that results from each experiment should continuously feed in new information to learn honestly about what is working and what isn't working to inform the experiments that follow. Along the way, you'll learn that some of these problem/opportunity areas aren't worth exploring further (as shown with Area 1 and 3 in Figure 3-4) and that some have great potential (as shown with Area 2).

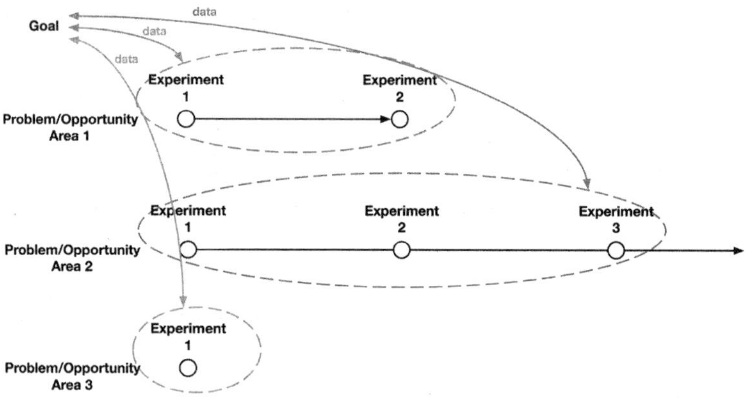

FIGURE 3-4.

Exploring problem/opportunity areas for experimentation. By exploring multiple areas in parallel through a series of experiments, we can use data to systematically determine which areas have merit and are worth continued investment (as in Problem/Opportunity Area 2), and which are less promising (as in 1 and 3).

You won't be able to learn everything that you need or want to know about your customers in one experiment. Being aware of how everything you're learning about your users is related, and how what you are learning contributes to a larger body of knowledge about them, is also useful. As part of adopting a learning mindset, you should think not only about honing your own instinct about your users, but also about sharpening the instinct of others at your company. We believe that a culture that supports learning, being challenged, failing, and ultimately gaining a more complete and accurate picture of their users will be most successful at leveraging data in meaningful ways, and therefore most successful at building useful, usable, and elegant experiences. We'll provide some concrete tips about how to create this organizational culture in Chapter 7.

Three Phases: Definition, Execution, and Analysis

Let's return to our summer camp metaphor. As we've established in Chapter 1, you're thinking of making enhancements to your summer camp experience so that you can ultimately improve your business. You've decided to take an experimental approach to find the best way to achieve your goal.

There are many different experiments you could run to achieve this goal, but first you'd need to get a little more precise about what your goal is. You'll have to *define* your goal and how you plan to measure your progress to it more clearly. First, are you interested in making more money from your summer camp or are you interested in building up the reputation of your camp? If you decide that you're going to focus on making more money from your camp, there are a couple of ways you could get there. Are you looking to make more money by increasing the number of campers at your summer camp? Do you want to instead focus on keeping the same number of campers but possibly charge more money per camper? Could you do this by adding more bespoke activities (nighttime kayaking, for example) that you could charge more for? Each of these paths that you could take will have different pros and cons. You'll need to weigh the importance of different factors into your decision about which path to take. What decisions will give the best outcome for your campers? For your business?

Once you decide which things to test for your summer camp, you'll then get to try some of those ideas out by *executing* against them using real campers. And, once you've set up a few experiments, you'll be able to start *analyzing* those results. You might learn things along the way, both about the ideas you test (it's actually pretty hard to navigate your kayak at night when you don't have a full moon) and about your campers (even though they say they're interested in nighttime kayaking, it turns out that they'd rather sleep or relax at the campfire). As you decide what you'll ultimately put into place, you'll be juggling all of these factors in your mind and might want to make adjustments along the way.

Thinking ahead of time and having a good overview of the different things you might try and the different factors that might affect your outcomes will help to keep you focused and on track as you work through your experimentation framework.

To get a little more concrete about the experimentation framework and how to apply it in practice, we'll break it up into three phases: definition, execution, and analysis. We'll dedicate a chapter to each phase and use examples throughout to help illustrate the concepts that we introduce. For now, we'll just give you a brief overview of each phase so that you know what to expect in the coming chapters and have a sense of the overarching structure of the framework.

THE DEFINITION PHASE

In Chapter 4, we focus on defining what it is that you want to learn. We again emphasize the idea of crafting a well-formed hypothesis, and expand on the process of setting measurable goals in the context of your business and the scope of what you want to accomplish. Here, we cover how to articulate your ideas and goals as well-formed hypotheses that capture the "why" and "what" of your test and what you ultimately hope to learn. Once you've developed a set of hypotheses that you want to test and learn from, we'll talk about how you might narrow them down to one or several hypotheses that you'll then design for and test "in the wild."

Because we believe that careful planning is an important part of experimentation, this phase is really about thoughtfully capturing what it is you want learn so that you can be more effective and efficient in the execution and analysis phases. Figure 3-5 shows the parts of the experimentation framework that we'll cover in Chapter 4.

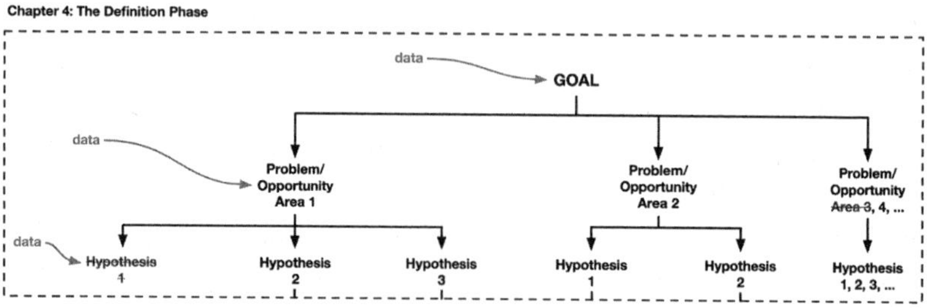

FIGURE 3-5.
Planning your experiment(s) to address your goal(s) by identifying problem and opportunity areas, and defining hypotheses.

THE EXECUTION PHASE

In Chapter 5, we get into the designing and building of your experiments so that you can maximize what you learn from your experiments. Now that you have just one or a few hypotheses that you are focusing on, we'll talk about how you'll want to make sure that the experience you design reflects your hypothesis. We'll also speak to the importance of having several design expressions or experiences for each hypothesis. We call each of these a *test cell*. This is the phase where you really get to practice the craft of design. We'll also talk about developing a designing-to-learn mindset and then how to select which test cells or experiences you'll ultimately want to launch to your audience. Figure 3-6 shows the parts of the experimentation framework that we'll cover in this chapter.

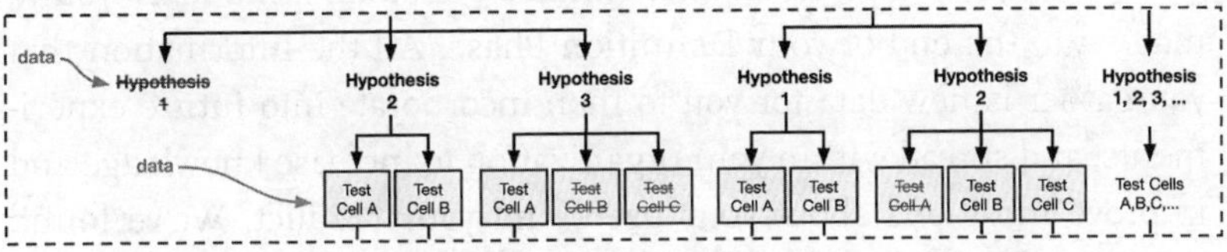

FIGURE 3-6.
Design your test cells, which are the treatments of your hypothesis or hypotheses that you want to launch to your users.

Although you're doing most of the design craft work in the Execution Phase, we deliberately choose not to call this the "Design Phase" because we wanted to be clear that as a designer you should be involved and active in all three phases. Designing an experiment is still design, and we believe that designers bring a unique perspective to each phase, which makes your input both necessary and invaluable.

THE ANALYSIS PHASE

Finally, in Chapter 6, we'll cover what you should be thinking about when launching your experiments to your users. With A/B testing, this is the first time that your users will be experiencing your ideas through your experiment. We'll then cover how to decide on your next steps once you've gotten your results and a few different common situations that you might encounter. We'll highlight a few pitfalls that you will want to avoid. The important thing to remember about this phase is that you want to make sure that you really learned what you set out to learn in the Definition Phase. The sections of our experimentation framework that we'll cover in this chapter are shown in Figure 3-7.

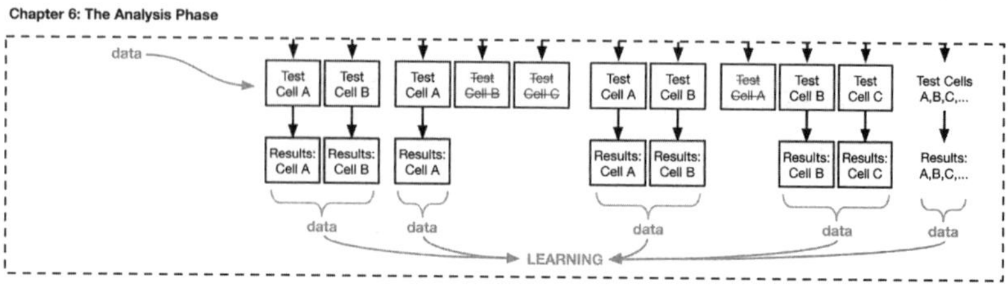

FIGURE 3-7.

Getting back results and learning from your experiment. These learnings are the basis of product decisions and future experiments.

Of course, your experimentation mindset shouldn't end after you've made it to the end of your Definition Phase. All the information that you gather is new data for you to then incorporate into future experiments, and spread within your organization to increase knowledge and improve intuitions about your users and your product. We've found that adopting this mindset can fuel increased creativity and curiosity to keep learning and experimenting. We hope that by the time you've run through one or a few experiments, you'll always be inspired by new questions and new things to learn as you wrap up the Analysis Phase.

Examples: Data and Design in Action

What we shared with you in this chapter might feel very structured. As we close out this chapter, we thought it would be nice to hear a real-world overview of how data and design work with each other throughout the development process at Airbnb and Etsy.

Katie Dill is the Director of Experience Design at Airbnb, where she oversees the designers that are responsible for defining Airbnb's digital products and services. Airbnb is widely recognized as a design leader that is especially thoughtful in their use of data when crafting their customer experiences. We thought it would be useful to share her anecdote, as it shows how you will ultimately need several forms of data throughout your design and development process. As we've tried to note throughout this book, it's important that you don't look at A/B testing as the sole method that you use in your design process. Katie starts by telling us how the team identifies the problem that they are going to address:

There are countless ways to learn about opportunities to improve products, including anecdotes directly from users, qualitative research interviews, and customer service FAQs. But it is data science that really helps us understand where the big opportunities for improvement are. Data showing the way people are using the product and purchase history can show us when and where there are recurring issues and negative trends. For example, we can look at our data and see that there are certain homes on our site that rarely get booked. We can then compare their characteristics and history to other homes to see where the issues might be. This can give us a hypothesis about the issue, but it's often not the whole story. We'll complement this insight with qualitative research to better understand the human behavior behind the issue. Quantitative data is very good at showing the what and where of the issue, but qualitative is often better at uncovering the why.

Based on our insights from qualitative and quantitative data, we'll develop product solutions. Design, user research, and data science continue to collaborate throughout the product design and development process. In the beginning the qualitative user research is foundational and helps us understand the problem. Once we have something on paper the nature of the research becomes more evaluative as we seek to understand users' reactions.

As the solution takes shape, it's time to discuss the testing strategy. If the team is really thoughtful about their rollout strategy, they are having conversations about where they want to be in the long run, and the steps they're going to take to get there. For example, the end solution might incorporate five new features. If they roll out all at once and there is an issue, they may not know where the issue is. Instead, they can choose to roll out each feature separately so they can study the effect of the feature in comparison to the old version of the product with clean data. Starting this conversation early helps us in our design process. If we know we're going to launch things separately, we might design them differently so the product feels complete even when it's delivered in pieces. That's pretty powerful, as it helps us be more efficient while still delivering a great user experience. These early conversations also help data science and engineering prepare for the things they will eventually measure in the new solution. For example, we might need to build tooling to take the measurements of interest, and we might need to start measuring certain things now with the current product in order to establish a baseline.

> By the time we're ready to launch a feature, we have a good understanding of what we're going to measure, for how long, and what success looks like. An in-house dashboard—an experiment framework—shows us all the metrics we're tracking across the product. There we can see what things are going up and what things are going down both in and outside the feature (e.g., number of users, clicks, purchases, etc.). This is important as the new feature may have unintended effects elsewhere in the product and we need to have a comprehensive view of the results. After the feature has run for long enough to gather meaningful data, we assess the results and make a judgment call as to the success or failure of the experiment. Typically, the rule of thumb is that if it achieves its goals and has a positive or neutral affect on all other key metrics, we keep it. And if it fails to meet its goals or has negative repercussions elsewhere, we'll roll the experiment back and remove the feature. However, there are times when a feature may have negative effects on our metrics, but we decide to keep it due to other benefits to the user experience and/or long-term plans.

Dan McKinley, formerly of Etsy, also shared a lovely example of how iterative A/B testing can fit nicely alongside a large piece of product work, such as a redesign of a page. His story illustrates well how a project might take a global approach at one point in time and then shift to a more local approach. He said:

> I think the best test and product release that we ever did at Etsy was redesigning our listing page. Etsy's listing page is super important. It's a really complicated page with a lot of edge cases. It has to work in many languages for many different kinds of items. Because it's so complicated, redesigning the whole thing is not the kind of thing that we could just iteratively get to, it would have been a thousand steps.
>
> So we designed the process in two phases. We said "OK, we're going to spend until July trying big changes to find one that's close. And after that, we're going to hopefully have a release candidate and we're going to do optimization on that."
>
> The first phase was to do some big redesigns of the page, and we spent the first half of the year doing big changes. To see if we got a variant that we're happy with and was even remotely close in terms of performance to what we had. We felt like we could devote 5% of traffic to a new variant without making people too angry. So that's what we did. We did 2 week iterations from January until July, trying all sorts

> of different things. We eventually found one which looks very close to what Etsy's listing page looks like today. Its performance was pretty close, but slightly worse than the existing listing page. So we said "OK, we're going to take that one and we're going to try and optimize it until it's better."
>
> We did that between July and October. We used optimization tactics as much smaller A/B tests on that variant until we felt like we could release it. When we were finally out of time for the year, we had a variant that was 5% better in terms of conversions on the existing listing page. At the time, it was like 50 million dollars. So that was the best release we ever did measure by the monetary yardstick.
>
> I think it was also the best product work we ever did. It was blending many different disciplines. So when we were doing the first phase, we were blending user feedback and qualitative research to try and figure out like why one would be better than the other. We got the release candidate and then we did A/B testing to get to the final thing.

As we conclude this chapter, we hope that these two examples have provided motivation for how powerful it can be to make data an essential part of the design process. In the next several chapters, we'll provide a greater look into how to build and apply these practices to your own design work.

Summary

Because Chapters 4, 5, and 6 are more focused on practical application, it's important to remember your business and experience goals, what you are designing for, and why you are testing at all. The aim of these chapters is to recognize that the main goal of gathering, analyzing, and contemplating all this data is to grasp a better understanding of your users so that you can learn to continually build better and more effective solutions for them. Adopting a data-aware approach to your design work and embracing an experimentation framework to structure your design process is fundamentally about adopting a learning mindset to your work. It is about becoming comfortable with testing your ideas and seeing if what you create has the effect or effects you expected. Even if the outcome in reality is different from your beliefs or expectations, adopting a learning mindset means you will capture and keep what you've learned for future work.

It is important to note that working with data as part of the design process is equal parts "art", "craft," and "science." Designing tests and interpreting results is not strictly science—it relies on the art and craft of applying science to the task of identifying and addressing important business and experience questions. We want to give you a flavor for how A/B tests play into a bigger program of research, and how determining which test to do, when to do it, how to execute it, and how to interpret results is a design problem, not simply an engineered solution to business questions. We hope that the next few chapters can help you understand how to balance art, craft, and science and translate those into actionable and informative A/B tests.

Questions to Ask Yourself

- What are some of the experiments that you would like to run?
- Are there areas of user behavior you have addressed using other methods in the past (e.g., user interviews) that you think could be further understood by designing an experiment?
- How much do you currently explicitly focus on the act of learning?
- What sources of data do you have at your disposal to help you identify goals, problem/opportunity areas and potential hypotheses?

[4]

The Definition Phase (How to Frame Your Experiments)

Now that you have the basics down, it's time to put them into action beginning in this chapter. Using the framework introduced in Chapter 3, we'll begin to flesh out each step in the process of designing an A/B test, and explain how the early and close involvement of designers is necessary to your team's success. We'll be discussing the activities shown in Figure 4-1 that are outlined in a dotted line. Throughout, we'll revisit some of the common themes we highlighted in the Preface and Chapter 1.

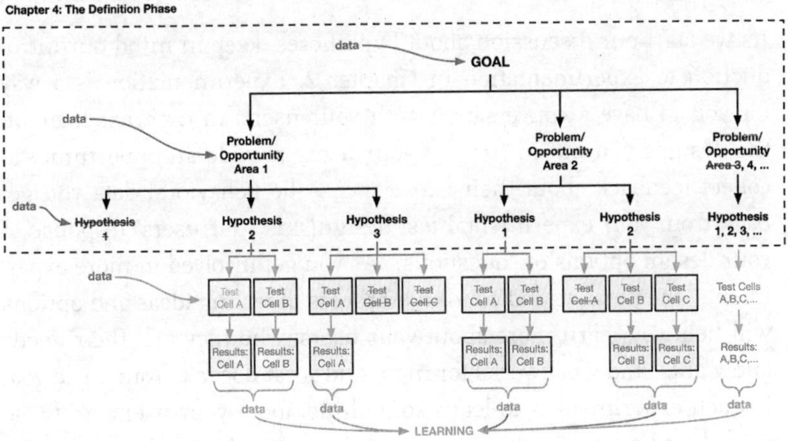

FIGURE 4-1.
"The Definition Phase" of our experimentation framework is where you frame the goal of your experiment and the hypotheses that you are interested in testing.

Taking a data-aware approach to design requires approaching your work with an open-minded attitude toward learning as much as you can about your users and which designs resonate with them. Adopting an approach of experimentation, and using data to explore and evaluate your ideas, will make you a better designer overall.

We're going to spend the bulk of this chapter laying out how you can define your goals, problems, and hypotheses to maximize your learning when designing with data. Recall that a hypothesis is a statement that captures the impact you believe your design will have on your users. In this chapter, we'll show you how to craft a strong hypothesis and how to "go broad" by generating as many hypotheses as possible. Then we'll discuss how to narrow down to one or a few hypotheses to focus on. You should revisit our discussion from Chapter 2 about how to formulate a hypothesis before diving into this chapter, but the most important thing for you to understand is that a key part of using a data-aware framework is articulating the "why" behind your design and stating clearly your expectations regarding the ways in which your design will impact users' behaviors and sentiments. Doing so is critical to using experimentation and data analysis successfully in your design practice, because it keeps learning central to every test you create and run.

As we start our discussion about hypotheses, keep in mind our introduction to experimentation in Chapter 2. Experimentation is a way for you to have a conversation with your users; in each experiment, the designs you put in front of your users provide an opportunity to collect feedback about their experience—the behavioral data you get back from your experimental test design(s) is your users' response to your design options or "questions." As you get involved in more experiments, the iterative and continual process of testing ideas and options will help you learn more about your users: who they are, their needs and wants, and what works for them and what doesn't. Your basic goal in each experiment is to learn something about your users. You also gain the advantage of demonstrating through behavioral data that the work you are doing has business impact. Having clear strategic business and user experience goals defined will help guide and prioritize the experiments you pursue.

Getting Started: Defining Your Goal

"Without goals, and plans to reach them, you are like a ship that has set sail with no destination."

—FITZHUGH DODSON

Beginning your experiment with a clear goal in mind is the first step to maximizing the learnings you'll get from your experiments. In this section, we aim to give you some helpful tips and questions to get started thinking about your goals. However, remember that we cannot be comprehensive—every circumstance, company, and design challenge is different. In your goal definition phase, maintaining close and collaborative relationships with product managers, engineers, and other partners on your team will help apply the initial thoughts in this chapter to your particular context.

We believe that first and foremost, you should focus your energy on things you care about. Experimentation as a framework and mindset can be applied to many types of questions; however, only your own personal curiosity and a true desire to learn will make your experiments a success. We invite you to think about the following questions:

- Where do you want to spend your time and efforts making an impact?
- What do you believe is good for *your users*?

Taking time to reflect regularly on these questions will help you put your own passion and desire to learn at the center of your goals and experimentation process—and will also help you communicate your perspective more clearly to others. We'll talk more about communicating your ideas and findings to others later in the book in Chapter 7. But for now, let's continue to focus on defining your specific design-related goals in experimental terms. Defining your goals is the first step in the broader experimentation framework we introduced in Chapter 3 (Figure 4-2).

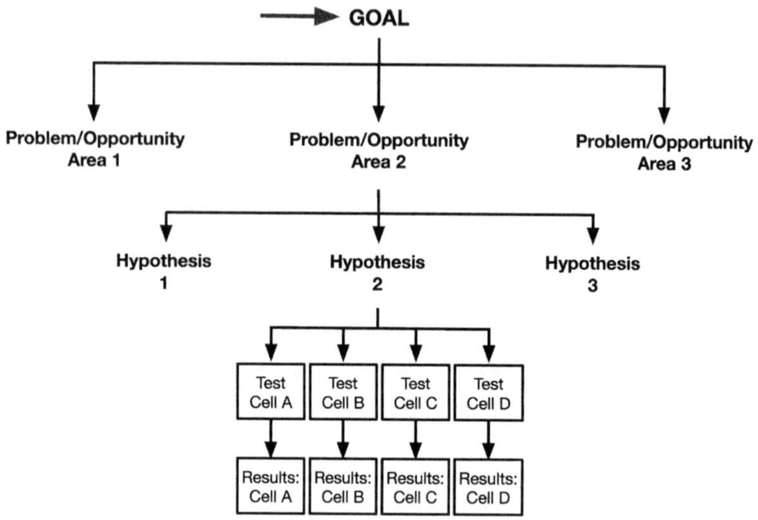

FIGURE 4-2.
Defining your goals is the first step in kicking off the framework for experimentation. Choosing goals you care about, and that make sense from an experience and business perspective, is crucial.

Beyond your own curiosity, we also encourage you to reflect on the following questions:

- What are the user and business-critical issues that get construed in your company as opportunities, or as problems and issues?
- Where are the biggest opportunities for you to improve upon your user experience?

Think about what investors, partners, colleagues, and customers value about your company and how you are currently measuring it. The best goals should articulate the impact you want to make on your product or user experience in a way that clearly ties back to your team and company's priorities.

Returning to our summer camp example, some goals are stated in terms of quantitative metrics. For instance: "I want to increase the number of campers who enroll at our camp." Other goals are more abstract or qualitative, such as: "I want to make camp more fun." Regardless of how you define your goals, you'll need a way to measure whether or not you're making progress toward them. Remember that all measurable things are rooted in human experiences, and most of the experiences you'll aim to impact are measurable in some way.

Often, a goal will have *both* qualitative and quantitative components. You shouldn't worry about classifying whether your goal is either qualitative or quantitative. For instance, think about the quantitative sign-up goal discussed before. If your goal is to increase the percentage of sign-up completions, you might also consider some of the qualities of the experience that would be important when getting more people through your sign-up process.

DEFINING YOUR METRIC OF INTEREST

Your goals should be measurable so that you can understand whether or not you're approaching or achieving them. In Chapter 2, we told you that metrics are evaluative benchmarks that meaningfully track your business's health. When defining your goals, you should also be thoughtful about choosing a *metric of interest* that tracks your progress toward those goals. We often hear designers worry that they'll become slave to metrics, and lose their ability to be creative. We want to take a moment to remind you here that designing with data is a creative process. You and your team should rally around both your metrics and your goal so that you have something to strive for. *How* you chase that goal is up to you. Making those decisions depends on design intuition and creative problem solving.

Although your company may have many metrics, you should strive to have a single *metric of interest* or each of the tests you run. This metric of interest will be how you measure the impact of a particular test. Remember that your metric of interest should be a reflection of the user behavior you're hoping to influence. To weigh in on this topic we spoke with Chris Maliwat. Chris has led product at a number of fast-growing internet companies, including Skillshare, Gilt Group, Vuze, and most recently, Warby Parker. In addition, Chris has product experience from large and established data-centric companies like Facebook, Netflix, and eBay. This means that he has broad experience across both smaller companies and established industry giants.

Chris shared an example of an experiment he ran at eBay that illustrates the importance of clearly defining your success metrics ahead of time, and then clearly relating those metrics to the user behavior you care most about. The test was about providing more information in the eBay bidding flow when there was a higher risk of the transaction being unsatisfactory for the buyer or seller. From past data, they knew that buyers were less likely to pay for their item in certain scenarios. Not all "fraudulent" transactions were malicious; for example, this could happen when a customer didn't realize that they were buying from someone in a different country, which could result in longer shipping times or higher shipping rates.

The team at eBay wanted to understand the trade-off between showing more information (and potentially adding friction to the purchasing process) and preventing "buyer's remorse," which could occur when expectations about shipping time or cost were violated. They found that showing additional information resulted in fewer total bids per item, perhaps because the additional information shown increased friction. However, their test was successful; they ultimately designed an experience that was more transparent for their customers, reducing the scenarios where buyers didn't end up paying, and ultimately increasing long-term customer satisfaction and retention by reducing "buyer's remorse."

There are a few user behaviors that eBay could have been focusing on: for instance, bidding on or purchasing items versus retention. The team was more interested in building long-lasting relationships with their users than optimizing for a single, in-the-moment, inadvertent purchase, which risked later product abandonment. The team chose metrics that aligned with this user goal, and assessed their test in relation to those metrics.

In practice, it can be a challenge to identify metrics that align with your goal. Recall that in Chapter 2 we gave an example from Coursera, and how they use proxy metrics such as test completion to anticipate one of their key metrics, credential completion. This is a great example of a practical consideration in choosing metrics: this proxy metric is necessary because credentials can take a long time to complete, and the teams at Coursera couldn't wait that long to collect data and learnings about their experiments.

Fundamentally, regardless of what metric of interest you and your team choose, a metric must always be measurable. Sometimes measuring the thing you care about can be challenging. We asked Jon Wiley of Google to tell us about how he approaches metrics that are more difficult to measure. His example of measuring "abandonment" shows how you may not be able to fully understand or capture everything you want to learn with A/B testing and it's therefore important to find other ways to get at the underlying data you seek:

> We have this notion of abandonment. Someone did a query on Google. Then, they did nothing else. They got there and they left. At the point that they abandoned, we don't know what happened.
>
> In those cases, what metric do you measure? How do you know whether they found what they were looking for? Maybe they found it on the search results page and they were happy, so they left. Or maybe they didn't think any of the results were good. Then, why didn't they refine the query? Maybe they just didn't think Google was very good at that particular query. There are a lot of questions we have at a moment like that that are very difficult for us to measure in terms of these A/B tests.
>
> We try to get at that in a couple of ways. We might bring folks into a lab and see if we can replicate what happens. We also ship surveys. You'll get a little survey in the bottom-right corner that'll ask, "Are you satisfied with these results?" We try to get some emotional or qualitative response from users and see if it matches up to the abandonment or if it measures abandonment, to try to determine what's going on here and why.

This is where a pitfall of A/B testing can emerge. Sometimes, it's impossible to measure the behaviors you care about only through the behavioral data of A/B tests. As Jon said, leaning on other forms of data is one great way to minimize or circumvent this pitfall.

Metric sensitivity

One consideration we haven't yet introduced when choosing metrics is *metric sensitivity*. Sensitivity refers to how much of a change in experience it takes to cause a change in the metric. For instance, net promoter score (NPS) is a common metric that many companies track. NPS ranges from –100 to +100 and measures the willingness of a company's customers to recommend the company's products or services to others. NPS is used as a proxy for gauging the customer's overall satisfaction with a company's product or service and the customer's loyalty to the brand, offering an alternative to customer satisfaction research. Proponents of NPS claim it is highly correlated with a company's revenue growth. However, NPS is a relatively insensitive metric—it takes a significant change in experience and a long time to change what users think about a company, and small changes like moving the placement of a button or tweaking the copy on a sign-up flow will not change such a holistic metric. It's important to select metrics that are capable of detecting and reflecting the change you're making. Otherwise, you may observe no change in your metrics even though there was a meaningful change in your user experience. For example, a copy change might actually lead to more registrations on your website, which you wouldn't know by tracking NPS.

How do you deal with these types of situations? Although you should always strive to impact business critical metrics, some of the tests you run will likely focus on specific metrics of interest that are designed to measure the particular goal you've set out to focus on. In these cases, it's essential to understand how other metrics you develop relate to, reflect, and influence your company's key metrics overall.

When your company metrics are insensitive, you may have to choose more specific or specialized metrics. We encourage you to collaborate with others, with your "data friends," to define the metric of interest that *best* tracks the causal impact of your experiment and help you measure success against your goals. As a designer, you should be involved early in the conversation about how you will define success for your projects—including helping to define metrics of interest. Defining your metrics of interest in advance will ensure that you and your teams avoid bias in the analysis of your results. When you have a clearly defined metric for design success—and therefore for business impact—against which to evaluate your test, it's harder to look for "other evidence" to call an experiment successful when it didn't actually have the desired user behavioral outcome or impact.

This speaks to a broader point about why picking the right metric of interest for your experiment is important to avoid bias. You'll want to be careful in structuring your test so that you don't judge the success of your design on a metric that "can't fail." You want your experiment to be fair. For example, let's say you decide to add a feature to your experience. During the course of assessing that feature's success, is it fairer to look at the number of clicks that it gets, or to measure the impact of adding that feature to your overall user experience (like impacting retention)? In this example, a feature will necessarily get more clicks if it exists than if it doesn't, so measuring "increased clicks" as your metric of interest will lead to an experiment that is not falsifiable. As you are defining your metric of interest, then, you should think about what you want to be different in your test group compared to your control group: Do you want these people to retain or subscribe at a higher rate? Engage with your product more frequently? It is these changes in user behavior that should be core to the metric of interest you choose to track.

Another example of this issue is when you measure the results from a self-selecting group as success. For example, let's say that you have a new feature where search rates for users who saved a song is up by 10%. If we were to claim that getting this group to increase search rates by 10% was a success, it wouldn't be quite fair. In this case, we aren't comparing two randomized samples, but rather we are reporting the effect on a self-selecting group of users—users who have saved songs have already demonstrated their engagement with your product. A better metric would have been to just look at the search rates of users with the feature versus those who do not have that feature.

Tracking multiple metrics

In many cases, making meaningful changes in your company's key metrics is a long-term game that is the result of many smaller changes. Even in those cases most companies are concerned with avoiding negative impacts to their key metrics. In practice, most A/B tests track several metrics: they make decisions about the "success" or "failure" of the test against the metric of interest, but may look to key metrics to make sure no negative change was made, and secondary metrics to gain a richer understanding of the impact of the test. *Secondary metrics* are less central to your business and experiment's success, but may still reflect important pieces of your experience or how your product is being used. Secondary metrics reveal positive side effects from improvement to the metric of interest. For example, your metric of interest may be increasing time onsite as a result of better content personalization, with a secondary metric tracking number of social recommendations made. These are great for exploring specific pieces and features or fine-tuning designs that might matter experientially without impacting your company's key metrics. Many feature teams define their own secondary metrics based on their goals; for instance, the iOS team at a social media company might measure how much content is created on iPhones. Although secondary metrics can be valuable and informative, one common pitfall we often see teams fall into is mistakenly targeting secondary metrics when they should be targeting key metrics or another metric of interest. In addition, secondary metrics are frequently targeted without teams thinking through how those metrics might impact the key metrics. If the improvement only affects a small subset of your user base or if you don't think your changes will affect important metrics, then it may not be the right place to focus your energy. Based on your particular circumstances, we encourage you to pause and confer with your team about whether exploring changes to secondary metrics is worthwhile; that is, should you invest the resources and time if you don't anticipate demonstrating a major impact on your company's key metrics?

To conclude this section, here are a few questions to ask yourself as you're thinking about which metric(s) to choose for the goal you have defined:

- If you were to ask everyone who is working on this project what the desired outcome is, what would they say?
- If you were to ask your colleagues how they expect to measure the outcome of your work, are you all in agreement? Are you all aligned?
- How are your metrics of interest related to your company goals?
- Are you focused on affecting metrics that will have a meaningful effect on your business? If you're also observing secondary metrics, what can you learn from them that you won't see in your metric of interest?

- Are the metrics you are targeting sufficiently ambitious? Are they too ambitious?
- Can you effectively measure a change in your metric within the timeframe of your project? If not, are there proxy metrics you can use instead?

These questions will help you choose appropriate metrics, in the service of measuring your progress toward your goals. Remember that in Chapter 1 we told you that one of the major benefits of using data in your design process is that it reveals the impact of design. We believe that articulating and justifying your goals in terms of your metrics of interest and company key metrics is one of the best and most empowering ways to advocate for your users when it comes time to make design and product decisions. In fact, you can think of metrics as one of the unifying languages within your company: it's one that will convey the value of your designs and your efforts to your key stakeholders and company investors most effectively. We believe that healthy and effective experimentation practices will add value to your company. Metrics therefore measure not only your success in that one experiment, but over time you'll know whether your data and experimentation practices are effective at your business in general.

To help illustrate the importance of metrics when defining goals, we'll share a few examples.

Getting the full picture

Katie Dill spoke to us about Airbnb's key metrics and how they are working to establish metrics that are reflective of the business needs and also customer happiness and quality. Because Airbnb's experience exists both online and offline, it can be harder to get a measure of the full experience. There is a transactional part of the experience where users are booking their stay online, but there is also an offline component where the "guest" and the "host" are actually interacting in real life as well:

> I'm quite proud of the fact that our company has acknowledged that while our business metrics (we use "guest arrivals") are the best classification for how successful we are, they can't be the only thing we focus on. We are now looking at quality measurements of various types, too. We're working hard to learn how they relate to each other, so we can use nights booked and quality metrics as complements to each other.

> Measurement is critical in experience design, but first we need to understand what we want to learn and what we want to accomplish so we know we're measuring the right thing. Measurement can shape your approach and cause you to focus on certain things over others. So before you settle on a metric you need to make sure it's also the one that best depicts what success is. Design can play a key role in this conversation and help ensure we're measuring what's key to a person's enjoyment and fulfillment with an experience. Over time, it's not just the purchases made on your platform, but the quality your customers experienced that will determine your success as a business and a brand.

As Katie highlights, having design involved in the conversation about what is going to be measured can be instrumental in making sure that you feel confident about what you are prioritizing in your experience and in judging whether or not it's performing.

Your metrics may change over time

To weigh in on how metrics can evolve as the business evolves, we spoke to Eric Colson. Eric is the Chief Algorithms Officer at Stitch Fix, where his team helps to redefine retail shopping using a unique personalized experience for their customers by leveraging data, personalization, and human curation. Stitch Fix sends their customers a personalized selection of clothes and accessories with every order, which they call your "Fix." As the business went from an "on demand" service to one which also offered an automatic cadence—something more akin to a subscription service model—their metrics needed to change to reflect the shift in their customers' behavior. His story also points out how a small change to the design manifested as a big insight that eventually affected their business fairly dramatically:

> Our business model was on demand; clients would schedule each shipment individually and whenever they wanted one. Early in 2012, we wanted to provide a way for clients to have a more effortless experience. So, we added the option to receive shipments automatically on a set cadence. Clients could opt in to this by checking an option box on the bottom of their account page. It was a subtle—we didn't think many would opt in; perhaps just those who loved the service so much that they didn't want to have to remember to request a shipment every month. But, to our surprise, tons of clients started ticking the box. We had underestimated the convenience automatic shipments

would provide. We later added different cadence options—every other month, quarterly, every two months, and so on. There's four cadences now and many of our customers opt in to this.

This merited a shift in how we view the success of our service. Our company was born out a transactional model. We cared about metrics relating to a successful transaction (e.g., the number of things sold, the amount of the sale, the feedback on the items, etc). But with so many clients interested in receiving shipments on an ongoing basis, we had to shift towards relationships. The outcome of each transaction/shipment is less important. What ultimately matters is the long-term relationship with the client. Are we adding enough value to her life to have her come back again and again? So we had to adjust our mindset and elevate retention to become our core-metric, rather than the transactional metrics we had focused on earlier.

Eric noted that the transition from focusing on one metric to the other took some effort for the team as well. At first, people were used to evaluating success based on which experience generated more transactions; it was very quick to see results because you could simply see how many things were purchased per shipment. The shift to retention required people to take a more long-term view when evaluating their efforts. You would have to see if customers continued to purchase from order to order and not just evaluate the experience based on a single transaction.

As an illustration of how key metrics are used to define a goal for your testing and experimentation, let's consider Netflix. Because it is a subscription-based business, one of Netflix's key metrics is retention, defined as the percentage of their customers who return month over month. Conceptually, you can imagine that someone who watches a lot of Netflix should derive a lot of value from the service and therefore be more likely to renew their subscription. In fact, the Netflix team found a very strong correlation between viewing hours and retention. So, for instance, if a user watched only one hour of Netflix per month, then they were not as likely to renew their monthly subscription as if they watched 15 hours of Netflix per month. As a result, the Netflix team used viewing hours (or content consumption) as their strongest proxy metric for retention, and many tests at Netflix had the goal of increasing the number of hours users streamed. Recalling our earlier discussion about metric sensitivity, you likely also see the parallel between Coursera's test completion metric and Netflix's viewing hours metric. Viewing hours is more sensitive and therefore easier to measure quickly.

Your company's key metrics should be aligned with your business goals. If your business goals change substantially, your metrics will change as well. As an example of how things can change over time as your business changes, consider Netflix's transition from focusing on the DVD-by-mail business to streaming. In 2011, Netflix was very clearly a DVD rental business. The key metric for Netflix was then, as it is now, retention, as defined by measuring how many customers renewed their subscription month to month. At that time, customers could add DVDs to their "queue." When they sent back a DVD that they had finished watching, the next DVD slotted in the queue would automatically be sent to them. If there were no DVDs in the queue, then nothing would be sent. Adding DVDs to the queue was an indication that customers were planning to continue using the service; receiving a DVD in the mail just a few days after returning the one that had been watched encouraged customers to continue watching movies from Netflix. The more they continued to watch movies from Netflix, the more likely they were to continue as a customer by continuing to pay their subscription each month. At that time, a common goal for testing was around encouraging customers to add DVDs to their queue, because this behavior was seen as being key to the success of the business. As Netflix changed into a streaming business, the key proxy metric for retention instead became how many hours of video people were streaming. Adding movies to a queue wasn't as important as it was in the days of DVD rentals. The proxy metric that tests aimed to shift thus changed to reflect the shift in business strategy. Likewise, the goals and metrics used to measure the success of tests also changed.

Competing metrics

In some cases, you might find that you have two teams that are working on metrics that feel like they are competing with each other. Katie Dill shared a story with us from Airbnb about how they handled a similar situation:

> We have a "List Your Space" flow where hosts can sign up and create a listing of their home. Two teams wanted to redesign this part of the product. One team wanted to improve efficiency and the conversion

of hosts signing up. Whereas another team wanted to improve the readiness and preparedness of the hosts that went through the flow. These teams' goals were potentially at odds. One team would benefit from a more concise flow resulting in more sign-ups, while the other would benefit from a more in-depth flow resulting in fewer sign-ups. To ensure both goals would be addressed, and team collisions avoided, the teams banded together. A composite team was created with product managers and designers from both teams. They used both goals as their guiding light—readiness and conversion—and in the end tracked both metrics. They needed to make sure that one metric didn't increase at the detriment of the other. It was a tough project but everyone is happy with the result that helps many hosts sign-up well prepared to host.

In Katie's example, you can see the importance of balancing metrics to deliver the best experience (e.g., host quality and host quantity have to work together). This is a good reminder for how it's important to find the right metric(s) of interest for the goal you're trying to achieve and how much those metrics might affect the behavior and incentive of the team to design the experience that can deliver those goals.

We fundamentally believe that successful businesses are built on successful user experiences. In other words, the best metrics will align well with both your users' needs and your business goals. Customers won't sign up for your service unless they believe that it has value for them. Customers won't stay with your service or use your products if they are too difficult to use or don't do what your customers want them to do. As you start to define how you will approach your goals, always ask yourself *why* you expect those approaches or solutions to positively impact your key business and experience metrics. And as you continue to learn more about your users and business through the data you get back from experiments, keep your eyes open for new metrics you could derive that are important to your business. This is where data, design principles, and business come together.

REFINING YOUR GOALS WITH DATA

As we started to show you in Chapter 3, data can be immensely useful even in the early stages of the definition phase. We really want to emphasize that data isn't only used at the end of an A/B test to see which test cell was most successful, but that it's used throughout the entire process of planning and executing your experiment. Data can be used to help inform and shape your goal and to provide you with insights into how you might go about achieving your goal via experimentation. In Figure 4-3, we show that data already plays a role even at the stage of defining your goal, even if only informally—we draw on prior assumptions and experiences to define goals.

As you consider and define your goal, think to yourself: what data do you have available to you right now? What evidence do you have about how people are currently using your product? Take stock of everything that you know about your experience currently and how users are reacting to it. Where do they get stuck? Where are their frustrations? How do your insights align with your company and business goals? If this is your first time really engaging with data, you will want to do a few things.

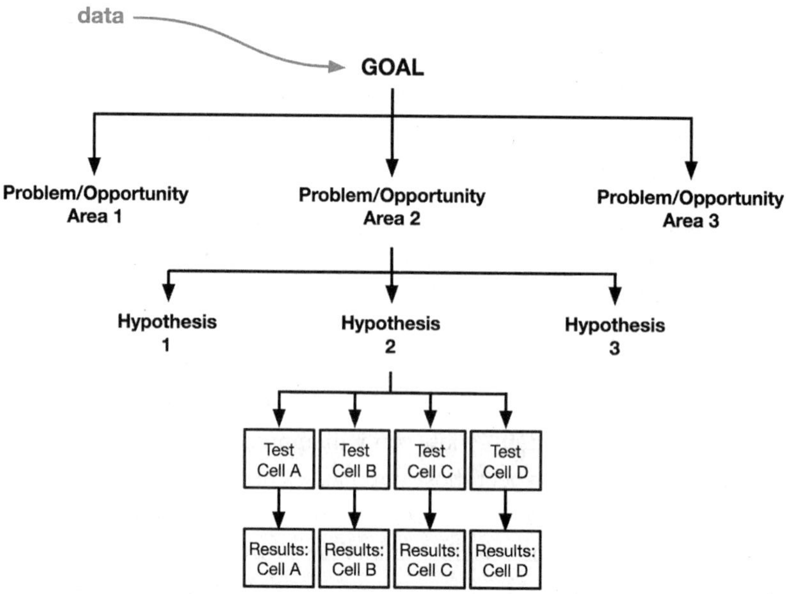

FIGURE 4-3.
Data should feed into the definition phase of your experiment, as you're defining your goals.

First, be as broad as possible about your definition of "data." As we showed in Chapter 2, data can come in many forms and be from many sources. Don't let your biases restrict the scope of the data that you consider in this phase. Being open-minded early in your process might allow you to stumble upon insights that you wouldn't have seen otherwise. Your user research, analysis, or marketing teams probably have many insights about your users that can help early in this process. Even if such teams aren't established at your company, though, there are other sources available that you might not have considered before—for example, if you have a customer support team, hearing what people are complaining about and praising is a great source of information and data.

Once you've gathered your data, remember that data has different levels of quality. So although we want you to be open-minded in collecting your data, you should be very disciplined and critical about deciding what data to leverage in making decisions. Here are some questions to ask yourself:

- Who or what does the data *represent*? Is it just from a specific segment of your user base or does it come from a sample of your users that resembles and represents the entire user base? Recall that certain kinds of data (like tweets) indicate only the happiest or the angriest of customers and experiences.
- Is it accurate? How has it been vetted for quality? Has the data been interpreted at any point, opening the possibility of bias?
- On what dimensions does the data fall? What are the strengths and limitations of that type of data?
- Was it collected recently enough to still apply to your company and business landscape today?

As we've said throughout this book, you can't think about data in isolation. Think also about how this data reflects what your users are doing and what it tells you about their behavior. What are they trying to achieve? Think hard about how human emotions, actions, and behaviors are represented in your data. By doing so, your existing data can inform the types of goals you'll pursue in your data and design process, and the types of things you hope to learn.

To summarize, here are some questions to get you started thinking about how to leverage existing data to refine your goals prior to designing and testing:

- What kind of data do you currently have access to that might give you insight into where you can make the most impact?
- How can other forms of data provide insight into where there is an opportunity to improve performance?

- What are some of your most engaged users doing? How can you encourage other users to do the same? What delights those users? Will the same things delight users you would like to attract to your service?
- Why do they do what they do and how does that behavior make them more likely to continue using your product or service?
- What do users who are most likely to convert do? What actions do they take?
- What are your users' biggest pain points? Do pain points vary across cohorts and segments of your users?
- What types of complaints do you hear in your customer service department, or through past user research?

Understanding this type of data can open your mind to possible problem areas and opportunities that will later help you to formulate different hypotheses and solutions that you might not have identified otherwise. If you don't have a lot of data available to you to help shape and inform your goal, you can also make a list of the kind of data you would like to have access to. You might find that you can invest in some user research or surveys within your company or through external agencies like UserTesting.com or UserZoom.com in order to gather some preliminary insights around your goal. Investing early and often in data will help you check your intuitions at every step of the process. The earlier you catch errors in your intuitions about your users or problems with your execution, the easier and less costly they'll be to change.

Returning to the summer camp metaphor, let's imagine that although your camp is doing well, you still have empty capacity and you want to get even more campers to enroll. You make a goal to increase the number of campers who enroll at your camp. Now that you have this goal, you want to start thinking about how you're going to get there.

Identifying the Problem You Are Solving

So, you've started thinking about a goal and how you're going to measure your success at moving toward that goal. Once you've articulated your goal, you'll have to think about how you will approach *achieving* it (Figure 4-4). Hopefully you had some data that helped you to refine your goal, and you feel excited about pursuing that goal. Right now, you don't need to know exactly how you're going to achieve that goal. However, in many cases looking at past data helps you refine your existing goal and spur some ideas about a few approaches you could take to achieving that goal (what we are labeling here as "problem/opportunity areas").

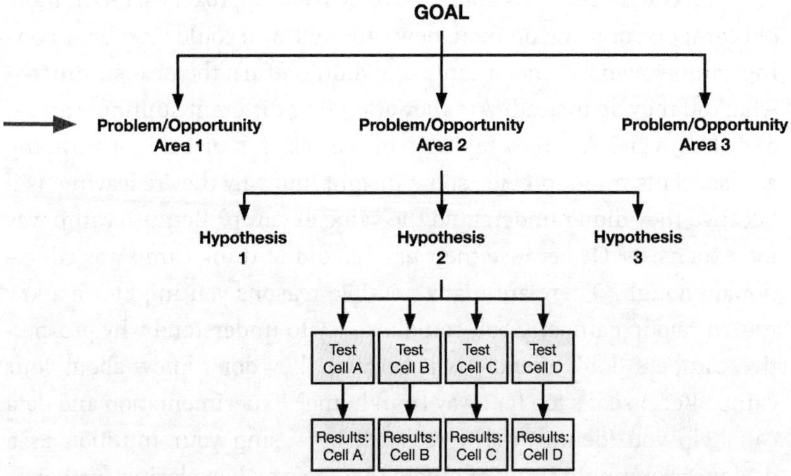

FIGURE 4-4.
Now that you have your goal, it's time to start thinking about different problems you could address or opportunities you could pursue in service of your goal.

Through analysis of the data and insights, you should be able to identify areas where there are problems that can be improved or opportunities to innovate toward your goal. For each of these areas, we can form a problem statement that explains it further and links it back to measurable criteria (usually the metric of interest you're using to measure progress toward your goal). We encourage you to take a two-pronged approach to thinking about these addressable areas, in terms of problems and opportunities:

- What are the biggest problems with your user experience that are impeding your goals? Where do users consistently have trouble? What are their biggest complaints?
- What are the biggest opportunities for you to improve your experience? What are your "power users"—those who quickly adopt and use your most advanced features—doing that might give you clues on possible opportunities?

Identifying a few problem/opportunity areas where your designs could make an impact is the first step in beginning to craft your hypothesis. For example, let's go back to the example goal of "increasing the number of campers." What might lead you to get more campers? You could break this out into two possible approaches: retain more old campers, or bring on more new campers. You could start by surveying campers who attended camp and didn't return the next summer—what did they do instead? Are they attending different summer camps, and if so, why? Are they taking summer classes instead, or traveling abroad? This might provide some insight into why they're leaving: is it because they didn't understand the value of camp? Because camp was too expensive? Or because their parents didn't think camp was educational enough? There are many possible reasons you might see a low return rate in campers. You could also try to understand why prospective campers don't attend—is it because they don't know about your camp? Because it's too far away from home? Experimentation and data can help you identify many reasons, but using your intuition as a designer you might think of others that are worth exploring further.

The following example, shared by Arianna McClain from her time working on an IDEO project focused on supermarket frozen meals, illustrates how looking at data in unexpected ways can help identify new design and business opportunities. She said:

> It was dinnertime, and my colleagues were staring into the freezer of a 48-year-old man named John. As IDEO designers, we were working with a client to develop a new line of healthy food products, and John was one of the people who had invited us into his kitchen for research.
>
> What we saw surprised us: stacked boxes of USDA certified organic, freezer aisle entrées intended for children. John was a bachelor with no kids, so why would he have kids' meals in his freezer? Simple: Because he wanted to eat healthy, and he believed that no company would make unhealthy food for kids.
>
> Why is that interesting? In data research, John represents the classic "outlier," a person who stands out from the other members of the group. From a traditional data perspective, people may by default look at measures of central tendency or how the majority of people

> behaved. However, as designers we seek these outliers. From a business perspective, outliers may provide a new design opportunity that we might not pay attention to otherwise.

The underlying principle in Arianna's comment is that looking for surprising behaviors can inspire new product directions regardless of the type of data you're using. In Arianna's words, learning from these "outliers" is a great way to inform potential opportunity areas or hypotheses to explore.

Another great example comes from Chris Maliwat, and his time at Warby Parker. Warby Parker is an eyeglass manufacturer that has both an online and offline component to their customer experience. Customers can browse frame styles online or in person in a Warby Parker showroom. Chris talked to us about how the team at Warby Parker looked at customer behavior in the retail experience and in the customer's home as a way to inspire experiences that they would then design and test online. At first, Warby Parker assumed that a customer who started in their retail store would purchase their glasses in the retail store and that a customer who started with Warby Parker online would then purchase online. They originally approached the customer experience by considering only "one channel" at a time. Instead they learned that their customers were "omni-channel" shoppers who would often go back and forth between the online and retail experience.

However, their qualitative research showed that there were certain behaviors that made their customers more successful in the retail store if they started online and vice versa. One of those behaviors was "list making." Their researchers saw that people were more likely to make a purchase if they made notes for themselves on Post-its, took screenshots that they then printed, or simply remembered the names of the frame. Chris explained that prescription glasses are a "high consideration" product where most people don't make a decision on what they want to buy right away. Chris said:

> We realized that every time we force a consumer to start over with the consideration process, it means that they have to virtually or actually go down a path that they've gone down before and remake three or four decisions they've already made. We wanted to reduce the friction, and help them pick up where they left off. We wanted to recognize

which real-life behaviors we could encourage by building features to bridge those gaps. So we made a list-making tool for people who were traversing from online to retail or from retail to online.

Looking at existing behaviors in the relationship between the online product and retail stores for Warby Parker helped the team uncover a major opportunity area: helping facilitate the decision-making process.

There is a danger in diving too deep or too quickly into problem-solving mode. By calling out "problem/opportunity areas" first, we hope to get you in the mindset of staying at the right level of thinking for this early stage in the process. Each "problem/opportunity area" should be broad enough that you might generate at least a few hypotheses to explore within it. As a designer, you may have been trained to dive into proposing and exploring potential solutions immediately. We recognize that it may be a difficult transition to resist the desire to start thinking about solutions in the form of wireframes, interaction logic, and action flows immediately. Our goal in giving you these frameworks and asking you to be explicit about your goals, problem/opportunity areas, and the scope of your project is to encourage you to remain broad and open-minded as you approach every new problem. By avoiding the common pitfall of honing in on a single solution too early, you are forced to be more creative. We believe this will push you to be a better designer, and over time help you work toward more optimal solutions for your users.

REMEMBER WHERE YOU ARE

As we close out this section, we want to remind you one more time to think about the space of design activities you might be embarking on. This is a good time to review for yourself the nature of the work you're taking on with each problem/opportunity area along the two dimensions we introduced in Chapter 2. You need to ask yourself whether your problem is of a global or local scope. Are you aiming to evaluate your ideas or explore more possibilities? In the next section, we'll begin to speak about generating hypotheses that align with the problem/opportunity areas you're thinking about. In Figure 4-5, we show that taking time to scope your problem carefully at this point will help you decide what data and hypotheses are most appropriate for the design activity you're working on, and being thoughtful at this point in the process will save you significant time later on.

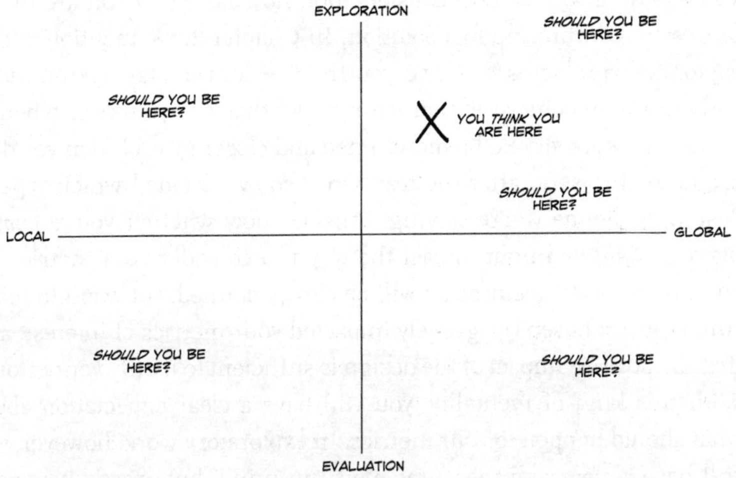

FIGURE 4-5.
Don't forget about where you are in the space of possible design activities, and think about how it might impact your approaches to data and your hypotheses.

When we talked about metrics, we expressed the idea that metrics help you measure not only your success toward your goal, but also whether your efforts were "worth it." Resource limitations and prioritization are realities at the vast majority of companies, and make it impossible to chase every idea. When you're thinking about global problems and opportunities, you may be looking to fundamentally change your approach. Deviating significantly from your existing experience requires more resources and effort than making small iterations. When you design in "unknown territories" (as you often do when working on a global scope), you can't be sure in advance whether these territories will be fruitful or not or whether there's a much better solution to be found. In these cases, you should look hard for existing data or signals that indicate that these efforts might pay off in larger metrics increases. You can think of global problems and opportunities as being more high risk and high reward than local when working on a local scope, because with local problems your proposed changes will be more similar to the existing solution. As you're scoping your problem or opportunity area, then, always consider how external sources of data can give you confidence (or counterevidence!) in support of your efforts. If you don't have signals to suggest that a global scope is worthwhile, consider whether you should be thinking about a local problem of opportunity instead.

You should also take into consideration how far along you are in the process of committing to a solution. In Chapter 2, we mentioned that exploratory problems can give you the freedom to stay open-minded without fear of being stuck launching work that isn't your best, whereas evaluatory work should be more vetted and closer to a solution you'd be proud to ship soon after the test. Once you've decided which type of design challenge you're solving, consider how whether you're *exploring* or *evaluating* might impact the way you consider your metrics. In an evaluatory test, your goals will be clearly defined: you want to make sure that you haven't negatively impacted your metrics of interest, and that the positive impact of the design is sufficient to justify your efforts. With this kind of mentality, you will have a clear expectation about what should happen to your metrics. In exploratory work, however, you still have a clear and measurable goal in mind, but exactly how your designs will lead to that impact might not yet be clear. You therefore will approach your metrics with the mindset of observing what happens (perhaps in several secondary metrics as well as your key metrics) rather than seeing if an expected change happened. These types of problems can help inspire further experiments to gain greater confidence in the phenomenon you observed.

By this point, we hope that you have a clear sense of your goals, and some ways to approach defining the different problem and opportunity areas you could consider in service of meeting those goals. Now, we'll launch into a deeper discussion about how you as a designer should be involved in crafting well-formed hypotheses.

Building Hypotheses for the Problem at Hand

In Chapter 2, we introduced the idea of a hypothesis as a testable prediction of what you think will happen to your users if you make a change to your experience. You now know that defining clear hypotheses is important to ensure that your designs express a clear intention that you can learn from. You can think of your hypothesis as a north star that helps you stay focused, guiding you toward valuable insights that will be actionable and meaningful to you as a designer, and to achieving your business goals. Having a clear hypothesis is also an essential way to keep learning at the center of your experimentation practice.

What we haven't covered yet is how to actually generate a solid hypothesis. In this section, we'll walk you through the key components of building a hypothesis. We'll also provide some secondary questions that will help you when crafting your hypothesis. You'll notice that we deliberately used language to reflect what designers are most familiar with: user behaviors and experiences. This should help to set the foundation for the way you will design your hypothesis statement and test cells, the material we cover in Chapter 5.

One way to construct a strong hypothesis is:

> For [*user group(s)*], if [*change*] then [*effect*] because [*rationale*], which will impact [*measure*].

We introduced a simpler version of this hypothesis framework in Chapter 2. Now, let's talk a little bit more about each of the components in turn.

In a hypothesis, the *user group* component indicates who you hope your change will affect. In Chapter 2, we told you about the diversity of your user base and how certain grouping strategies can help you start to understand and represent this diversity. Based on previous data, you may be focusing on your entire population of users or only a subset. Here are a few questions to get you started thinking about the user group(s) you're aiming to affect with this hypothesis:

- What do you know about them as a demographic? Their habits?
- How are you targeting these users in relation to your business?
- What relationship do they have with your company?
- Are these existing users? New users? Power users?

You'll need to do *something* different to impact the user group(s) you've defined. Recall from Chapter 2 that the *change* component is a broad statement of the types of changes you'll be making to your control (current) experience to encourage the user behavior you're aiming to impact. This doesn't have to be a perfect expression of exactly how you'll design or implement the change; rather, it should represent the change abstractly while still leaving room for you to design several possible treatments of the hypothesis. We'll discuss how to design different treatments of the same hypothesis in Chapter 5. As you're thinking about the change your design will bring about, consider the following questions:

- Are you introducing something completely new to the experience, or removing something?
- Are you changing something about the existing experience?

Your goal in making a change to your experience is to impact your user's behavior in some meaningful way. When you define the *effect*, you're explicitly articulating the *desired behavior* you hope to bring about in your user group(s). This *effect* part of your hypothesis will probably be directly related to the problem or opportunity area you already defined, since your hypothesis represents an idea you have for targeting that particular area. The effect essentially calls out the specific behavior that will help you address that. As you revisit your problem or opportunity area, think about the following:

- What was the problem you identified? What user behaviors can minimize or address this problem?
- What was the opportunity area you identified? How can you incentivize behaviors that make this opportunity a reality? What are your power users doing?

In Chapter 3 and earlier in this chapter, we discussed how data can help you identify effective problem areas and ways to address them. The *rationale* part of a hypothesis is a statement of the evidence you have to support your hypothesis, *or* the common sense reasoning why you think your proposed change would drive the desired behaviors. In other words, why do you think that the change you make will have the desired outcome? By including your rationale in your hypothesis, you're giving the reasons you believe your efforts will be justified. This is one way for you and your team to make sure you're prioritizing hypotheses that will give you the most effective learning and the best shot of a successful test. Get started by asking yourself the following questions:

- Does your rationale speak to your customers' motivations or does it leverage a tactic or mechanism to make that change?
- What kind of data have you seen to support this hypothesis and how consistent is that data?

Finally, the *measure* is the metric or metrics that you will ultimately try to impact. These describe how you will measure your success. You need to have your success metrics defined upfront, so that after you launch your tests you have an objective way to track their performance, therefore maximizing your learning. One more important note is that tracking your business success metrics is important, and the best business metrics will consider customer experience; however, you should also be thoughtful about whether you should track a qualitative measure of user sentiment as well. This is one way to triangulate your findings and ensure that your data reflects a holistic image of how your design changes affect your users. We already provided an in-depth discussion of choosing appropriate metrics (refer back to "Defining Your Metric of Interest" as well as Chapter 2), but here are a few more questions to put it into the context of hypothesis generation:

- Which metrics are you going to look at to understand if the impact you are making is the right one or big enough? How are these metrics related to the goal you've already defined, and your business's goals?
- Will you measure or factor in user sentiment, and if so, how? Will you use surveys, focus groups, and interviews?

As you continue to develop hypotheses and run more experiments, you might find that a number of these building blocks tend to be the same from hypothesis to hypothesis. For example, if you are consistently working with the same user group(s) every time, you might find it getting redundant to state the specific user group(s) in every hypothesis statement. It might occasionally make sense to create hypothesis statements that don't include every single one of these items, but we believe it's important to periodically revisit all five of these areas in the course of your work to make sure that you remain aligned with the other folks you might be working with and the larger company goals. Our opinion is that the minimal good hypothesis will include the change you're trying to make and the metric you will track to observe its effect. This is in service of holding yourself and your team accountable to your goal and knowing very concretely whether you have achieved it, which is at the core of making data-informed decisions.

EXAMPLE: A SUMMER CAMP HYPOTHESIS

Now that we've introduced each of the building blocks in depth, let's apply them to an example of a well-formed hypothesis. Let's imagine that for your summer camp, you're hoping to put to action your goal of enrolling more campers. You've noticed that historically only a small proportion of campers have come from urban areas. You wonder if offering a bus from major metropolitan cities to your camp will improve camp attendance from city children, as you believe that urban-based families are less likely to own cars than suburban-based families, making it harder for them to drop off their children at camp. You might say:

> For new potential campers from the city (*user group*), by providing free buses from major cities to camp (*change*) we will increase camp sign-ups from a previously underperforming population (*effect*) because the friction to go to camp will be lower (*rationale*). We will know this is true when we observe more urban campers at camp (*measure*).

You might want to learn whether or not providing a bus service will increase the sign-ups from potential city-based campers. You might have questions about whether different metropolitan areas will utilize the buses differently (you might expect that a two-hour bus ride from a nearby city is more appealing than an eight-hour bus ride from a city far away). You might also want to learn to what degree buses impact sign-ups to camp at all. Is the potential difficulty of simply finding transportation to camp a real reason why prospective campers might not sign up? Are there other reasons why urban interest in camp might be lower (including less comfort with the outdoor activities, less familiarity, or a higher density of city-based camps)? Considering all the different things you might want to learn, you can start to imagine how you might sequence different series of tests to build out your understanding of what works or doesn't work.

There is no strict way to formulate a hypothesis. The structure we described earlier was merely illustrative. As long as you capture the most important and relevant building blocks for your situation, your hypothesis will be clear and well formed. Here is another example of a format that might work for a hypothesis that is similar to the template that many tech companies use:

> We predict that [*doing this/building this feature/creating this experience*] for [*these people/personas*] will achieve [*these outcomes*] because of [*these reasons*]. We will know this is true when we see [*this impact to our metric of interest*].

Notice that our language is very specific here—we say "predict" rather than "believe" because while a false belief can make you wrong, a prediction can be false without any reflection on you. This is the mindset you should take when experimenting: your experiment may reveal evidence against your hypothesis or prediction(s), but *you* didn't fail in your reasoning process nor did your predictions fail. This is an important principle to remember throughout the experimentation. Though many experiments may reveal data that counter your initial intuitions or your well-formulated predictions, the outcome is a critical learning you can use to make the process of experimentation a success for you, regardless of the specific outcome.

Hypotheses can be narrow or broad. Much of this might depend on the nature of the goal you are trying to achieve and how mature your product/experience is. Here are some examples of hypotheses that different companies could pursue, based on their specific business focus and their specific offerings:

- For a photo-sharing platform a hypothesis could be: We predict that by giving all users a way to add effects and filters to their photos, more people will use our product because it makes their pictures look better and is more fun to use. We will know this is true if we observe increased user engagement with the app.
- For an online professional networking platform, a hypothesis could be: We predict that by adding a progress bar showing users how much of their profile they've filled out that more users will complete their profiles because they feel a need to accomplish the task. We will know this is true when we see a higher percentage of completed profiles in our service.

- For an online social networking platform also interested in supporting real-time communications, a hypothesis could be: By making a separate experience focused only on text messaging, we will attract more users to our messaging service because the app can be more targeted and simplified.
- For an online flight comparison service, a hypothesis could be: Because we know that users in Japan more often make a decision to purchase a flight on popularity than price, we predict that ranking flight results by popularity for users in Japan will increase user confidence in recommendations, thereby decreasing bounce rate (defined as the percentage of users who leave the website). We will know this is true when we observe a statistically significant 2% decrease in bounce rate in that market.
- For an ecommerce platform, a hypothesis could be: We predict that providing more information about shipping costs, and making that information salient through design, we will decrease unwanted orders and increase customer satisfaction.

In addition to using your own internal data, thinking more broadly about the competitive landscape of your product (including offline experiences!), your user group(s), and other trends can help you identify particular hypotheses to pursue within your target problem/opportunity areas.

Asking some of the following questions might help you as you look for ideas:

- Are there any emerging trends that could inform, affect, or change your customers' behavior in a way that you are not considering now?
- Who are your users? Do they match the users you would like to have in the future? How are they similar or different from each other? (Think back to our discussion in Chapter 2 of new versus existing users.)
- What are some of the current gaps in your product, experience, or service that you can fill?
- What are competitors or other companies in the space doing that is successful but different from your experience?

Now that we've introduced some concrete thoughts on how to go about building a hypothesis, we want to walk you through a concrete example of how this played out at Netflix.

EXAMPLE: NETFLIX—TRANSITIONING FROM DVD RENTALS TO STREAMING

As an example of creating a hypothesis, consider this example from Netflix when they were transitioning from a company that was known for its DVD rental business to one that would lead the market in video streaming. The Netflix website was divided up into several major areas—the first two tabs in the navigation were "DVD" and "Watch Instantly" (Figure 4-6). At that time, the "DVD" tab had been the first and default tab for many years. A lot of work had been done to optimize that experience for first-time use. There was a lot of testing around what behaviors were important to encourage right after the user had signed up (e.g., "Add 6 DVDs to your queue") and on welcome messaging (Figures 4-7 and 4-8). Because the "Watch Instantly" tab was not the default tab, it hadn't received the same degree of optimization.

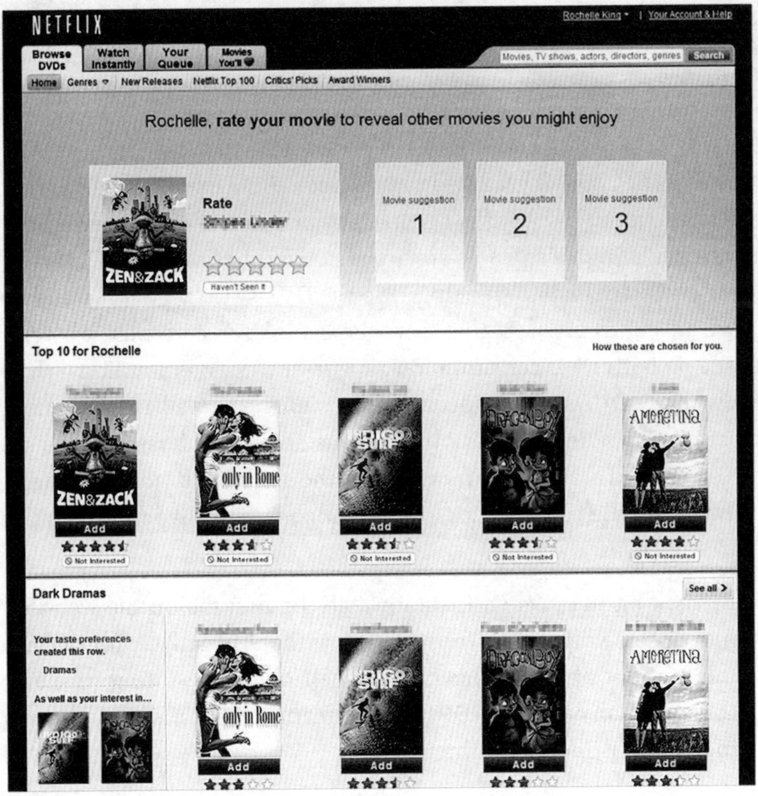

FIGURE 4-6.
"Browse DVDs" and "Watch Instantly" were the first two tabs on the Netflix web experience.

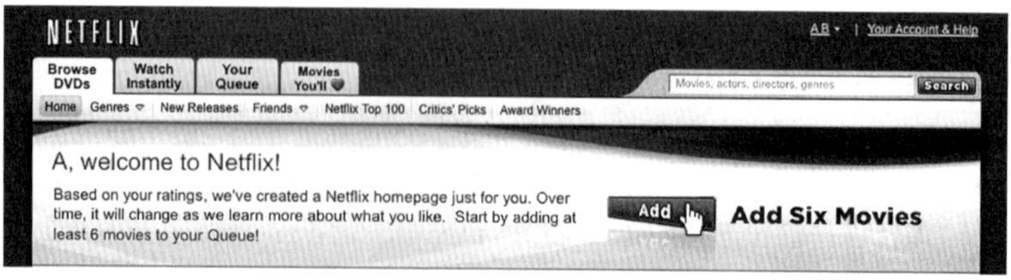

FIGURE 4-7.
Because "Browse DVDs" was always the default tab, it received a lot of optimization.

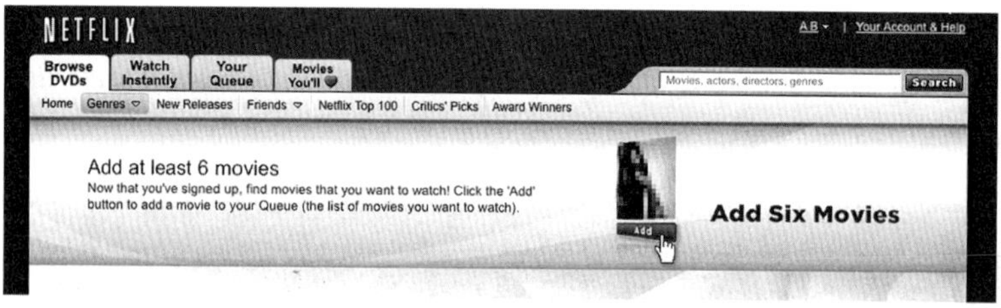

FIGURE 4-8.
Another way in which the "Browse DVDs" tab was optimized.

Given that the company wanted to understand the extent to which the tab placement could both affect people's impression of the company and the number of movies people streamed, a hypothesis was put forward to change the first tab from being "Browse DVDs" to "Watch Instantly" (shown in Figure 4-9). At that time the company's core metrics were focused on both DVD consumption and streaming consumption—that is, how many DVDs were added to a user's queue as well as how much they streamed. The belief was that because the DVD business was so well established at the time, moving it to the second tab would not negatively impact the core metrics for the company. This hypothesis could be formulated as:

> By making the "Watch Instantly" tab the first tab on the website, more users will stream from Netflix without negatively impacting the number of DVDs they add to their queue, resulting in more consumption of Netflix (DVDs and streaming) because the streaming option is more prominent.

Though we are focused simply on creating hypotheses in this chapter, it's worth sharing the results of this test with you now. In this case, the hypothesis performed well enough that Netflix was able to keep "Watch Instantly" as the first tab. It increased streaming hours, allowing Netflix to start reaping the benefits of making a bold move toward a streaming value proposition despite not having optimized the streaming service as much as the DVD service at that point in time.

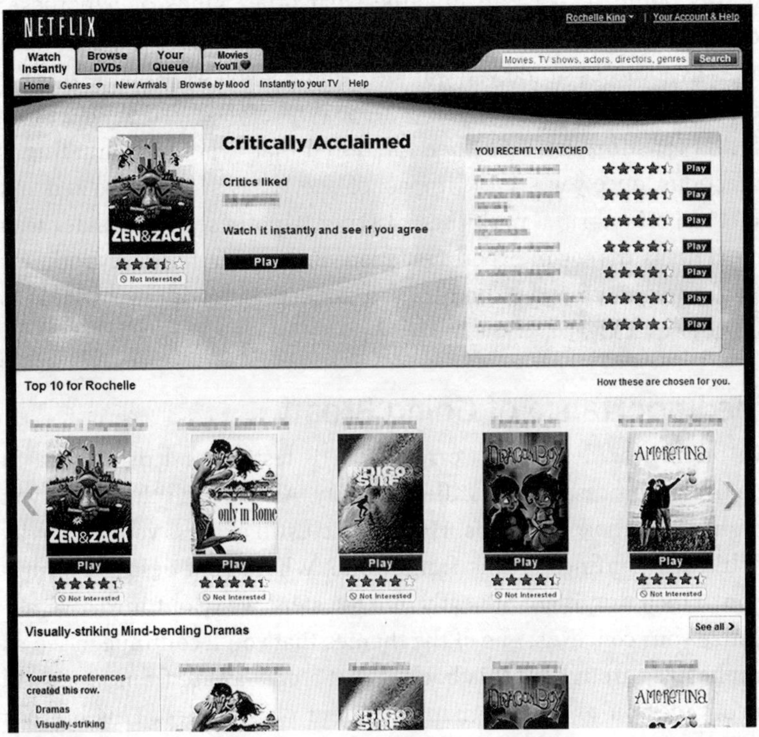

FIGURE 4-9.
After their A/B test, the Netflix team decided to put "Watch Instantly" as the first tab.

Having this data confirmed that they could move forward without negatively impacting the business and this allowed Netflix to move faster on a large, strategic decision than they might have otherwise. Now, though the overall results were positive on the test cell with the Watch Instantly tab first, it's hard to pinpoint whether or not there were any negative effects because that treatment didn't have any optimization for first-time messaging. It's hard to know, but we can conclusively state that putting the "Watch Instantly" tab first moved metrics in the desired direction. Knowing how unlikely it is that you crafted the best experience and design with your first go, it's a fair bet to conclude that further iterations could only improve the streaming numbers even more.

At this point, it's easy to imagine what other kinds of hypotheses could be crafted, knowing that first hypothesis tested well. What other hypotheses would you want to explore if you were on the team at Netflix and wanted to find more ways to impact your goal of increasing Netflix consumption? We hope you'll find that hypothesis building is infectious: once you see the impact of one, it's easy to get excited and start to brainstorm a multitude of other hypotheses to consider testing. This is the joy of experimentation. Because building hypotheses is lightweight, creative, and fun, you can come up with many ideas to consider quickly.

The Importance of Going Broad

We often hear designers worry that A/B testing and using data in the design process might stifle creativity. As you read this book, you might share those concerns. How can you still express your creativity within the confines of this framework? What about designer's intuition, which might not fit neatly into the steps we've outlined? We recognize your concerns; one of the themes that you'll continue to see us emphasize throughout this book is that a data-aware framework will encourage you to explore many different possibilities. This breadth is the ultimate way to bring creativity to your process, and encourage others on your team to get onboard with this creative approach to design and problem solving.

Up until now, we've shown how you can use data to identify your goals and understand the nature of your problem/opportunity area. We've also talked about how to structure and craft a hypothesis statement. So although the process we have covered so far looks something like Figure 4-10, where a problem/opportunity area lends itself to a single hypothesis, in actuality it's more like Figure 4-11, where there may be multiple hypotheses that address the same problem or opportunity area. In this section, we'll talk about how to go broad in your generation of hypotheses.

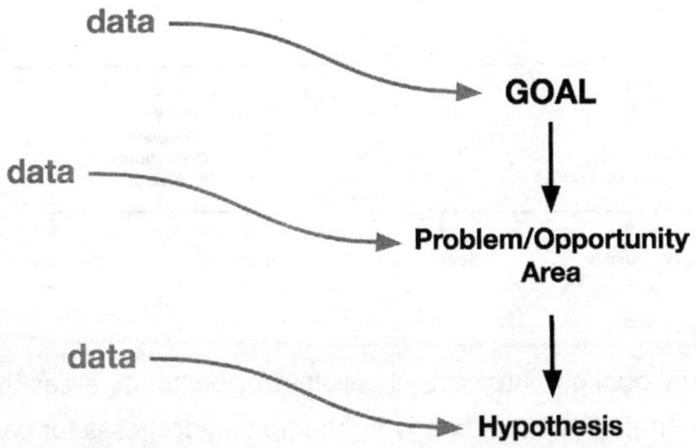

FIGURE 4-10.
Generating a hypothesis based on a problem/opportunity area to address a specific goal.

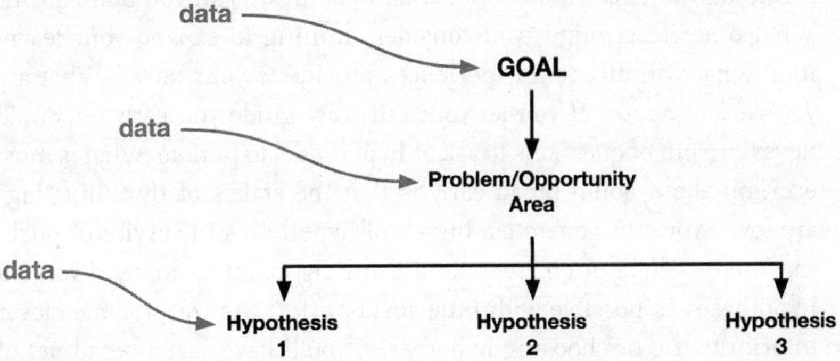

FIGURE 4-11.
Generating multiple hypotheses for a problem/opportunity area to address a specific goal.

As part of ensuring that you are constantly learning from your designs, we believe that generating a large variety of different hypotheses prior to designing forces you and your team to be more creative. This will force you to think about very different ways to solve your problem, and therefore help you to generate a greater diversity of solutions. In fact, you could have also identified a number of problem/

opportunity areas that might each generate more hypotheses, so Figure 4-12 could be a more accurate representation of the way we'd want you to work with data.

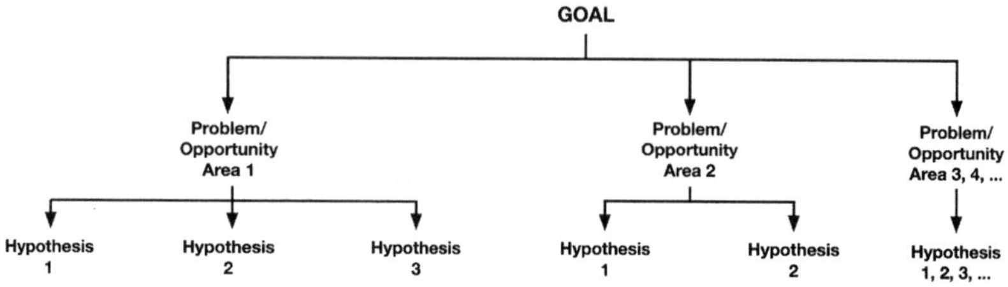

FIGURE 4-12.
Breaking a key goal out into several problem/opportunity areas that could have impact on that goal, and deriving multiple hypotheses for each.

As a designer, you're probably already familiar with this kind of "going broad" process. Brainstorming and exploring many divergent designs is common in design practice. We want you to do the same thing in the framework of experimentation: what hypotheses can you brainstorm? What other tests might you consider running to expand your learning? What will different experiences provide to your users? What are you *curious* about? If you let your curiosity guide you early on, you'll never run out of questions to ask or hypotheses to pursue. What is most exciting about going broad early is that the stakes of thinking "big" are low—you can generate a bunch of hypotheses in service of pushing the envelope of creativity and thinking about as many divergent hypotheses as possible with little cost or effort. As you become closer to prioritizing or choosing hypotheses, you'll have cast a broad net of ideas letting you and your team make thoughtful choices about the best hypotheses to further pursue.

Notably, though we've reiterated the importance of allowing data to feed into your hypothesis generation, it is important to remember that this is *in service of being data first* but not *data only*. Design intuition is a powerful tool for generating hypotheses in unexplored territory; this is especially the case where there may not be strong evidence for which hypotheses are the most critical to test. At the hypothesis generation phase, you need not weed out these hypotheses. They are worth noting and considering alongside other data-backed hypotheses later on, and you can always decide not to pursue them due to potential risk later on. Remember that hypothesis generation is meant to be lightweight and nonbinding, so you shouldn't restrict yourself or your creativity too early on in the process.

Now we'll share just a few thoughts on how you might generate many divergent hypotheses at this stage in your process. Once you've identified a problem area or an opportunity, the easiest way to generate multiple hypotheses is to keep some of the building blocks of your hypothesis statement constant while brainstorming other possibilities for other pieces.

MULTIPLE WAYS TO INFLUENCE A METRIC

As you may have already seen in your experience as a designer, there are often many behaviors that can drive the same eventual result. For instance, think back to the summer camp example from before. Remember that your goal is to increase enrollment for the camp's upcoming summer session. You've identified several problem/opportunity areas toward that goal, but now you're going to focus on one specific opportunity area: increasing the number of new campers. We built one hypothesis earlier—that providing buses to camp would increase registrations from urban campers—but we can build more by thinking more broadly.

Start by brainstorming a list of all the possible desired behaviors (effects) that might impact your goal. Each of these could be the seed of many new hypotheses, because for each behavior there are many changes that could encourage that behavior. In this way, you can generate hypotheses both iteratively and in parallel. For instance:

- We predict that by providing a discount to families who refer new campers to camp, *existing campers will tell their friends about camp*, which will lead to an increase in new campers. We will know this is true if we observe an increase in the number of campers next year.
- We predict that by advertising in parenting magazines, *more families will know about camp*, which will lead to an increase in new campers. We will know this is true if we observe an increase in the number of campers next year.
- We predict that by offering a discount to first-time campers, *more new families will be able to afford sending their children to camp*, resulting in an increase in new campers. We will know this is true if we observe an increase in the number of campers next year.

All of these examples speak to different behaviors (in italics) that might lead to reaching the same goal—increasing the number of new campers. You might have different guesses for which hypothesis is most likely to give you the best results or you might find them equally compelling. We'll talk more about how to narrow down your choices to the hypothesis that you want to test later in the chapter.

We're sure you can imagine that even for the preceding hypotheses there are multiple changes you could make to encourage the same behavior. Taking just the first example, where the desired behavior is that existing campers will tell their friends about camp, you could probably begin to brainstorm other possible changes beyond just offering a referral discount: what if camp was more fun? What if campers got "swag" like sweatshirts that they could wear when they returned back home from camp, prompting conversation with friends? What if you posted photos on social media and tagged the campers so that their friends would see? As you can see, brainstorming different behaviors and different changes can occur in parallel. Changing these two factors is often the easiest way to generate many hypotheses, and we'd encourage you to start going broad by focusing on these two building blocks.

FOCUS ON NEW AND EXISTING USERS

Thinking about the user component of your hypothesis can be more challenging, but has the potential to make huge impacts to your metrics. Recalling our conversation about different cohorts and segments in Chapter 2, there are a few ways you could approach hypotheses regarding different users or user groups:

- Broaden your user base by targeting new users (e.g., by opening new markets, expanding advertising efforts to new populations, etc.)
- Provide a better experience to an existing set of users (e.g., to improve retention of those cohorts or segments)

Speaking to the first point, we want to take a moment to pause here to remind you that though it's important to consider your current users, you should be equally thoughtful about who your future users may be. The users you currently attract and target may be very different from the users that you would like to have in the future. The success of your business depends heavily on you continuing to attract and retain new users in the future. For instance, early adopters of new technologies are often more tech-savvy than the average person, and are more tolerant of poor experiences because they're highly motivated to use your product. As you try to grow your user base, you might find that a broader or different set of users will have different behaviors, needs, or abilities than your initial user group. Another example might be a company that initially launches in the United States but then decides to expand internationally. While it might turn out that the experience you are designing has broad appeal right from the start, it's rare that an experience won't need to take into account different needs from an evolving and growing user base. One rule of thumb is that if your business is fairly mature and you've saturated a market then you should focus on your existing users, but if you're at the early stages of growth as a company, then you should focus on new/future users.

Remember the three Coursera segments that we introduced in Chapter 2? Recall that Coursera thinks about lifelong learners, seasoned professionals, and unseasoned professionals as three segments with very different needs who are *currently* using their product offering. John Ciancutti also shared an example from Coursera about how there is potentially a fourth segment that the company might not be thinking about just yet, but that could be very promising for the business in the future. According to him:

> Most of the world hasn't spent the last 200 years building universities. Developing markets would need 10,000 more universities just to get to the baseline of first-world post-secondary education. They would need a million more instructors than they have today. But in fact, they're losing instructors and colleges there because there's a global competition for that talent. Structurally, they're not going to do it the way the United States did it. They don't have those 200 years; they want to do it now.
>
> If you're at Coursera, today there's not a business model that's going to meet the developing markets segment. You have to make choices. The easiest way to make money in 2016 is to go after those affluent lifelong learners who want to give you money. There's a lot of temptation to do that, but if you're going after the biggest possible future demographic, you go after the people who want the credentials. 93% of humans never get a post secondary education of any kind, but middle-class jobs today require it. So there's a gap. The question is, are we going to roll the dice and go with the big thing?

As John shared, considering a new segment of users is potentially a great way to open new doors for a business. However, the types of people who would use Coursera in an emerging market are very different than the lifelong learner segment. You can imagine that if Coursera decided to explore these emerging market learners, they'd need to be thoughtful about using data to understand how those folks react to their product offering.

With these factors in mind, consider how the selected users or user groups might affect your hypotheses. Will your business be more successful if you start to target a new set of users or a different set of user groups, or should you iterate on the experience for existing users? Is your demographic currently shifting, resulting in new confusions or opportunities to improve?

As a very simple example, consider Facebook. When it first launched, Facebook was available only to college students at a select set of universities. In order to register, a user needed to be part of the college community. In 2005, when Facebook expanded to high schools, it required an invitation to join. Then in 2006 when Facebook was opened to anyone, the requirements changed again—users simply needed an email address and verification that they were 13 years or older. As Facebook grew in size and became more open, users became more concerned about privacy. The needs of the users also changed as the user groups who were interested and or were targeted for company growth evolved. In 2007, Facebook had 100,000 company group pages focused on attracting customers. Recognizing that many businesses saw Facebook as a place to promote their companies, Facebook created Pages in 2009, an offering specifically designed for businesses. "Users" of Facebook for Business had then, and still have, different interests, needs, and goals than the average person on Facebook. You can see how shifts in the company's user base to include new user groups with different needs may have large or small but significant effects on requirements of the product. These changes present new opportunities for different hypotheses to be formed over time as well. A concept like "Pages" may not have made sense for design exploration and experimentation when Facebook first launched, but it made a lot more sense to test and explore once they saw that businesses were using their platform. An area for exploration for them might have been, "How can we adapt our current interface, which is very consumer and individual focused, to be used for businesses?"

To the second point, you could also think about how to improve your experience for an existing group of users. We discussed that your user base of urban campers is small at camp. This might be an issue of awareness or "fit" for camp, but let's say you've realized that campers who grew up in the city are not *retained* as well as campers from the suburbs once they've come to camp. You want to figure out how to keep these city campers coming back to increase the number of campers who are at camp next year. Figuring out what isn't working about your existing experience for users you already have is a great opportunity to collaborate with your user research or data analyst friends—they probably have interesting insights about the challenges your current users face, which might prompt new hypotheses about how to improve things. For instance, maybe city kids don't come as prepared to camp because they don't know about the importance of bug spray and good hiking boots. Providing a packing list is one concrete and cheap way to address this problem, and a hypothesis you might pursue.

We don't need to tell you that what is the right experience for your users will change over time. Users and user groups change, technology changes, and business strategy changes will all impact what your customers expect from you and what their needs are. Keeping abreast of these external changes might mean that you need to come up with new hypotheses to test in order to reach your goal or that some of the assumptions you had about former hypotheses that tested well have now changed and you need to rethink those ideas. One benefit of the experimentation mindset, rather than just running one-off A/B tests, is that once you become comfortable and excited with this way of thinking, you'll always be ahead of the game forming new and testable hypotheses as the market evolves. And an important implication of this is that as the world around you changes, the hypotheses that have the potential to succeed may change as well: hypotheses you've tested might perform differently under these new conditions. We encourage you to keep records of old hypotheses, even if you don't pursue them straight away, as they could encourage experiments you run somewhere down the line.

REVISIT THE SCOPE OF YOUR PROBLEM

Just now, we spoke about how you could vary the *change, desired behavior,* and *user profile(s)* to generate more hypotheses. One rule of thumb to remember is that the scope of the problem you are trying to solve could impact how many of these hypothesis dimensions you vary away from your control experience. For instance, for a local problem, you might be making a different *change,* but otherwise focus on the same users, desired behavior, or metrics. However, for a more global problem, your hypothesis might deviate away from your control in more than one way: maybe your hypothesis has to do with changing or expanding the users or user groups in which you are interested, or targeting a new behavior, or measuring additional or different variables, as opposed to just making different product changes.

As we discussed in Chapter 2, local problems are generally ones where you have decided to focus on one area of your customer experience. You are already familiar with the territory, and are looking to optimize the existing experience by making only one or two small changes to your existing experience. You can think of local problems as those where the different hypotheses represent smaller changes to the user experience, giving you more trustworthy data about exactly how the small changes impact your users and your metric of interest. In global changes, remember that you're trying to come up with the best possible solution by being open-minded to radical changes that might dramatically alter your user's experience, the user groups you are serving, or your business model.

Earlier, we told you that for local problems, your hypothesis might only reflect a different change relative to the control experience, keeping the users, measures, and desired behaviors the same. However, though we've often heard concern from designers about these "local optimizations," in practice such changes can have huge measurable impact on the health of an experience and business. In other words, small changes to the experience don't necessarily imply small impact. And, local experiments are often the only way to be very confident of the impact about specific components of the experience, since they let you "tease apart" the causal impact of each individual change.

By contrast, your hypotheses for a global problem should be much more diverse. Even though your intuition might tell you that thinking narrowly enough for a local problem is more challenging, we would contend that thinking as broad as you should for a global problem is actually much harder. We encourage you to challenge yourself and think deeply about how you could leverage each component of the hypothesis. How can targeting different users or user groups help you address your selected problem or opportunity area? What different behaviors can you encourage in those different users or user groups and with what incentives? What might you change about your experience to drive the behavior you'd like to see? As you can see, you might have an exponential number of different hypotheses you can generate by targeting each of the building blocks of your hypothesis in turn.

In the next example from Netflix, we will look at a global experiment that tested highly divergent hypotheses.

EXAMPLE: NETFLIX ON THE PLAYSTATION 3

When Netflix first launched on the PlayStation, the experience was fairly basic (Figure 4-13). Users had to click through one title at a time, making it challenging to evaluate many possible movies to watch, and the experience generally didn't scale well to a growing catalog of streaming content.

FIGURE 4-13.
The original Netflix design on the Sony PlayStation.

When A/B testing capabilities came to the PS3, the Netflix team was eager to get to work on optimizing their experience. This was the first time that the team had the opportunity to experiment with a TV interface, and they acknowledged that they had yet to develop a well-honed instinct about what works and what doesn't work in that environment. They didn't feel confident that the current design was the right one and knew there was a strong chance that the "right" design was significantly different from what was in market. Therefore, it was important to try some different ideas.

If you recall, earlier in this chapter we shared the example of how "viewing hours", or the amount of Netflix content that was consumed, was the strongest proxy metric for retention for Netflix. So the team starated by rearticulating that the goal on the PlayStation was the same as the goal for all other Netflix devices—to maximize the number of hours of content consumed. Getting customers to watch more TV and movies through Netflix was the key measurement of success for the team.

In order to solve these problems, the team started by brainstorming different hypotheses for what was most important to address in the new user experience. Design worked closely with product management and gathered cross-functional teams from across the company. They defined different hypotheses for various design concepts based on their understanding of the limitations of the existing design. Although more initial hypotheses were generated during the project, we'll share just four of them here:

Hypothesis 1

"By clearly giving users easier access to the entire catalog, they will be more likely to explore the breadth of the catalog and find a movie that they like, which will result in more hours of content consumption."

In the original experience, many users expressed a concern that they were only getting access to a limited part of the catalog. The basis for Hypothesis 1 was to ensure that the user felt confident that they had access to the entire catalog. The downside of allowing users to browse the entire catalog might result in a more complicated experience.

Hypothesis 2

"By providing users with a simple interface that replicates the website experience, users will apply their existing understanding of how Netflix works, which will result in more hours of content consumption."

In the second hypothesis, the team strove to focus on simplicity as the core basis of the hypothesis. Rather than focusing on providing users with depth of access to the catalog, they thought about how to make things easier. One aspect of this hypothesis was that the website was an understood paradigm for Netflix users and replicating that interface on the TV would result in more streaming due to the familiarity and ease of navigating through the experience.

Hypothesis 3

"By separating the act of navigation from the act of browsing for a movie or TV show, the interface and experience will be simpler, which will result in more hours of content consumption."

Here the driving concept was that you could simplify the experience more by separating the navigation from the content itself. This was based on the insight that people generally know that they want to watch a "drama" before they even launch Netflix. By simplifying the available choices based on this knowledge and guiding them through a step-by-step process to select the movie, the team assumed the process would be faster and easier. The team took away as many distractions of choice as they could at each step along the way.

Hypothesis 4

"By replicating a TV-like experience where discovery is based on video streaming, users will serendipitously find more things to watch, which will result in more hours of content consumption."

In this final hypothesis, the team started to think about how people watch TV today. In other contexts, people are used to turning on the TV, sitting back, and just flipping through channels to serendipitously find something to watch. This hypothesis aimed to replicate that experience within Netflix, by allowing customers to decide what to watch through the act of watching.

The team believed that by launching these different experiences to their users, they would get directional guidance about what the potential impact was for what each of the four hypotheses represented. This example illustrates how even when tackling a large global problem, A/B testing and experimentation can be used to explore the impact of a few concrete hypotheses against a specific metric (consumption time). We've intentionally not shown you the designs that were created for each of these hypotheses because we wanted to make a point of abstracting the work of making a hypothesis from the work of designing it. We know and understand that for most designers a natural way of working is to design and craft a hypothesis or set of hypotheses at the same time. This is, of course, completely fine. However, we have found it helpful to at least consider each of these as a separate step so that you are conscientiously making sure that you are not jumping too quickly to a specific solution that you get attached to before exploring all the other possibilities that you might be able to explore.

We'll take a deeper look at this example and the different designs that were made to represent each hypothesis in Chapters 5 and 6. For now, we hope you can see how each of these concepts tried to serve the same goal (increasing the amount of time people spend watching Netflix) even though the approaches were different. To really learn the most from this A/B test, the team also explored secondary metrics in order to understand the strengths and weaknesses of each version. When there are many different ways to reach your goal, your job will be to find out which approach will help you achieve that goal in the best possible way.

INVOLVE YOUR TEAM AND YOUR DATA FRIENDS

We hope that this chapter has empowered you to start generating many hypotheses to address your design goals and problems. We want to take a quick moment here to remind you about other members of your team and organization who can bring their own superpowers to the process of building hypotheses. This is valuable not only to build team consensus on hypotheses that will shape the team's work going forward, but also because different members of your team have unique expertise that can inform your hypotheses.

If you work with product managers, they will often have unique insight into the business or strategic goals. These strategic goals should inform the metrics that have the highest priority in your hypothesis, and have the potential to shape what behaviors you consider encouraging in your users. Similarly, these strategic goals may put limitations on what you can and can't change based on the strategic priorities of your company.

Anyone on your team who focuses on working with data, such as user researchers or data analysts from across the organization, have specialized knowledge about your users. One point we want to emphasize is that past learning should inform future hypotheses. By partnering closely with all kinds of data specialists, you can apply that past knowledge to your hypothesis generation, inspiring you to think of alternative hypotheses that you otherwise would not have considered.

Finally, your engineering partners can help you understand the potential engineering impact of different hypotheses. Although you don't need to nail down exactly what the implementation will be while generating hypotheses, your engineering friends will be able to clue you into roughly how much work different ideas take to pursue. Sometimes these are obvious (of course, redoing a whole home page is harder than changing the size or color of a button), but they may be less obvious as well.

Which Hypotheses to Choose?

The bulk of this chapter so far has focused on going broad, and by this point, you should be excited about the many potential hypotheses to explore. But as we've reminded you throughout this book so far, one of the main decisions you'll need to constantly make when designing with data is determining when your efforts are worth it. Will you learn enough to justify the time and resources it takes to collect that data? Is it appropriate for your current goals and needs?

Similarly, these questions apply to selecting which hypotheses you should pursue. You've mostly been reflecting and working with your team to scope and define your goals, identify problems and opportunities to address, and generate hypotheses. Selecting appropriate hypotheses to move forward designing and A/B testing is important because from here on out, every additional step requires making the time and resource investments we've started to allude to earlier.

In this next section, we'll explore some of the main considerations when selecting hypotheses. You'll first need to determine which hypotheses you can remove and which you can refine and tighten, at which point you'll need to prioritize the ones you've narrowed down to. As you begin to reduce the number of hypotheses, you might find that as you explore the ideas you've generated, many of them are impossible or impractical to execute due to past data or the realities of pursuing that hypothesis. Of the remaining hypotheses, your decisions about which ones to pursue might depend on which hypotheses have the strongest evidence in favor of them already, or which will be most helpful for learning or pursuing your strategic and tactical goals. In this way, you'll be able to decide on one or a small set of hypotheses to start designing and testing.

CONSIDER POTENTIAL IMPACT

One lightweight way to help prioritize potential hypotheses is by doing small or rudimentary calculations about the potential impact of your hypothesis. These small calculations require only a little bit of arithmetic but can help you see whether learning that your hypothesis is true will have impact.

For instance, in his talk "Data Driven Products Now!" Dan McKinley shares a couple of examples from his time at Etsy of how simple estimation (what he calls "applied common sense") could help project the potential value of different hypotheses before building anything.[1] He shares two examples of reasonable-sounding product ideas that turned out to have very different potential impacts: building a landing page for local furniture, or emailing people that give up in the middle of purchases.

By looking at some metrics they already tracked, McKinley found out that the furniture landing page would have nominal impact for the business, and the experiment would need to run for more than six years to reach sufficient power—hardly feasible at all, and not worthwhile! Comparatively, emails to people who gave up in the midst of a purchase had much bigger potential impact to the business: due to the promising estimations, the team rolled out the feature and it wound up contributing to 1.5% of Etsy's total sales in a year (a huge success for such a seemingly small feature!).

The point we're trying to emphasize here is that making some ballpark estimations early on is a great way to vet potential hypotheses to understand their impact. You might only be thinking of orders of magnitude ($10K potential revenue versus $100K potential revenue versus $1M potential revenue?), but this is often enough to give you a sense of whether to further explore a hypothesis or not.

USING WHAT YOU ALREADY KNOW

At the end of our hypothesis generation section, we closed with a note reminding you to involve other members of your team and your "data friends." To be clear, your team is not only helpful in generating hypotheses, but they can be invaluable in selecting them as well.

1 *http://mcfunley.com/data-driven-products-now*

Your "data friends," in particular, may have many types of data and past insights available at their disposal: past A/B tests, user research, surveys, and market research, among others. This expert knowledge can start to provide a lens through which you can start pruning some hypotheses and prioritizing others. Selecting the best hypotheses is another instance where past data should inform future data.

Start by sitting down with your data friends to discuss the hypotheses you've already generated. You might want to ask some of the following questions to begin your conversation:

- Have we conducted research about any similar hypotheses before?
- Similar users or user groups? Similar changes? Similar desired behaviors? Similar rationales?
- How have these types of hypotheses been performed in the past?
- What types of changes have successfully impacted this metric in the past?

Remember to be open-minded about the types of data that inform your hypotheses; sometimes you might have weak signals from previous tests that were not relevant at the time, but apply well to your current hypotheses. Insights need not map one-to-one in order to be useful or worth considering.

That said, you should always be cognizant about *confirmation bias*, or the tendency to look for evidence that confirms your existing thoughts or beliefs. Even if your company does a good job of documenting past research in reports or other formats, we strongly encourage you to take the time to collaborate with your data friends, since they can put the findings in context and help you avoid confirmation bias. Plus, your data friends can help you look for evidence that disproves or contradicts your hypothesis, which is an important part of a balanced approach to using data to explore hypotheses. Being balanced with the data you explore early on requires skill but will pay off later.

So how should you actually go about leveraging past data in service of slimming down hypotheses? Strong contradicting evidence and data might suggest that you should prune that hypothesis: perhaps it's not worth exploring further because you've already been down that path and found it fruitless. Further investment might be a waste of time. However, as we mentioned earlier in the chapter, you might also be curious about how to prioritize different hypotheses. The questions we introduced before can help you prioritize based on expected payoff: if you already have some evidence that supports your hypothesis, you might have more confidence that your test will be successful (that your results will show a positive change in your metrics of interest).

There's another way to use past data to prioritize hypotheses that might be less obvious. Throughout this book so far, we've tried to emphasize the importance of approaching design with a *learning mindset*. With this in mind, remember that while you should always be aiming to make positive changes in your metrics, that shouldn't be your sole purpose; you also want to make sure that for every test you clearly learn something about your users and the types of designs and experiences that work, because it is *this* type of knowledge that will carry forward and hone your design intuition in the future.

To that end, you might want to also ask data-focused folks at your company about open questions they still have that align with your general goals and problem/opportunity area. Aptly chosen hypotheses can help you triangulate with past research findings, or understand confusing previous results. Consider also asking the following questions of your data friends:

- What have you found in past similar research? Is there an opportunity to triangulate with or strengthen those previous findings?
- Have you seen any surprising results in similar research? Can pursuing this hypothesis provide clarity into that past finding?

We hope that in this way, you're able to begin collaborating with your data friends and past research to inform future data and designs. This is one essential step in both pruning and prioritizing your hypotheses as you move forward toward the design and execution stage of an A/B test.

USING OTHER METHODS TO EVALUATE YOUR HYPOTHESES

Your company hopefully already has past insights available that can guide your hypothesis selection process. However, in certain cases, you might also want to invest in evaluating your hypotheses using other research methods, which may be lightweight or (what have been called) "quick and dirty" methods or through "pilot studies." *Pilot studies* are small-scale preliminary studies that you carry out prior to a full-scale study. Pilot studies allow you to iterate on your study design through evaluation of feasibility, time, cost, and sample size, likely effect size or statistical variability, and, most importantly, potentially have adverse effects on your users. Putting effort upfront into these kinds of explorations means you can assess whether your expected payoff executing, launching, and analyzing a large-scale A/B test is worth it. Oftentimes, collecting feedback from smaller groups of users and assessing sentiment toward or usability of your proposed hypothesized design(s) is well worth it. This is especially true if you find yourself in situations where you're about to embark on a very large and costly global test, and you want stronger signals before making that commitment. Another method you can use to start evaluating your hypothesis is a survey. *Surveys* allow you to collect small to medium amounts of data from users about their attitudes and emotions (but not, importantly, their behaviors). In this method, you can collect self-reported data, which can be both quantitative or qualitative.

In 2014, Spotify was looking to redesign their interface with the goal of unifying the design and experience. In the past, the interface's dominant color varied significantly across platforms, and the team wanted to take a united stance on whether to pursue a light UI or a dark UI, while ensuring that existing users would be OK with the change. They crafted two hypotheses to address this concern:

Hypothesis 1

> "By unifying the Spotify experience using a dark UI, users will feel that the music and content are more central, and therefore will perceive Spotify to be more accessible and attractive."

Hypothesis 2

> "By unifying the Spotify experience using a light UI, users will feel that the app is fresher and more consistent with the existing experience, and therefore will perceive Spotify to be more accessible and attractive."

To assess these two hypotheses, Spotify conducted a survey using the different design prototypes with 1,600 people from the United States and Germany, and measured self-reported attitudinal data around the different designs. From this, they found that one of their dark UI iterations performed much better than the light UIs, and the team decided to move forward with the hypothesis of uniting under a dark interface.

Additionally, generating low-fidelity mocks or prototypes (e.g., wireframes, sketches, or noncode prototypes such as those built in InVision) to collect a pulse check on your hypothesis is a great way to get insights from other sources prior to your A/B test. You need not focus yet on optimizing or perfecting design ideas. These mocks don't need to be the same design you ultimately launch in an A/B test, but they should help convey the hypothesis you're planning to convey so that you can get quick feedback about those ideas before you invest in an A/B test.

With such low-fidelity mocks, you can use other methods to evaluate your hypothesis. *Usability studies*, for instance, provide observed, behavioral, qualitative data from a small sample of users to help you identify possible usability issues. Many companies utilize usability tests to help eliminate possible hypotheses that don't perform well in lab settings. However, usability testing is also extremely valuable in ensuring that you give the A/B test you ultimately launch the best chance of succeeding, by avoiding results that fail due to usability issues rather than due to inherent issues with the hypothesis itself.

Similarly, small-sample user research methodologies like interviews and "card sorts"—a method of helping to design or evaluate information structures where people organize topics into categories that they label based on what makes sense to them—can help explore and validate concepts surrounding a hypothesis. These moderated methods let you dive deeply with your sample of users in order to understand the reasons behind their answers to your questions, and gain a nuanced understanding of their needs and desires. This kind of depth provides a valuable jumping-off point to evaluate hypotheses, since you'll be able to collect a signal about *why* the hypothesis might be consistent or inconsistent with your goal so you can improve it or select hypotheses that better align.

Using other methodologies to explore and vet your hypotheses ahead of time can help steer you away from hypotheses that are not as promising as they seemed prior to testing. They can also help you prioritize hypotheses by signaling the likelihood of success or the possible magnitude of success of that hypothesis. By using supplementary research methods to evaluate your hypotheses, you can make the most informed decisions about which hypotheses are worth pursuing through a proper design and test phase.

CONSIDER THE REALITY OF YOUR TEST

We've talked a lot about how you can make informed decisions about which hypotheses to pursue, by leveraging your broader team and their knowledge of existing data, and collecting further data to help evaluate your hypothesis. Our discussion of hypothesis selection has focused on selecting hypotheses that maximize the potential for learning and that give you the greatest chance of having your efforts pay off. However, the practical considerations of launching your test will also dictate which hypotheses you can pursue through to a completed A/B test. This is because you need to make sure that the data that you'll get out of the test is hygienic and actionable. In other words, you need to make sure that you can reasonably collect the data that you need from the appropriate and representative group of users, in a reasonable length of time, and in a way that you can reasonably detect a meaningful effect if there is one. Here, we'll walk you through a few key considerations when thinking about whether you can realistically test a particular hypothesis.

How much measurable impact do you believe your hypothesis can make?

Recall that in Chapter 2 we introduced the concept of statistical power. *Power* is the ability of your test to measure an effect, if it exists in the world. If your A/B test has insufficient power, you won't know whether your result is because no difference between your test cell and your control exists in the world, or because you just didn't have a strong enough lens to see it.

We want our experiment to robustly test our hypothesis so we need to have sufficient power to detect a difference in the control and treatment when a difference actually exists. A power analysis will determine the *minimum detectable effect* (MDE); this is the minimum change you'd need to see (this can be positive or negative) in the metric to have a chance to observe a change with statistical significance. So, for instance, a power analysis might reveal that the minimum detectable effect would require that you observe at least a 10% increase in the number of campers next year to conclude that the difference is statistically significant.

Why does the minimum detectable effect matter in the hypothesis selection phase? Let's continue on with the example of a 10% minimum detectable effect in the change in how many campers you have.

You'll need to ask yourself for each hypothesis whether you *really believe* that the change you're proposing can make that big of an impact. This is where design intuition becomes critically important, because you'll have to make a judgment call about this. In some cases, you'll conclude that your hypothesis doesn't "think big enough," giving you the license to consider more ambitious changes to your existing experience.

Can you draw all the conclusions you want to draw from your test?

Making sure you have a big enough sample size to detect an effect is an important part of considering whether you can test a hypothesis. It is best practice to run experiments with a small percentage of your users to ensure that you don't disrupt your user's experience by changing the experience and design of your product too often. This puts a practical limitation on your hypotheses, because you can only test hypotheses when you have a big enough user base to generate an appropriate sample. When might this matter for the hypothesis selection process?

Sometimes, one metric is constrained by another. If you're trying to evaluate your hypotheses on the basis of app open rate and app download rate, for instance, app download rate is the upper bound for app open rate because you must download the app in order to open it. This means that app open rate will require a bigger sample to measure, and you'll need to have at least that big of a sample in your test. This is important to think about from a methodological standpoint, because hypotheses that target app open rate can only be tested with that bigger sample. Knowing this, you'll have to decide whether pursuing those hypotheses is worthwhile—larger samples mean you have to run your test for longer and require introducing your experimental experience to more users, which means taking on more risk. You should have a clear reason to care about app open rate in this type of test that justifies that additional cost and risk.

Similarly, if you plan to segment your results you'll have to keep that in mind too. Let's say your experiment is focused on testing the user experience on all the devices for which you have designs but you particularly care about users who primarily use your mobile device experience(s)—let's call those users the "mobile" user group. When you analyze the results for all devices combined, you'll have a larger sample size and more power. But you'll also need to make sure that you have a large enough mobile-only sample to draw conclusions about the mobile device user experience specifically. Again, this involves taking on more cost and rolling out an experiment to a bigger constituency of your users. Plus this constitutes more risk to your experience, since you're exposing more of your users to an as-yet-unproven, experimental design. In this kind of situation, you should very carefully vet hypotheses that target your mobile users specifically.

Balancing learning and speed

One more important factor to consider when you think about power and minimum detectable effect is how long you're willing to wait to get that learning. The principle here is that users are allocated to your experiment over time because best practice is to launch the experiment to only a small sample of your user base. Say you need 1,000 people in your sample. You're trying to follow best practice, so you decide to allocate 1% of your users to the experimental condition. The trouble is that if your website only has 1,000 unique visitors per day then you'll only allocate 10 users each day to the test cell, and it will take 100 days to gather enough data to draw conclusions.

In those cases, you'll have to ask yourself: Do you have enough time to wait for the results to come in before you make a decision? Or, do you have enough users that you can collect enough data in a short length of time? (The previous example wouldn't be an issue if you had 1,000,000 unique visitors per day—you'd have enough data after one day!) If you can't answer "yes" to these questions for a given hypothesis, you might not be able to collect clean data about it through an A/B test, and you might want to dismiss that hypothesis for now.

The second consideration for balancing learning and speed is how long you will need to keep your test user group living with the test experience. It will often take time for your users' behavior to change, and depending on the behavior that you are hoping to impact, you may need more or less time depending on the details of the test you are running. Recall that some metrics may take longer to measure than others. It is in this situation that having good proxy metrics will help to minimize the time you need to keep a test running. A clear example of this is offering something like a 30-day money-back guarantee to your users. You would need to leave this test up for at least 30 days to see how many of the people who bought your product or service actually end up returning it within the 30-day period. Although you may have increased the number of purchases (and can measure those results right away), you won't know whether the purchases you added will actually contribute to the bottom line until after the 30-day period is over.

The third consideration is that you'll want to run your experiment for at least one full business cycle in order to minimize bias in your sample. Depending on the nature of your business, your cycle may be a day, a week, or longer. The intuition here is that your product may be used differently at different points in your business cycle: on weekdays or weekends, for instance. Having an experiment that runs only during weekdays could cause bias if the product usage or users are very different on weekends (consider parents, working professionals, etc.) You may need to let your experiment run longer in order to get learnings that generalize and are free of bias.

In this section, we showed you how our abstract conversation about statistical power in Chapter 2 becomes more concrete as you generate and select hypotheses. We encourage you to be proactive about considering the minimum detectable effect and whether you have sufficient power to evaluate your hypotheses *early* in designing your A/B test. All too often we see teams invest heavily into A/B tests, only to reach the heartbreaking conclusion at the end that they weren't able to see an effect if it existed. Remember, even if you have to abandon an exciting hypothesis now due to practical considerations, there's always the hope that you could evaluate it in the future when your user base grows or you have more time to explore.

KEEP YOUR OLD HYPOTHESES IN YOUR BACK POCKET

We've given you some considerations on how to select hypotheses in this chapter, by prioritizing hypotheses that give you a greater chance of success over those that don't and pruning hypotheses that don't currently make sense to test due to practical considerations about your launch and past research and insights. However, we want to take a second to remind you not to give up on the hypotheses that you really believe in, even if you can't test them immediately.

Experimentation is a mindset and an iterative process, which means that it is constantly building on itself and improving. As your experience evolves, experimentation will allow the data and insights that guide your future design directions to be crisper and more relevant, bringing to the foreground hypotheses that you might have had to table at first due to lack of evidence or even counterevidence. Who knows what the future of your experience and product will be? By hanging onto hypotheses that you didn't pursue before, you'll make your next iteration of generating hypotheses easier and faster, and you'll always be ready to learn when the next opportunity arises.

This holds even when your hypothesis fails. Remember, A/B tests are run in the real world rather than in isolation. This makes them sensitive to the changing nature of your evolving user base and trends in design, technology, and the world. You simply can't hold these factors constant, and sometimes they'll impact the performance of certain hypotheses. For hypotheses you really believe in, it's possible that exploring that hypothesis again in the future will lead to a different outcome. We encourage you to hang onto those ideas—they just might be what you need someday in the future.

Summary

This chapter illustrated the importance of creating a strong hypothesis statement and the value of tying that statement back to your company's key metrics and overarching business goals. We also talked about the importance of "going broad" and trying to generate as many different hypotheses as you can before you embark on the process of designing how those hypotheses are represented or manifest in your experience, and then slimming down to select one or a few hypotheses to move forward with.

Throughout this chapter, you might have sensed similarities between generating many hypotheses and your existing design process, where you likely develop many possible designs. These processes are nearly the same, but in hypothesis development you think about high-level goals you want to achieve and the underlying user behaviors that will get you there rather than the way they manifest as design. That being said, we firmly believe that your existing skills as a designer are critical to hypothesis generation and can allow you to be more creative in how you craft your hypotheses.

It's a surprisingly common mistake for teams to move too quickly past this first stage of clearly articulating what it is that they are trying to accomplish. Often people fall prey to this because of eagerness; we all want to roll up our sleeves and build, whether that means designing or implementing engineering solutions. Having a clearly defined hypothesis that the entire team is aligned around can help you to avoid the frustration of finding out late in your test process that you are focused on the "wrong" things. Having several strong hypothesis statements that you can revisit again and again throughout your experimentation journey will give you a north star that you can check yourself against along the way. Understanding what it is that you want to learn from your statement and how you'd measure the outcome of your work in the beginning will help to ensure that the results you get at the end of the process will be both actionable and useful. By rallying around well-crafted hypotheses you'll foster a mindset of designing to learn rather than designing to ship, letting you be successful in every test even when the test itself fails.

Questions to Ask Yourself

- What are the goals that you want to achieve for your company and how do they align with the experiences that you are going to be designing in your product?
- What are the things that are most important for you to learn from your experiment(s)?
- If you break down your hypothesis into the different parts—change, effect, users or user groups, measure, and rationale—what are the things you would hold constant and what are the kinds of things that you would change?
- What data have you leveraged in generating and getting inspiration for your hypotheses?
- Have you generated the full range of possible hypotheses before narrowing down? Will these hypotheses broaden your understanding of your product, experience and users?

[5]

The Execution Phase (How to Put Your Experiments into Action)

IN CHAPTER 4, WE focused on the importance of generating multiple hypotheses and also showed you how to evaluate and select the hypotheses you want to focus on. In this chapter, we will focus on the discussion of how to "design" hypotheses. Before we dive into the main part of this chapter, we want to underscore a couple of points.

First, we want to reemphasize the importance of not jumping too quickly to narrow and specific solutions; hastily moving to premature solutions is a common problem we've encountered time and again in the design process. This is a natural tendency for us all—we want to dive in and get working on the problem, designing elegant solutions, as soon as possible! And, of course, this tendency is exacerbated by pressing project timelines.

Second, we note that, even though we've separated hypothesis generation and designing your hypothesis into two separate chapters in this book, these two activities often go hand in hand.

Following the framework for experimentation outlined in Chapter 3, this chapter is focused on the execution phase (outlined in dashes in Figure 5-1).

This is where we take the hypotheses that you've defined and selected and then craft them into the test cells, which will make up the core of your experiments.

Through experimentation, in design practice we can test out a broad range of ideas that we may otherwise dismiss too early in more traditional product development processes. Premature commitments and unwarranted dismissal of ideas with great promise plague many design and development processes.

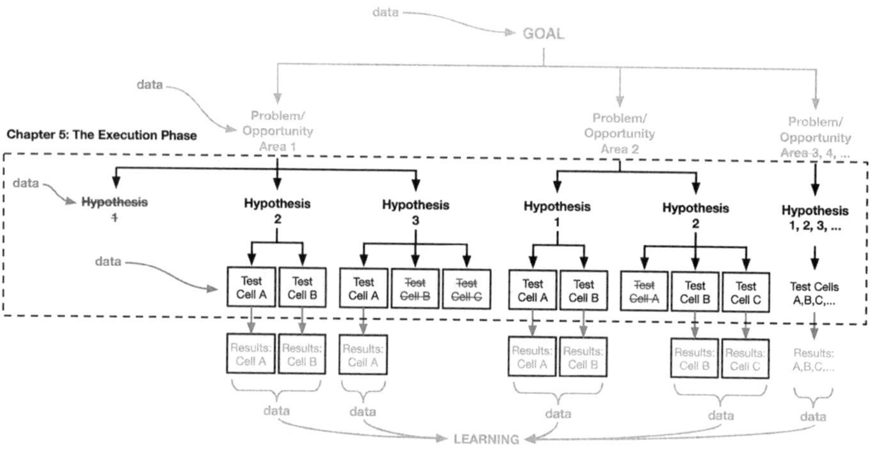

FIGURE 5-1.

This chapter focuses on the execution phase of the experiment: designing the treatments of your hypothesis or hypotheses that you'll launch in your A/B test.

As the goal of experimentation is to test more than just one idea, we now have a mechanism to get many ideas and many possible solutions in front of real users to see how they react to them. As you can see in Figure 5-1, each of these solutions results in a test cell.

"Testing" your ideas on a small group of users means that you are able to try bolder and more wide-ranging design solutions because you don't have to be as confident about being "right" in the same way that you might if you were going to ship that solution to everyone and only had one chance to do it. In fact, testing solutions that are more divergent and different from each other can sometimes result in deeper and broader learning.

We believe that you can apply a data-aware framework to a full range of problems that you may want to solve or areas where you would like to understand user behavior and the impact of your designed solutions much more deeply. This can range from very tactical and small things ("What is the most effective layout of this page?") to much larger and more strategic questions as well ("What is the relationship between qualified customers and retention?").

We recognize that for designers who haven't worked with data before, there are cultural challenges of incorporating data and A/B tests into your product development process. We've heard that it can feel to some people like leaning on data requires giving up control of determining your user experience. Chris Maliwat talks about this transition within the team at Warby Parker:

> Culturally, at companies that are focused on brand, you want to put the best brand forward and what that generally means is you (not your consumer) are the editor and curator of what you think is best. Particularly for folks in our marketing and brand team who didn't have experience with A/B testing, it was challenging to say we're going to design some stuff and end up launching whatever works best. That ceding of control culturally was actually a bit difficult. We involved the brand team in the test cell design and ensured that the test cells were all within the brand constraints. The conversation then became "these are all within the brand constraints, but we're still not sure which one works best so we're going to test it and the one that wins, we should do."

Here, Chris argues that data still needs to be balanced with design considerations like creating a brand. We believe that in this way, the designer's intuition is a natural complement to data. By designing with data, designers should feel emboldened to take bigger risks in service of learning, which in turn can further hone their instincts. In the next section, we'll dig deeper into this topic of how data can help put learning at the center of every design exploration.

Designing to Learn

One of the main reasons to bring data into your design process is so that you can begin to get a sense of how well your designs are performing. Another way to think of this is measuring how quickly you, as a designer, are learning how to most effectively meet your users' needs. Over time, are you getting better at creating experiences that have the impact that you predict they will have on your users' behavior? Do you find that you can predict the outcome of your experiments with better accuracy as you do more of them?

We want to convey two important points. First, that you approach your design work with the mindset of trying to understand how your craft will impact customer behavior rather than focusing on shipping a final product experience that is "done." Understanding that you are engaging in an iterative and ongoing design process will help you focus on the act of learning along the way. Second, that your designs need to be effective representations of the ideas that you want to test with your users.

We first introduced the hypothesis in Chapter 2, and noted that it should capture "what you are going to do and what you think the effect will be." We also said that you should have a clear "plan that addresses what you would learn by testing" your hypothesis. So in this chapter our aim is to demonstrate how you can approach experimentation and design as a way to get better and better at evolving your ability to serve your customers' needs over time.

ENGAGING YOUR USERS IN A CONVERSATION

A good way to approach this is to start by considering the difference between writing a book and having a conversation with someone. Let's say that you've been recognized as an expert in your region and you've been asked to write a guidebook to the area. You'll want to convey your take on the region to your readers, highlighting some of your favorite attractions, restaurants, and activities. However, with a book, the form, packaging, and content of your thoughts is fixed and static. As people read your book and have reactions to what you've written you can't change the words that you wrote or react to their feedback. For this reason, you will spend a great deal of time perfecting your writing, polishing the book, and making sure that you're picking just the right places to spotlight.

For your readers, there is also no easy way for them to give feedback to you about what they like or don't like in the book. They might have wished that you spent more time highlighting outdoor activities, that you covered more of the "cheap eats" in the region, or that you had clearer maps in the book. But even if these readers took the time to write to you and give you suggestions on how to make your guidebook better, you would need to go through all the work of rewriting and republishing the book to incorporate their feedback. This is all just to illustrate that you will put a lot of extra effort into polishing and perfecting every aspect of your book, thinking of the final product as exactly that: final.

In our summer camp example, the relationship you have with your summer campers is different. You can engage in regular conversations with your campers, and those conversations will be different than if you were to write a static book for them. You can ask them a question, propose an activity, and then see how they react in the moment. As you speak back and forth you'll learn more about what motivates them, how they think, and how they react to the ideas you're sharing with them.

Because you know you'll have many opportunities to talk to the campers about the ideas you have, you'll also become more comfortable with *not* having to polish your thoughts ahead of time. ("I'm thinking of doing something around a new water activity... What about something with boats?" can lead to "OK, I'm really focusing on the boats now, what do you think about sailing?" or "Last time you said you don't like the water, what if we did a hiking activity instead?")

Quick and frequent conversations will allow you to get feedback on some of your ideas from your campers. You can then react to their feedback, and re-engage with them once you've evolved your thinking to see if your refined ideas are meeting their needs and desires more closely. Having as many conversations as you can in quick succession with your campers is more convenient than polishing your ideas to perfection and instead taking a really long time between each conversation. Again, this is very different than the mindset and approach you might take if you were working on a book where you *only* have one opportunity to communicate with your readers.

The conversation is a great metaphor for how we see working with data. Ideally, you are trying to build a long-term relationship with your customers and both data and design can help you have those conversations with them. Your design allows you to present your ideas to your users. Letting them interact with your design is your way of asking, "Does this work for you?" The data you get back is their response to you. As we've said before, behind every point of data is a user, and behavioral data is the "language" that they are using to tell us if what we presented to them is working (the data shows positive results) or not working for them (the data shows negative results).

HAVING QUALITY CONVERSATIONS

Conversations are most interesting when people are able to voice a strong opinion. This is also when you learn the most about what matters to them.

For example, let's go back to the idea of introducing a brand-new activity for the campers. If you start your conversation by asking "Should I add kayaking as an activity or should I add crew as an activity?" you may not get very insightful answers because the difference between those two activities isn't very large: they are both on the water and they both involve rowing. If you were instead to ask, "Should I add kayaking as an activity or should I add orienteering as an activity?" or "Should I add kayaking as an activity or should I add painting as an activity?", you might get more interesting answers and learn more about your campers. The differences between these two sets of activities are more pronounced and that means that this question might be a more effective vehicle for you to learn about their interests than the first question. They can talk about whether they are more interested in a water or land activity, whether they're more interested in problem solving or physical exertion, or whether they'd rather take part in activities with a targeted goal or something more leisurely. On the flip side, if you jump too quickly to asking about water-specific activities, you may learn that campers would prefer kayaking to crew without realizing that in reality, they aren't too excited about either activity at all.

It's the same thing when you're having those conversations with millions of people through data. If you're trying to figure out what is going to work with your users, you'll want to design experiences that elicit clear responses. Presenting your users with as many feasible and differentiated solutions as possible—with differences that *they* can recognize—helps them articulate what is *important* to them.

Designing to extremes to learn about your users

Eric Colson had a great example from Stitch Fix where they evaluate the feedback from "polarizing styles" to better understand their customers' preferences:

> We have a notion of a "polarizing style." This is a piece of merchandise that clients tend to either love or hate. There's no one in-between; no one just "likes it a little"—it's one extreme or the other. We detect which styles are polarizing by studying the feedback data on our styles

> and applying measures of entropy. It's hard to predict a priori which styles will be polarizing. It's also hard to know which clients will be on the love side or hate side for a particular style. But after the fact, it's obvious—they explicitly tell us. And this can be useful information. Each client's response to a polarizing style reveals information about their preferences. The people who hate the style tend to share certain preferences. Likewise, people who love the style share similar preferences. So, regardless of whether or not the client loved or hated the polarizing style we now know more about them. This means we can even better serve them on their next fix. It's about setting yourself up for long-term success by continually learning more about your clients' preferences.
>
> It reminds me of what I learned about baseball during the 2014 playoff series. I am a passive fan of the San Francisco Giants. But of course I get more interested during the playoffs. I happened to watch a game with a friend who was much more of an expert on baseball. It was not looking good for the Giants. The opposing team's pitcher was on fire. He had the Giants shut down—no one was hitting off him. But the tide turned after a "great" at-bat by the Giants. I didn't initially see it as "great"—he had struck out! Yet as he returned to the dugout, all the players were high-fiving him. I turned to my friend and said, "He struck out. Why the high-fives?" He explained to me that it was a productive at-bat: he took up nine pitches (pitchers are only good for 100 or so). And each of those pitches revealed information to the next set of batters watching from the dugout. That was nine more times that they got to learn from watching the pitcher's timing. They got to see his slider, his fastball, the curve—even the sequencing of pitches is valuable to learn. So he revealed information that would benefit the next batter. It felt very similar to the value we get from our clients' feedback to various styles; we learn for the next time.

This story is a great pointer back to the story we shared from Eric in Chapter 2, which illustrated how the key metric at Stitch Fix had to change as their business model changed. In a similar fashion, if the goal of the team was to optimize for purchasing activity in a single "Fix," then there would be no incentive to risk an item that might be rejected. The stylists would only want to fill the box with items that were likely to be accepted. But once the incentive or the goal was changed to focus on building out a long-term relationship with their customers, the value of having a polarizing style in the box that better reveals the customer's preferences becomes a clear long-term benefit, even if in the short term it decreases the likelihood of purchasing.

As we've noted before, data can be used to shape the experiences that you are building (through algorithms, recommendation engines, personalization) and it can be used to help inform decisions that you are making as a designer about building your product (through A/B testing, qualitative studies, surveys, etc.). Eric's example isn't exactly about A/B testing; he wasn't describing a specific A/B test that was run where some users got a polarizing style and others didn't. However, we thought it was a really great example of how the experimental mindset should be applied and how it's important to think about what you can learn over time about your customers in a series of interactions. Every Stitch Fix box is an opportunity for the company to interact with their customer, learn more about him or her, and continue to evolve their conversation and relationship with the customer for the long term.

Revisiting the minimum detectable effect

You might remember that in Chapters 2 and 4 we introduced the concept of minimum detectable effect (MDE). Recall that this is the minimum difference we want to observe between the test cells and the control. The question you'd ask on an A/B test is for the metric(s) you'd be measuring, do you *really* believe that your design is capable of making an impact at least as big as (or bigger than) your minimum detectable effect? Colin McFarland, Head of Experimentation at Skyscanner, uses the example of changing the color background on your company's home page to explain this concept. Say you're trying to impact a harder to move metric, such as retention. You've formulated a hypothesis, and now you're evaluating whether to pursue it. Your hypothesis is: "By changing the background color of our home page from red to green, users will be more likely to find our site more relaxing and enjoyable to use, which we will measure by an increase in retention."

In the spirit of having effective conversations, we urge you to ask yourself whether you really believe that changing the background color will result in a measurable impact in your customer retention (or whatever your metric of interest is). Assessing whether you believe that your hypothesis can have the measurable impact that you set out to make is one place where the designer's intuition and the science of experimentation must come together. By framing your hypotheses in terms of their potential and quantifiable impact, you're forced to reflect on how substantial of an impact you really believe that hypothesis can make. If you don't believe that you can create such an impact with your hypothesis about changing the background color, for instance, you might consider looking at your other hypotheses to see which of them are likely to have a greater impact, or think about different ways you could design your test cells for a single hypothesis to be more impactful.

It might seem daunting at first to try to make judgments about the size of the impact just on the basis of intuition, especially if you haven't worked with A/B testing data before, or aren't yet familiar with your company's metrics and the types of things that affect them. However, as we said in Chapter 3, experimentation is a process that will help build these intuitions. These types of judgments about potential impact will become easier with time, and at the beginning, relying on your data friends who are more familiar with these metrics is a great place to start.

Designing the Best Representation of Your Hypothesis

Once you have a strong hypothesis statement (or a few) that you want to test, you'll want to make sure the designs you create are truly representative of those statements and that the information that you gather from the results of your experiment will give you information that you can act on and learn from. This is the art of designing in a data-aware framework. We want designers to inspire small and large changes to your experiences and to test how effective those changes are. Your design will influence both what you can measure and what you can therefore learn.

In Figure 5-2 you'll notice that our framework assumes that each hypothesis might have several different ways that you could represent it. Here, we show that Hypothesis 2 has four different possible ways of being treated—versions A, B, C, and D. To put this into A/B testing language, each of these "treatments" would be a test cell that we measure against the control. Each of the four test cells has the same measure of success, the same metric that we are judging them by, and every test cell has the same underlying hypothesis, a statement that captures our belief around the behavior we can incentivize and the result it will have.

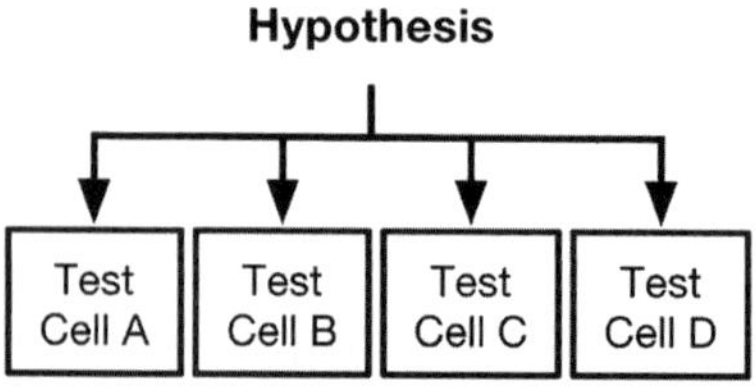

FIGURE 5-2. A single hypothesis may have several representations, or "treatments."

However, each test cell represents a different approach to how we might represent that hypothesis. Because it takes time to craft and build each test cell, you want to make sure that you can clearly articulate what it is that you will learn if that test cell either increases or decreases the metric you are measuring when compared with the control.

UNDERSTANDING YOUR VARIABLES

To illustrate this, let's start with a very simple example from Netflix where they explored surfacing different amounts of content in different ways. Their slimmed-down hypothesis was the following:

> By giving users more choice in the selection of movies and TV shows on their home page, we will increase consumption of content (hours viewed).

In the control experience, there were 25 rows on the home page and 75 titles in each row (Figure 5-3).

There are two simple ways that they could "put more choice" on this page:

- Add a wider selection of movies in each category (add more options to each row)
- Add more different genres and categories (add more rows)

One variable is the breadth of movies represented on each page (adding more rows, which allows a user to browse through a wider range of movies), and a second variable is the depth of selection (the number of movies in each category, which allows a user to dig deeper within a category). Essentially, this test was constructed to get some sense of whether it's more important for you to provide more depth for your customers or more breadth or a little bit of both.

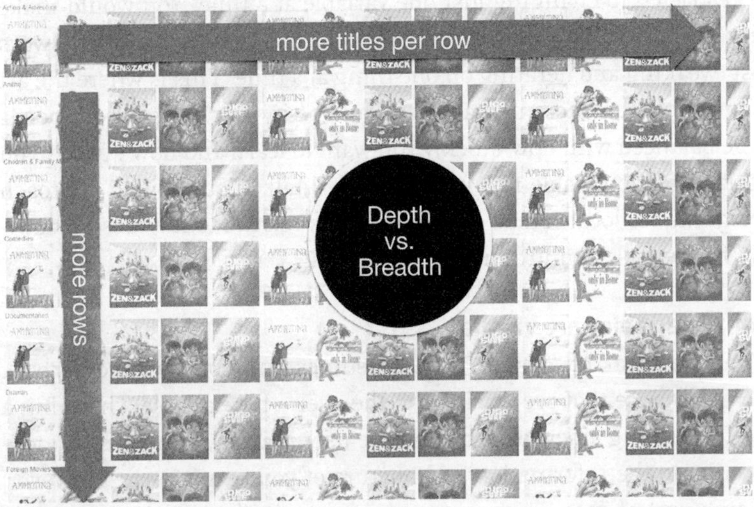

FIGURE 5-3.
The Netflix home page at the time of testing.

The control had 25 rows × 75 movies per row. The team tested three test cells against this control:

- Cell A: 25 rows × 100 movies per row
- Cell B: 50 rows × 75 movies per row
- Cell C: 50 rows × 100 movies per row

It turned out that the winning test was Cell B and the team learned that allowing customers to dig deeper within a category was not actually that important, but giving them more choices of different genres was. In many ways this would make sense because if you haven't found a movie that you're interested in out of 75 movies, it's unlikely that you'd find a suitable movie if that list of movies were expanded to 100. It's more likely that you would find a good movie by looking at a completely different genre.

A good experiment will balance the number of variations or test cells that you create with the level of detail that you are trying to learn. Like a good science experiment, you'll obviously have a cleaner test if you control your variables so that you are only changing one thing at a time. This way you can isolate and understand what it was that impacted your results. In this example, the impact of adding movies to a row versus adding rows is pretty clear. However, not every experiment you run will be restricted to changing just one variable at a time. You would make very slow progress in your larger product experience if you were always just tweaking and iterating on one thing at a time. This is where the art of knowing how incremental you should be in your design work needs to be balanced with how quickly you want to learn and how quickly you want to get actionable results. Later, we'll talk about how to approach designing for local versus global problems relative to the "design activity" framework we introduced in Chapter 2.

Not all variables are visible

When we speak of "design," we sometimes only consider the parts of the experience that are "visible" to the user—for example, changing a layout, creating a new workflow in the user journey, or making a modification to the information architecture of your experience. However, a large part of many experiences nowadays is "invisible" to the user. Recommendation and personalization algorithms play a big role in creating a good or bad experience for your users.

Sometimes the variable in your test cells might be different versions of those algorithms. One version of the algorithm might weigh "popularity" more strongly than another, which might instead focus more on someone's past history with your service. You might make these changes "visible" to your users by calling them out in the design (e.g., saying "Recommended to you because these are popular") or you might do nothing at all and see if the invisible experience changes will be reflected in your customers' behavior.

Another example might be that you are changing something about the algorithm that increases response speed (e.g., content download on mobile devices or in getting search results); users see the same thing but the experience is more responsive, and feels smoother. Although these performance variables aren't "visible" to the user and may not be part of visual design, these variables strongly influence the user experience.

Jon Wiley spoke to us about how Google approached testing the perception of "speed." According to Jon, "speed" has long been one of the core principles that defines a good experience at Google. Whenever Google makes improvements in speed, it results in a lift in their key metrics.

Although one might consider speed to be purely technical, Jon and his team worked on understanding the effect that the perception of speed had on the user experience. Here Jon talks about how they use both behavioral data from A/B testing and feedback from the usability lab to measure something that is more nuanced like the perception of speed:

> We started to investigate the perception of speed. We discovered that if there was a little bit of a delay, people thought it was faster, which is counterintuitive. There are tons of studies on people's perceptions of time in terms of waiting. It's like if you drove without traffic for 10 minutes versus if it still took you 10 minutes, but you were blocked in traffic—your perception of that would've been much slower even though it took you the same amount of time.
>
> There is this interplay between people's expectations of what is going to happen, and what actually happens, for example, the delay in the response of the server having to fetch it and render it. A great way of doing this, particularly on mobile devices, is to have a transition animation that carries you from one place to another so that you can see this is part of this continuous process. It's not just a jump to the next thing. We're trying to bring more of this into our software (in our web applications, in our native applications) so that people feel like it's a smooth experience rather than a choppy one—even if it took exactly the same amount of time.
>
> With an experiment, we can look at the amount of time it takes per action or between actions for a user in the lab. We can say, "They scroll down. They've gotten a result. That takes *X* amount of time on a typical basis. What if we added this animation, or what if we added this transition?" We can see what impact that has on the timing of it. We're trying to match what we see in the lab up against what we see in the environment. If we can correlate behavioral changes on the experiment side with perception changes that we basically ask people about then we feel pretty strongly about it.

Think about playing your role as a designer in shaping these kinds of experiences and using experimentation to understand their impact on your customers as much as you do about the kind of design work that you might more traditionally associate with our craft.

YOUR DESIGN CAN INFLUENCE YOUR DATA

So far we have been talking about the importance of making your designs a good representation of your hypotheses. However, it's also important to understand how your design might influence the data that you collect.

We like the experiment Gaia Online ran many years ago as a tongue-in-cheek home page test (Figure 5-4). One of the ways that people often try to "game" test results is by simply making the thing you want to measure as prominent and large as possible. But sometimes doing this increases one measure of success (clicks on the feature you are focusing on) to the detriment of the overall user experience.

FIGURE 5-4.
Gaia Online home page experiment.[1]

Designers often complain about being asked to make really big buttons to drive more traffic to a feature because simply making a huge button will definitely result in more engagement with that feature. However, the feature that you are driving that traffic to may not be the most important thing on that page or may not be "worthy" of such a strong presence. You want to be cautious of creating a design that optimizes for "winning" a single test instead of thinking about creating the right balance for the *overall* experience of your users.

1 *http://gaia.wikia.com/wiki/File:GaiaOnline_Homepage_2010_-_Big_Red_Button.png*

If you're not careful, the designs you create might impact or influence the data that you can and will gather. We want you to always be aware of this relationship between your designs and the data because sometimes we forget to see how one can influence the other.

Example: Netflix Wii

When Netflix first launched on the Wii, the wand was a relatively new input device and gesture a new input mechanism. It was most common when using a remote on other devices, to use the LRUD input (left-right-up-down buttons) to navigate TV interfaces. The team wanted to understand whether people preferred using the wand or the LRUD buttons on the remote control to navigate the Netflix UI.

A quick analysis showed that the vast majority of users were navigating the UI using the LRUD input. The most obvious conclusion might have been that the majority of users preferred to use the LRUD as input over the wand or that the wand was still not widely adopted enough. However, on reflection, the team realized that the UI of Netflix on the Wii mirrored its design on other devices; it was a simple grid. Perhaps if that UI were instead a random scattering of movie images on the screen or maybe arranged in a circle, then people might have used the wand to navigate the UI instead of the LRUD buttons.

This is a pretty clear example of where the design had a strong impact on the data that was collected. You can imagine that the conclusion that team drew might not have been an accurate representation of how users might naturally choose to navigate the Wii interface because there wasn't a competing design that was optimized for using a wand instead of the LRUD buttons.

To this end, you can easily see how this might expand to other situations. At the most basic level, if you choose to have engagement with a particular feature as the predominant metric of success and your design makes that feature difficult to find on any given screen, then it's likely that the design will have influenced the outcome of that test as much or more than the desirability of that feature itself.

REVISITING THE SPACE OF DESIGN ACTIVITIES

In Chapter 2, we introduced a framework for the different ways you might think about design depending on where you are in the space of possible design activities. Figure 5-5 was used to show how the nature of your design work and the type of feedback you are looking for in your experiments might vary. Most importantly, it's not about thinking about solving either a "global" or a "local" problem or about looking to either "explore" or "evaluate" the merit of your ideas—it is about working across this spectrum of activities and being thoughtful about where you are (and where else you might be) at any given point in time.

To revisit the concepts quickly—*global* and *local* refer to the scope or approach you are taking to addressing your problem/opportunity area. Will your designs change multiple variables in each test cell (global) or will you be focusing on just one or two elements (local)? *Exploration* and *evaluation* are good ways to articulate how far along you are in addressing your problem/opportunity area. Are you in an exploration stage where you are crafting your experiments so that you can get directional feedback on your designs (e.g., "Should we keep working on this feature/does this feature matter at all?")? Or are you looking to evaluate your design, changing as few variables as possible to gather the strongest evidence and establish causality (e.g., "Is *X* better than *Y*?"). The nature of the design work that you do and the way that you leverage your designs to answer the problems you are looking to solve will vary depending on where you are on the diagram shown in Figure 5-5.

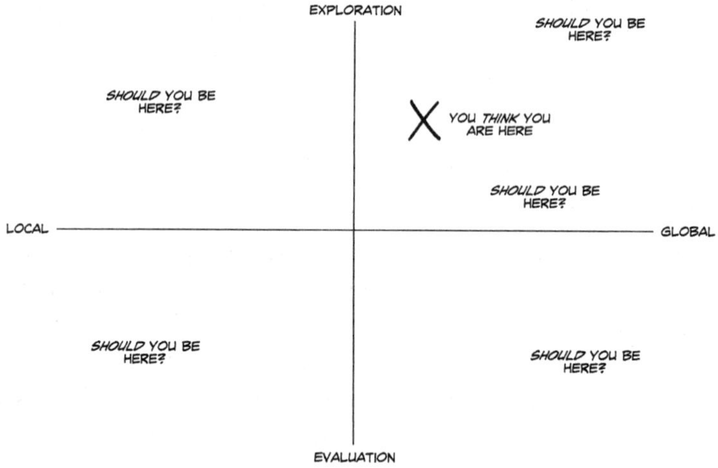

FIGURE 5-5.

Consider what kinds of designs you should be producing relative to where you might be on the spectrum of local–global and evaluation-exploration.

When you are on the global side of this diagram, you are generally operating under the belief that there might be a very different experience from what you have today that will result in big gains to the metric(s) of interest that you are looking to impact. Remember that in Chapter 2, we introduced the concept of local maxima and global maxima. Global design gives you a greater opportunity to try out all of the possible design solutions to your problem at hand, to see whether there are solutions out there ("other mountains") that are more promising than the one you've landed on now. In those cases, it would make most sense to do design explorations that are not just very different from your existing experience but also very different from each other. You can see this illustrated in Figure 5-6.

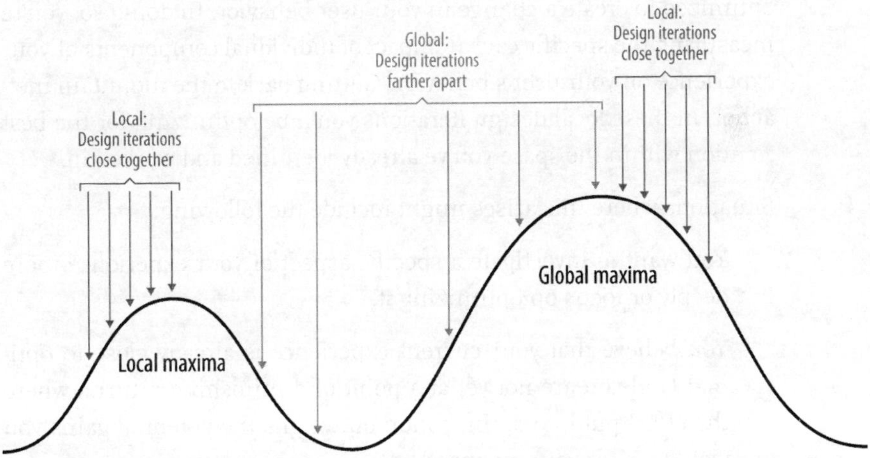

FIGURE 5-6.
Global experiments might involve designs that are very different from each other, whereas local experiments normally have less variation between the designs.

Doing this type of global exploration makes most sense when:

- You are developing for a new space that you don't have pre-existing expertise or experience in.
- You are interested in making a big strategic shift that would require foundational shifts in your experience in order to execute.

- Your existing product/experience has been static for a long time and you now have access to new technology that will allow you to try things that were previously not possible.
- You feel like you have reached a local maxima and any further optimizations on your product or feature won't give you significant increases in performance.

When you are on the local side of the diagram in Figure 5-6, you are looking to optimize your existing experience. Here, the difference between each of your design iterations or test cells will not be as different from each other and also are not likely to be that different from your current experience. You'll need to be much more precise in what it is that you are designing and which components of that design are being optimized to create a change in your user behavior. In doing so, you're measuring the specific causal impact of individual components of your experience on your user's behavior. Getting back to the mountain metaphor, in these local design iterations you'll be optimizing for the best solution within the space you've already identified and worked in.

Situations where this arises might include the following:

- You want to investigate a specific aspect of your experience more deeply or focus on optimizing it.
- You believe that your current experience is already close to optimal (and you are not yet at a point of diminishing returns where the effort put into optimization outweighs the potential gains you would get for your business).

AVOIDING LOCAL MAXIMA

It's risky to do the type of global design we've proposed, where you test with multiple variables altered at once. More often than not, any change to a variable is more likely to result in a negative result than a positive, and the more variables involved, the less likely to find a win.

Sometimes, however, the win you seek may not be reachable from the place you are in single steps. As we've discussed, with local design you aim to take small steps up the mountain you're already on. This practice of "hill climbing" one step at a time, however, won't get you to the top of the peak next door if you are climbing a mountain surrounded by valleys. It's perhaps only by taking multiple large steps in different directions that you can discover whether the landscape that isn't contiguous to your current product may have a higher peak (refer back to Figure 5-6 to see this in action).

A note: when probing for adjacent non-local peaks, it's rare to have the insight to stumble directly upon a higher piece of the landscape. However, if you do a handful of tests with simple variations near the one big leap you are studying, you may find that the land surface isn't too much lower, but that it has a steep gradient, as indicated by differences in the test results between your small differences tests, and that steep gradient might indicate that there is a promising destination to be found nearby.

It's important to remember, however, that the impact of your experiment on metrics might be either large or small, regardless of whether you are running a local or global test. For example, you might classify introducing an "Other users also bought" feature as a local test, since you are simply introducing this feature to one page. However, that recommendation feature might have a big impact on your metrics by introducing a new user behavior. It might be that you learn that you begin to move a metric that you weren't even considering before. For example, this feature might negatively impact conversion by adding a distraction, but increase average basket/cart size. That could be a much larger learning and have the impact you would expect from a larger redesign. Sometimes small changes can also have big adverse impacts. LinkedIn learned this when they found that introducing only 5px to the header (shown in Figure 5-7) resulted in a sudden drop in advertising click-through metrics on advertisements, perhaps because of fewer accidental clicks on the ad.[2]

Another example might be making a change to a call to action, but if that call to action appears on every page in your experience then the ramifications of that experiment might be quite large in some areas of your product.

---

2 *https://building.coursera.org/blog/2014/09/11/talks-at-coursera-a-slash-b-testing-at-internet-scale/*

FIGURE 5-7.
Slide from Ya Xu's talk on A/B testing show that a mere 5px had a large measurable impact on LinkedIn's advertising click-through metrics.

Of course, the inverse can also be true: a "global" change may not lead to the positive change you'd expect in metrics despite how big of a change to the experience it might be. This illustrates the point that the return on investment of experiments is not relative to the nature of the change. It's important to use this global versus local metaphor as a tool to think about how much of a change you're making to your experience, rather than as an indicator about the potential impact of the change. Also consider whether you are exploring or evaluating your solution. How far along are you in your design process? What will your next steps be after your A/B test? The way you will approach your designs and what you'll learn from your tests depends on whether you are exploring or evaluating.

If you're taking an exploratory mindset, you and your team have the license to think big. You need not feel constrained by product ideas you would be proud to ship, since your goal is to learn from your designs rather than to create a "finished" product. Your aim is to get directional feedback about where to push harder, and which ideas you can probably abandon without too much more investment. You are probably exploring if:

- You have just kicked off a new long-term project and want to start to build up your knowledge about different possible approaches.
- You and your team are aligned on taking more time to investigate a bunch of directions and iterate over time.

If you instead at the point of evaluation, you're looking to quantify whether your design had the intended impact. Did you move your metrics in the way you had hoped? These types of tests are candidates for rollout, if you and your team decide based on the results that you feel comfortable launching at scale. One important impact of this is that your designs should feel polished—work you would be proud to make your default experience in the future. You are probably evaluating if:

- You and your team have already aligned on a particular direction, and now you want to see whether you made the impact you had hoped.

As you can see, how far along you are in your product process will have material impact on the types of designs you product, and also what you'll learn from your A/B test.

Different problems for summer camp

As we go deeper into our discussion of designing for different types of problems, we wanted to walk through an example from the summer camp metaphor for each of the four quadrants. Remember that these are spectrums rather than binary classifications; however, for the purposes of simplicity we won't specify where on the spectrum these different questions fall.

	LOCAL	GLOBAL
Exploration	**Goal:** Make camp more fun **Questions:** Which activities should we pick for our outdoors-focused camp? Kayaking, orienteering, yoga, painting, rock climbing?	**Goal:** Increase revenue **Questions:** Should I move to a new location? Target a new audience (moms instead of kids)? Move to a new value prop—like yoga camp instead of general summer camp?
Evaluation	**Goal:** Make camp more fun **Questions:** Do kids enjoy kayaking more than rowing crew?	**Goal:** Increase revenue **Questions:** Should I stay in the camp business? Is this the best way to maximize my revenue?

We hope that this helps make the framework we've been discussing feel more concrete. We encourage you to refer back to this as you're thinking about what type of problem you're most similar to at any given point. As a thought exercise, you might also consider drawing out a similar chart for a problem you're working on. What are the different ways you might approach the same goals, depending on the type of problem you're solving? What creative ideas can you come up with?

Directional testing: "Painted door" tests

Recall that exploratory tests provide directional input about whether you should pursue a particular idea. Ideally, you'd want to understand whether something is directionally worthwhile *prior* to investing any resources. One example of a way you could test a concept pretty bluntly to understand whether you should follow a particular direction is a "painted door" test. In this kind of testing, you have a feature or an idea that might take a lot of time to build out but you want to learn whether your users have interest in the feature first. Building a new door is costly (you have to cut into the wall, buy the materials, etc.), so you don't want to do that without knowing whether your users want a door there at all. Instead, you can first paint a fake door on the wall and see how many folks try to open it. This will give you some signal about the interest in that feature and perhaps the potential addressable audience.

In a painted door test, you might tell your users about a particular feature or offer, giving them the option to select it. However, when they do click on it, they get a message saying that there was an error and the feature isn't available for them. By tracking the number of people who clicked on that offer, you could gain a rough sense of whether it would ultimately be worth building out. Although this is a common practice, we recognize that it is nevertheless a bit questionable—it is misleading to tell your users that a feature exists and to then deny it to them because it never existed. We will discuss the ethics of A/B testing in more detail in Chapter 8, to help you think about the ethics of these types of experiments.

Let's take a simple example that could illustrate how a "painted door" test might be used to explore a pretty large change to a business proposition. Let's go back to that summer camp example. You're working on a website for your camp. You want to know if you can make a big shift in your business by broadening your customer base. One idea that you have is to move from offering a camp for just kids to now offering a "family camp" where the parents and kids could get away together. However, building out all the services needed to make that change in your business is likely costly and time consuming, since it fundamentally changes the experience of camp. Before you do that, you could put an offer on your website that gives people the option to sign up for the family camp. You might measure how many people click on the offer and you might even ask a few questions as the first step of that flow to find out which activities they want to do as a family. However, when it comes to the final step where they need to choose which week(s) to sign up for, you could give them a message that there is no more availability. This would give you a fair amount of data to inform the decision about whether to invest further in this idea. You'd have to take into account a few things—like the fact that you might have gotten more sign-ups if you had advertised properly or that you are only hearing from folks that are already looking at your website for your kids' camp—but the signal you get from this limited audience is likely still useful.

As you can imagine, the downside of a painted door test is that it can be very frustrating for the users who were hoping to get that feature. You risk alienating them in order to get the information back. For this reason, you should keep the test group for your "painted door" tests as small as possible and use them sparingly. You should also avoid any types of painted door tests that could be physically or emotionally harmful to your users or detrimental to their relationships with others.

Picking the right level of granularity for your experiment

Picking the right level of design polish is a function of where you are in the diagram in Figure 5-5 as well. For example, if you are working on a local problem/opportunity, you might want to further understand the causal impact of each component of the experience by refining and optimizing your:

- Language
- Stylistic elements and visual representation
- Algorithmic testing (e.g., testing different algorithms for recommendations)
- Activity flows and changes to user paths

It's often the case that focusing on this level of detail will result in more test cells. However, these variables are also usually "cheaper" to test because they are isolated and therefore easier to build.

When you are executing a lot of different variations it will be easy to be drawn into the idea of testing everything you've come up with. You'll still need to use your design instinct to filter down your test cells into the ones that you truly believe in and into the ones that you think will actually have an impact on your users. If you can't quickly see a difference between one test cell and another, it's worth questioning if your users will either and whether it will in turn result in a change in behavior that could actually impact your metrics.

You can also take advantage of the sequential nature of experimentation. For example, if you're testing sizes of buttons, you could consider just doing small and large in your initial test, to see if changing button size makes a difference at all. If you find that changing the button size does indeed have a measurable effect on your user's behavior, then you might want to continue to invest time into exploring different button sizes more granularly to optimize, but you will eventually need to balance testing something like button sizes against testing other parts of your experience that might have a bigger effect on customer behavior and therefore more potential impact on your metrics.

EXAMPLE: NETFLIX ON PLAYSTATION 3

To illustrate the way in which your design reflects your hypothesis, let's look at an in-depth example. You can always do parallel testing where you are exploring multiple hypotheses at the same time and for each hypothesis you might find that you can design multiple treatments of each hypothesis. This is what happened when the Netflix team launched their experience on the PS3. The team focused on four hypotheses, which we introduced in Chapter 4 to build out and test. Now, we'll show you what those hypotheses looked like when visualized:

Hypothesis 1

In the original or the control PS3 experience, many users expressed a concern that they were only getting access to a limited part of the catalog. The basis for Hypothesis 1 was to ensure that users felt confident that they had access to the entire catalog. By providing a menu, they were trying to give the user an overview of all the areas of the catalog at Netflix and allow the user to drill deeper either through the menu or via the box shots at the left (Figure 5-8). This design was predominantly focused on making it apparent to the user that they had access to the full catalog of movies and TV shows.

However, one of the downsides of a design like this is that it can also be quite complex. The user can easily see that they have access to a lot of functionality, but it might feel like more work to get through the full catalog.

FIGURE 5-8.
Hypothesis that browsing more titles using a flexible menu system and hierarchy will lead to more viewing.

Hypothesis 2

While the first hypothesis traded simplicity for depth, in the second hypothesis, the team strove to simplify the design (Figure 5-9). Everything from using a flat hierarchy (no drilling deeper) to having the entire experience in a single view was a means of simplifying the prior design. There were no categories to drill into. Only a few ways to navigate—up, down, left, and right. This concept also most closely mimicked the successful website interface.

FIGURE 5-9.
Concept for a simple, flat interface that focuses on content.

Hypothesis 3

The argument was made that the team could simplify the design even further. And in this hypothesis, they attempted to challenge a core design principle at Netflix, which was that you needed to show users box art from the very first screen (Figure 5-10). This kind of exploratory testing can be a really great mechanism for deciding whether long-established beliefs should still stand.

Here the driving concept was that you could simplify the experience more by separating the navigation from the content itself. Many people seemed to know that they wanted to watch a "drama" before they even launched Netflix. If you could give them even fewer choices and guide them through a step-by-step process to select the movie, it would make the process faster for them by presenting less along the way. The team took away as many distractions of choice as they could at each step in the process.

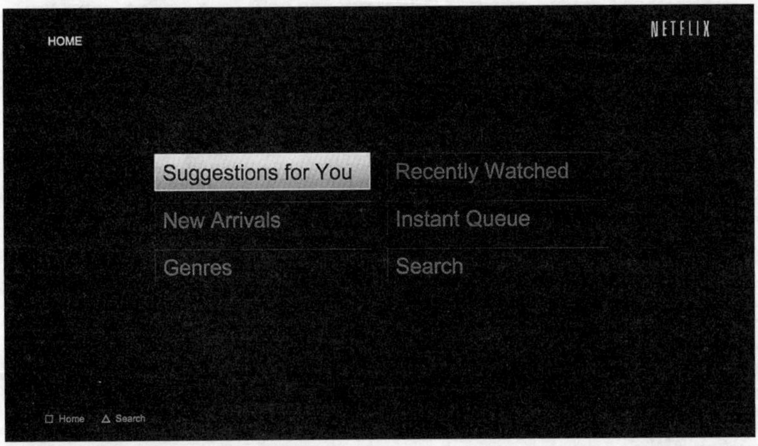

FIGURE 5-10.
Hypothesis to simplify by separating navigation from content.

Hypothesis 4

In this final hypothesis (Figure 5-11), the team started to think about how people watch TV today. People are used to turning on the TV, sitting back, and just flipping through channels to serendipitously find something to watch—why not replicate that experience? Let customers decide what to watch through the act of watching. In this design, as you clicked through each box shot, video would start playing. The idea was that you might stumble onto an interesting moment of a TV show or movie and then keep watching. The differences between this design and the others was that you had to significantly limit the number of box shots that were on the page since so much of the real estate was taken up by the video.

FIGURE 5-11.
Hypothesis of a video-rich browsing experience.

These four hypotheses were A/B tested against each other and though there were many variables that were different from concept to concept, the belief was that by launching these different experiences to their users the team would get directional guidance about what the potential was for each of these different ideas.

Within each hypothesis, minor differences or variables were also tested so that each hypothesis had perhaps four or five test cells within it. For example, in Hypothesis 4, the variation was whether or not the video started playing automatically.

This example illustrates how it's possible to be working on a global problem while also using A/B testing to validate a few concrete hypotheses against a specific metric (consumption time). Each of these concepts tries to serve the same goal—so while the design may differ dramatically, they share the common goal to "lead to more viewing hours." At the same time, the teams also looked at the resulting data and tried to drill into all the other metrics in order to understand where the strengths and weaknesses were in each of the versions. So to that end, you could say that both exploration and evaluation were being done using this set of A/B tests. We wanted to include this example to show how adopting A/B testing doesn't mean that you need to be restricted to small changes. We believe tests like these "large-scale concept tests" can provide a lot of directional information for you as a designer.

EXAMPLE: SPOTIFY NAVIGATION

Let's look at another example of how designing for A/B testing can work in practice. In 2016, the existing Spotify navigation on the mobile application was in desperate need of a cleanup. It had grown organically over the years and become confusing and cumbersome to use.

While everyone in the team instinctually knew that the navigation could be improved, there was also evidence from research that indicated that simplifying the navigation and restructuring it to more clearly reflect what a user could do in Spotify could significantly improve the user experience. For example:

- In usability testing, the task completion rate for the existing navigation was very low. For example, if a researcher asked a user to complete a core task for Spotify's product, such as "find some music to dance to," only 30% of the users could do so successfully.
- A previous test that performed poorly indicated that one of the reasons it did so was because of some changes to the navigationt—the team thought would not have a sizable effect. (This is also a good example of how you can learn from "failed" tests as well as successful ones.)
- Finally, there was also a lot of discussion in the design community about UX best practices around avoiding the "hamburger" menu, which created an "out of sight, out of mind" navigation structure[3,4] (circled in red in Figure 5-12).

---

3 *https://techcrunch.com/2014/05/24/before-the-hamburger-button-kills-you/*

4 *http://blog.booking.com/hamburger-menu.html*

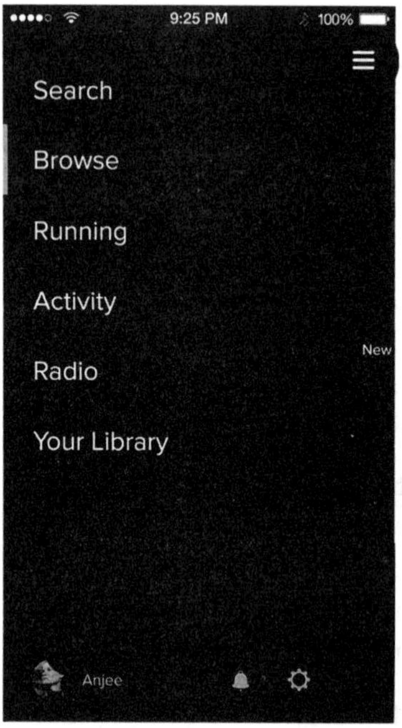

FIGURE 5-12.
The Spotify navigation with the "hamburger" menu.

The team believed that if they could successfully improve the user experience by fixing the navigation, they might ultimately have a positive effect on "second-week retention," which is the number of users that stay with Spotify (or "retain" two weeks after signing up) Second week retention is often a good prediction of long-term retention (and is this used as a proxy metric for long term retention). Therefore, looking at retention just two weeks after a user signs up allows the company to get a perspective on how their test is performing fairly quickly.

In Figure 5-13, which shows how this example maps to the framework that we introduced in Chapter 3, you can see that one of the problem/opportunity areas identified is navigation. There certainly might have been other data that would have pointed to other areas of focus aside from navigation (e.g., ease of use), but for the sake of simplicity, we'll only focus on one problem/opportunity area. The team decided to approach this problem/opportunity area using iterative A/B testing to understand what changes within the navigation space could improve second week retention.

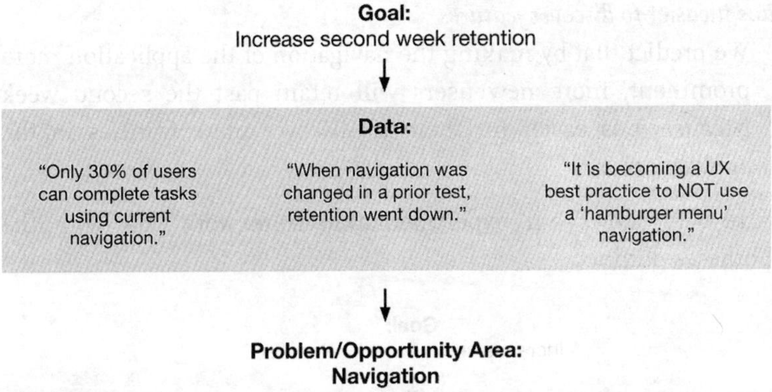

FIGURE 5-13.
Spotify navigation example using the framework introduced in Chapter 3 showing the data that led to the "problem/opportunity" area of "navigation."

Experiment 1: Defining the hypothesis to get early directional feedback

As the team broke this problem space down, they came up with two different hypotheses to test. One was around restructuring the information architecture of the navigation to make the "value proposition" (or what Spotify offers) more clear. A better organization of the navigation could clarify the main activities and areas in Spotify:

- Access to the large catalog of music ("all the world's music")
- Access to the music saved and earmarked by the user ("my world of music")
- The intersection of the two preceding bullets ("music I like and might like")

The other hypothesis was around making the navigation more prominent in the UI so that it would be easier for users to discover the features that were in the Spotify app. Using the formula introduced in Chapter 4, you could articulate this as:

Clarify the value proposition

We predict that by simplifying the information architecture of the navigation, more new users will retain past the second week because the organization of the features will be more logical and therefore the value of Spotify's services will be more clear.

Make it easier to discover features

> We predict that by making the navigation of the application more prominent, more new users will retain past the second week because it is easier for them to discover more features in the application.

Figure 5-14 shows our experimentation framework now with the hypotheses outlined.

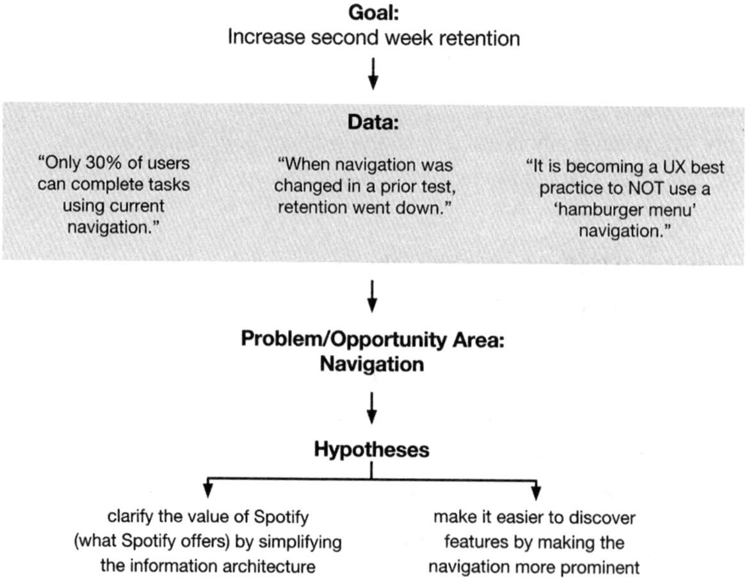

FIGURE 5-14.
Spotify navigation example showing the two hypotheses that were being explored.

Experiment 1: Designing the hypotheses

Figure 5-15 shows two examples of designs the team created to represent the two hypotheses that they came up with and compares them to the control. Here you'll see that in the treatment of the first hypothesis, the content of the navigation has changed, but the mechanism to get there (the "hamburger menu") is still the same. We are just showing one treatment here for simplicity, but the team also tried different treatments with different information architectures as well.

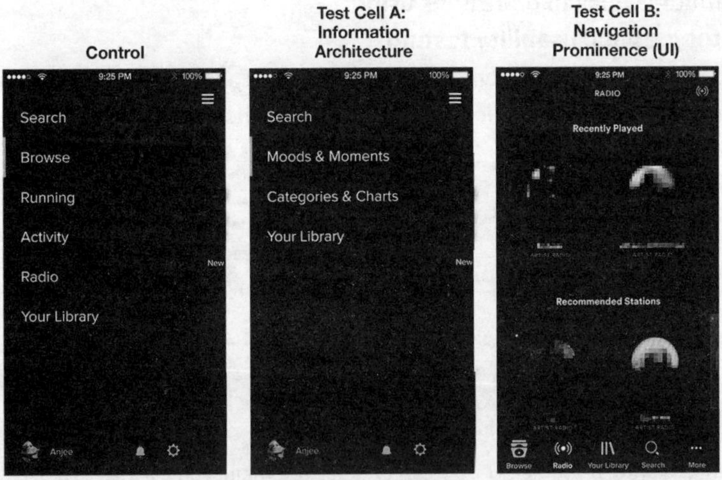

FIGURE 5-15.
The Control navigation shown next to two examples of hypotheses for improving it by either simplifying the information architecture (cell A) or by making the navigation more prominent (cell B).

If you look at the treatment for the second hypothesis, the team had to make some decisions about which tabs to set as the first four and which to put behind the "ellipses" tab, in order to keep the same basic grouping as the control.

This first round of A/B testing was done to get some directional learning on a large sample before the team invested heavily in one direction or another. Because this was an early and informational test, the team didn't spend as much time on fine-tuning the design . Since this was a test intended purely for learning, they never intended to fully launch either of these cells to the entire user base.

The results of this initial test showed that there wasn't a significant effect on second-week retention for either of the treatments. However, the treatment with a more prominent navigation (test cell B) improved some of the secondary metrics that the team was interested in. Users who experienced test cell B tended to explore more of the application. The team knew about some evidence from a separate piece of analytics research that showed increased exploration of the application was tied to retention. Being aware of this older data helped the team decide to invest further in exploring a more prominent navigation.

Interlude: Quick explorations using prototypes and usability testing

In Chapter 3, you might remember that we talked about taking an iterative approach to experimentation. Figure 5-16 shows how we described this.

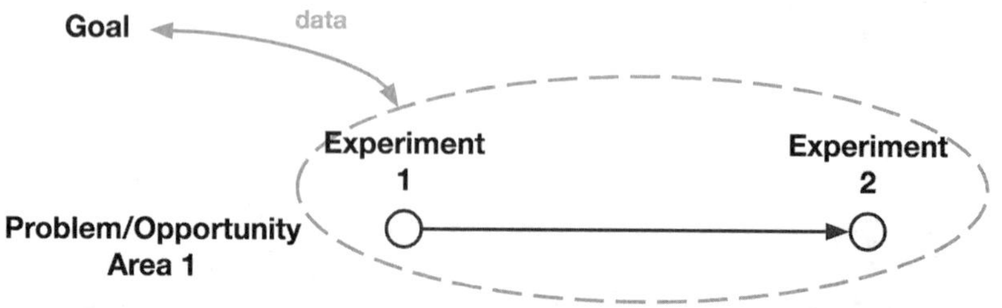

FIGURE 5-16.
When exploring a problem/opportunity area, you might run a series of experiments. Each experiment can provide new data that informs your goal.

Before jumping into another round of A/B testing right away, the team created some quick prototypes to explore different ways to make the navigation more prominent. You could say that they were moving down the spectrum of "global" to "local" and from "exploratory" to "evaluatory." Some of the things they explored included placing the navigation at the top and bottom of the screen, more prominent directory structures, as well as tab variations that included fewer items, different icons, and icons with and without labels. Usability testing showed that explorations that used the tab structure were generally more successful than the other explorations. Triangulating methods by conducting lightweight usability testing early on made it clear that the team should focus in that direction.

Although we are focusing on A/B testing in this book, we wanted to highlight how using different methods can be beneficial to getting different kinds of data and information at different stages in your design process.

Experiment 2: Refining the "tabbed" navigation

With this information in mind, the team went into another set of A/B tests focusing on the bottom tab bar. In Figure 5-17, you see the next iteration of the A/B test. You'll notice that the team was now testing two different treatments, each with five tabs, against a new "hamburger" menu control which had fewer navigation items. Two versions of the information architecture were being tested (remember in Chapter 4 when we suggested you keep some of your old hypotheses in your back pocket?). In test cell A, the "Profile" page had been combined with the "Your Library" tab; in test cell B, "Radio" had been combined with the "Browse" tab.

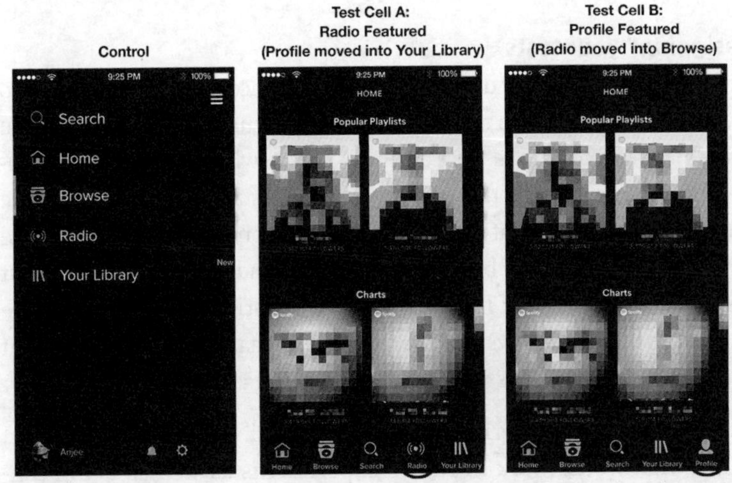

FIGURE 5-17.
Design treatments for Experiment 2 showing the "hamburger" navigation control versus the two versions of the tabbed navigation.

EXPERIMENT 2: INFORMATION ARCHITECTURE		
Control	**Cell A**	**Cell B**
Search	Home	Home
Home	Browse	Browse
Browse	Search	Search
Radio	Radio	Your Library
Your Library	Your Library	Profile

Now, all of this was being tested on iOS and on Android, and this time the new designs resulted in an improvement to second-week retention. Cell A had the added benefit of also increasing another proxy metric that the team cared about—and so it made sense to launch that one to all users.

After this, the team continued to run experiments to further refine the experience. They experimented with things like number of tabs, labels for the tabs and icon treatments. When it no longer seemed like the experiments they were running were yielding the results they were looking for (impact on key metrics) they determined that they had reached a local maxima in the navigation space. Then, the team was able to move on to other problem area/opportunities to experiment in.

"Designing" your tests

As much as we talk about designing the experiences that you are going to test, it's also important to think about the structure of the test itself. We sometimes refer to this as "test design." This is where you take into consideration the set of cells that you are testing. As a team will you be able to get the information that you are looking for from this experiment? Are there any cells that might be extraneous or redundant? Are there any test cells that would be better in the next set of experiments rather than the one you are running now? Are there test cells that are missing, but that would address other ideas your team is thinking about?

You should see each experiment as an opportunity to build your instinct around what would work in future experiments as well as being concerned about the results for the experiment you happen to be running now. There are two things that can help at this stage:

- Articulating a strong list of things that you hope to learn (both in success and failure) *before* you invest in building out your current solution and testing it on your users.
- Asking yourself "If *X* succeeds/fails, what experiment would I run next? What is the next set of experiences I would design?"

This can help you to take a step back and consider what you might choose to amplify differently in each test cell for your current experiment. It might also result in you choosing not to bother with refinements that you might make later because those refinements don't contribute to learning that would affect your decision on "what to design next."

It's useful to think of all of your test cells as part of a larger portfolio. Any given experiment is just one in a series of experiments that you might run. In this way, just as the design process itself is iterative, so is A/B testing. One tangible benefit of this is that you can feel free to exaggerate features of a test cell with the intention to learn about the impact that it has on user behavior, rather than the intention of shipping that as a polished design, letting you take more risks that better inform your knowledge and understanding.

Let's return to our camp metaphor. Let's say that you have a hypothesis that you can increase enrollment by offering some new activities. Our hypothesis is:

> We predict that by adding new activities to our program, more campers will enroll because we will be able to engage a wider range of interests and attract a broader group of kids.

It's your first time experimenting with this idea, so you cast a wide net and decide to offer kayaking, orienteering, bird watching, studio painting, and hip-hop dance. The "control" in your test would be to not offer any new activities. Thinking back to our conversation about asking meaningful questions in Chapter 4, you choose activities that give you a nice range of variables that you can learn about.

WHAT DO WE WANT TO LEARN?	WHAT EXPERIMENT WOULD WE DO NEXT?
Do campers prefer outdoor activities to indoor activities?	Do people prefer outdoor water activities or outdoor land activities? Depending on what we learn, we could also optimize to figure out which indoor or outdoor activities perform best.
Do campers prefer strenuous activities or relaxing ones?	Try other strenuous or relaxing activities depending on what we learn to see which specific activities perform best.

You have both outdoor and indoor activities, you also have activities that take place on land and in water and you have some activities that are relaxing and some that are more active. Sometimes it can be helpful to organize your test cells into a table as shown here.

	INDOOR VERSUS OUTDOOR	WATER VERSUS LAND	ACTIVE VERSUS RELAXING
Cell A: Kayaking	Outdoor	Water	Active
Cell B: Orienteering	Outdoor	Land	Active
Cell C: Bird watching	Outdoor	Land	Relaxing
Cell D: Studio Painting	Indoor	Land	Relaxing
Cell E: Hip-Hop Dance	Indoor	Land	Active

If you were just thinking about this single experiment, then the likely next step is that you would just take the "winning" activity, the one that had the highest enrollment, and offer it to your campers in the coming year. However, if you were proactively thinking about refining your hypothesis through a few more experiments, then you could begin to plan some of your next steps right away. For example:

- If all the "active" test cells (A, B, and E) perform well, then you might want to try another experiment with only different kinds of strenuous activity. Would you offer activities that are even *more* strenuous than the ones you tested in this experiment?
- If you see a trend where the "indoor" activities (cells D and E) seem to perform better than the "outdoor" ones, then you might want to explore adding other "indoor" activities, like drama or arts and crafts.
- If you find that both of the "relaxing" activities (cells C and D) and the "outdoor" activities seem to perform well, an option might be to offer outdoor painting in the next experiment.

At this point, you might even decide that it's not worth differentiating between land and water activities, so you might put off Test Cell A off until the next round. Also, based on the results you get from this experiment, you might consider looking for other areas where you can apply your learnings. If it seems that your campers would prefer more outdoor activities, then you might think about what activities you currently have that you might want to move outdoors to see whether it's the location of the activities or the nature of the type of activities you've offered outdoors that caused that preference. Let's say you already have a yoga class which is in the auditorium, maybe you'll see if your campers would prefer to do yoga outside instead? What would you learn if the outdoor yoga class did not perform as well as expected?

OTHER CONSIDERATIONS WHEN DESIGNING TO LEARN

There are a few traps that you might fall into when you are in the design phase. We'll point out some of the most common ones in this section. We'll also highlight some of the other things you could take into consideration during this phase as well.

Polishing your design too much, too early

At the beginning of this chapter, we talked about the importance of designing to the right level of granularity for the stage of experiment that you are in. A fairly common pitfall is getting too detailed too quickly. For example, if the second or third experiment in the Spotify navigation example was five different test cells where the icon styles were varied, instead of considering if the navigation structure could have been simplified further (from five tabs to three tabs) then it might have felt like the team leaped too quickly to testing an execution detail. You would want to prove that your hypothesis was worthwhile first before investing more time in polishing your treatment of it.

On the other side of this issue is the risk of only releasing design work that addresses the MDE (minimum detectable effect, first introduced in Chapter 2). Many designers worry that once they "ship" a version, they'll never get the chance to revisit or polish it. We already talked about the importance of building alignment within your team about whether you are "exploring" or "evaluating" your hypothesis, as a way to help determine how close you are to finishing, and therefore how much polish your design work should have. Beyond that, having a clear plan of next steps as you're experimenting can help to combat that kind of behavior, so that designers always have the opportunity to feel proud of finished and launched work. To do so, consider highlighting not just what you would learn, but package it along with a series of additional things that you might have planned, in order to get it to a stage where you feel comfortable with launching it to 100% or your user base.

A helpful tactic is to keep a list of the things you would refine or investigate further as you are designing your test cells—you could call this your *100% launch plan,* which gets its name from the notion of rolling out an experience to 100% of your users. This way you already have a number of ideas around where you would invest further. If your experiment is successful, then this list might include things like:

- Visual and language polish
- Refinement of edge and corner cases
- Variations on visual treatments

Now, depending on the kind of test that you are running, what you are trying to learn, and how mature your product is, it could also be the case that having fine-tuned language or visuals might play a significant role in your results and should be taken into consideration early on.

You will need to become a good judge of how much you need to refine the execution of your idea in order to be effective at getting a response from your users. If you've done usability studies or used prototyping extensively, you should be familiar with finding this balance. Fundamentally you want to be able to understand if the idea/feature or concept that you have resonates with your users in the way you expect it to. Ensure your design communicates that proposition effectively enough to get a response. As we've stated before with respect to the MDE, if we can't measure the impact of our design work, then we can't learn from what we've done. You should feel that your design does a good job of expressing your hypothesis such that if it were correct you would have seen a response. The question to ask here is "If this test cell doesn't perform as well as the control will I blame the design for not being effective *or* will I dismiss the core concept instead?" If you think you might blame the design for not being a good treatment of the hypothesis, then you may want to do more work on it.

Underlying all of this is the notion of prioritization. You'll have to use your design intuition, your interests, and negotiations with your team and other data sources as you navigate a way to balance providing the "best" treatment of a hypothesis with polishing individual A/B test cells. This is another point where all of those factors will have to come together.

Edge cases and "worst-case" scenarios

As you are designing different treatments of your hypothesis, you'll want to ensure that none of the designs are at a disadvantage because of edge cases that could break the experience for your users. One approach is to exclude edge-case scenarios from the experiment so that you can keep your data clean. This means, of course, that you will need to design for them later—but only if your experiment is successful. This is one of the advantages of experimentation: you get to decide who is "in" the test groups, so you can ensure that it works for the majority and see how the design lands with some users before fixing those edge cases for everyone.

Another philosophically distinct approach that we learned about in addressing those edge cases, is using "worst-case" data. Josh Brewer, former Principal Designer at Twitter and currently a cofounder of the design tools startup Abstract, shared with us how it "became a necessity" at Twitter to use and consider the messiest possible tweets in their designs: tweets with authors who have very long names with wide letters, geolocation information, broken images, a whole bunch of favorites, and so on. Using the real worst-case data from your company (What *is* the longest name in your user database? How many favorites does the most favorited tweet have?) is one way to make sure you stress test your designs rigorously and steer away from wasting time testing work that is slated to fail at the outset.

At Airbnb, they also incorporate the notion of worst-case data in their design by including it in their mocks and prototypes. The goal is to ensure the product is well designed for the best- and worst-case scenarios. For example, they make prototypes showing a listing with low-quality photos and incomplete information, as well as a listing with high-quality photos and in-depth information. And they make prototypes for a host with one listing and another with 50 listings so they know that every user will be supported.

As the company grows, international considerations become even more important. At Airbnb, it was a big realization for the design team when they learned that the majority of the interactions between hosts and guests were not in English. Hearing that data helped provoke the team to recognize how they needed to broaden their thinking around the experiences they were designing. The copy, layout, and overall utility of the product needs to be thought through for a global audience. Simple things like word length and line breaks in different languages become problematic if not addressed early in the design work. Now designers are expected to create mocks and prototypes in a variety of languages to ensure the product will support the differences between them.

Addressing these edge cases could become another part of your *100% launch plan* along with design polish.

Taking advantage of other opportunities to learn about your design

Every time you run an A/B test, it's a good opportunity to learn things about your design beyond whether it impacted the metric you were looking to affect. The design phase is a great time to get involved in the discussion around instrumentation and measurement. Think of this as designing the measurements for the change you expect to see as a result of your design.

You might be pinpointing a very specific thing that you want to learn or you might be taking more of a shotgun approach where you are trying many different design techniques. Think in advance about what kind of data you would like to see from your design and work with the partners you are building the product with to ensure that you have the right kind of tracking on your data:

- What are the elements in your design that you want to understand? What data will best help you learn about those elements? (Some examples might be the number of clicks on a particular element, how many times something is seen before it's clicked, how much of a given feature does someone see—page scrolls, or how far down a process the average user gets.)
- Aside from tracking elements on a particular view, what are other things about the users' path or journey that you would want to understand? (How did they get there? What are the demographics of the people who use it? Where do they go next? How often do they use something over the course of a session or over the course of their time as a user?)

IDENTIFYING THE RIGHT LEVEL OF TESTING FOR DIFFERENT STAGES OF EXPERIMENTATION

In the Spotify navigation example we shared earlier in this chapter, you saw that there were a couple of different directions that the team was exploring. The very first exploration was around the impact of information architecture on the user behavior versus the impact of the user interface (how prominent the navigation was) on the navigation. They had two hypotheses they were exploring simultaneously to improve the experience for all Spotify users:

Hypothesis 1

"We predict that by simplifying the information architecture of the navigation, more people will retain past the second week because the value proposition for Spotify will be more clear."

Hypothesis 2

"We predict that by making the navigation of the application more prominent, more people will retain past the second week because it is easier for them to discover the other features in the application."

Each hypothesis might have multiple treatments, each becoming a single test cell. This would look like Figure 5-18.

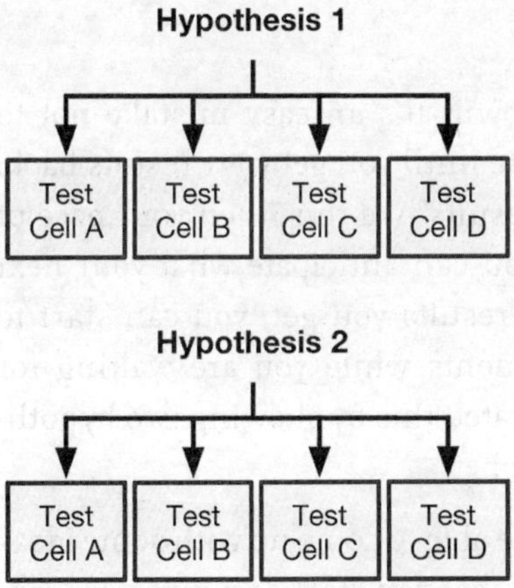

FIGURE 5-18. An experiment might have multiple hypotheses; each hypothesis can have multiple expressions or test cells.

We've already highlighted the trap of prematurely testing designs that are too specific, which could result in narrowing down your explorations too soon. We also talked about the importance of thinking of your experiments as a sequence of events, and thinking about which tests you might run next depending on the results you get. Figure 5-19 illustrates this concept.

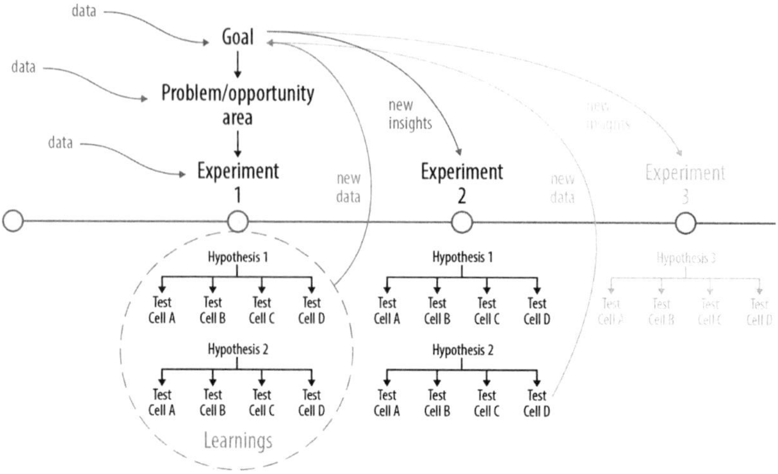

FIGURE 5-19.

Thinking about your experiments as a series can help you be proactive about how you design.

A/B testing shouldn't slow you down. It's an easy mistake not to think about what your next steps are until you get your results back. But if you are always waiting for results like this, then your pace of improvement will be limited. If you can anticipate what your next steps might be depending on the results you get, you can start to design your next stage of experiments while you are waiting for results. In Figure 5-19, we've illustrated this by showing two hypotheses that are being tested in parallel.

In this manner you might already be able to come up with some ideas for Hypothesis 1 and Hypothesis 2 that you start designing or "concepting" right away. If the actual results from your test come back, and you see that Hypothesis 2 is more successful than Hypothesis 1, you might abandon some of the exploratory work that you were doing on Hypothesis 1. However, you will also have a head start on some of the work on Hypothesis 2 and might have uncovered some new ideas in Hypothesis 1 that you could still use to inform the next round of design. This is shown in Figure 5-20.

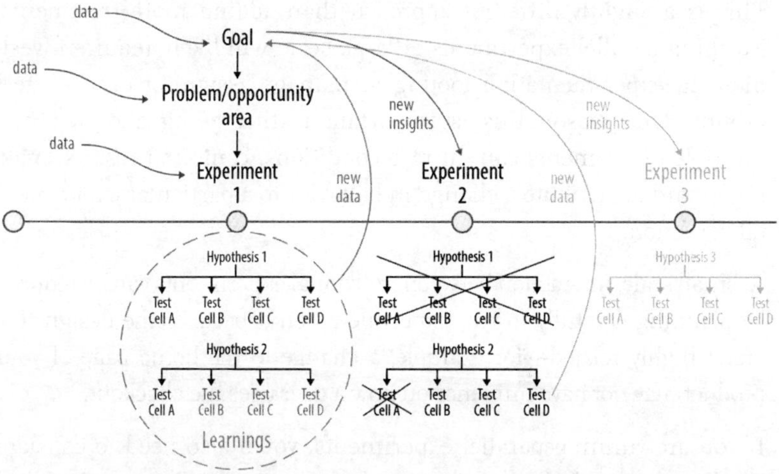

FIGURE 5-20.
As you learn from your experiments, you can adjust future experiments accordingly.

Running parallel experiments

Running parallel experiments is another way you might think about sequencing your tests. This approach can bring local/global experiments together. For example, we could run various overlapping experiments instead of individual experiments. In Figure 5-21, we show how if a number of these individual overlapping experiments won, it could be another way of getting to the global result in Figure 5-6.

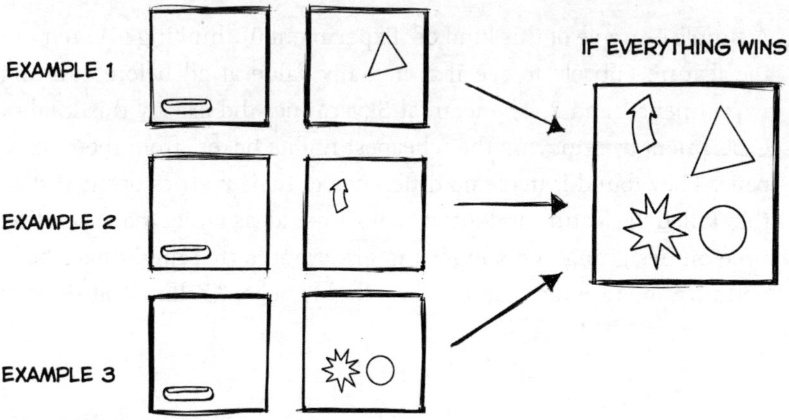

FIGURE 5-21.
How parallel experiments can work together.

This is a slightly different approach than adding more treatments. Running parallel experiments at large scale will likely require investment in experimentation tooling to manage assigning users to test groups. One reason this is important is that being allocated into multiple experiments can, in rare conditions, confound results, making it hard to attribute a change in behavior to a particular experimental condition.[5]

At small scale, interaction between individual experiments can be reduced by planning carefully to run experiments on aspects of the design that aren't highly related—for example, a change to the home page of your product may not have influence on how a user uses the checkout.

If you are running parallel experiments, you'll also need to consider whether the results you get from each experiment will be compounded when they are combined or if there were some aspects of the experience that might impact or cancel each other out. If you get two "winners" at the same time, validate how they work together with a new experiment.

Thinking about "Experiment 0"

Now, we want to introduce one more consideration when you are at the design phase. Before you get too attached to running the first experiment in a new problem/opportunity area, a good question to ask yourself is, "What is the experiment I might have run *before* the one that I am planning now?" (see Figure 5-22). This is a way to determine if you've jumped prematurely to a set of experiments that are too detailed for the phase you're in.

A simple example of this kind of "Experiment 0" thinking is to remove the feature entirely to see if it has any value at all before running Experiment 1 and 2. The team at Skyscanner did exactly this kind of experiment by removing the "cheapest flights ticker" from their home page. They found it made no difference to their metrics of interest so they killed the feature and moved onto other ideas rather than spending time on designing and supporting experiences that might have been optimizations around that "cheapest flights ticker." Killing features can

5 *http://research.google.com/pubs/pub36500.html*; *http://www.exp-platform.com/Pages/ControlledExperimentsAtLargeScale.aspx*

be a great way to save resources because it means you don't have to maintain them. This can be an added bonus, especially in teams where you tend to focus on adding features rather than removing them.

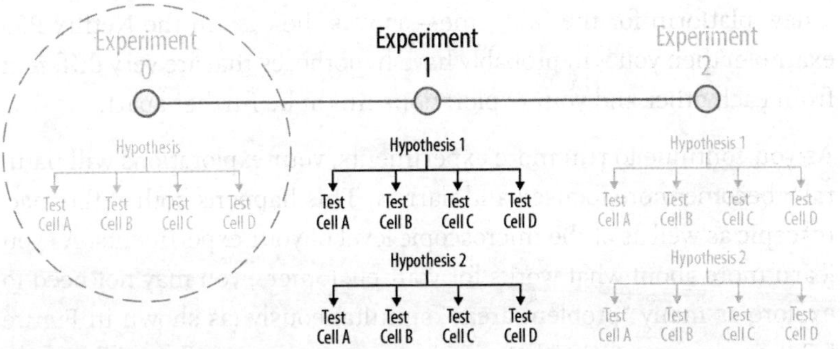

FIGURE 5-22.
Questioning what experiment you might have been able to run prior to the experiment you're currently running.

The strategy of using "painted door" experiments (discussed earlier in this chapter) is also another way of accomplishing an "Experiment 0." Before you build out the feature or invest a lot of time in crafting it, a "painted door" experiment can help you do something quick and easy that gets you some initial metrics. Ronny Kolhavi gives an example where before investing engineering effort to improve performance, Microsoft ran a latency experiment (adding various delays) to see how much speed mattered.[6]

Where you are in the product development cycle (whether you are at an exploration stage or an evaluation stage) will affect:

- The breadth or narrowness of your hypotheses
- The number and nature of variables that are being considered in your experiment
- The questions and solutions that you are investigating in your experiments

6 *https://www.quora.com/How-would-you-design-an-experiment-to-determine-the-impact-of-latency-on-user-engagement*

If you're working on a product that is fairly mature and been around for a while, you probably already have a good handle on what is and isn't working, and your experiments will be more focused. If, however, you are earlier in your stage of product development (e.g., launching on a new platform for the first time—as was the case in the Netflix PS3 example) then you will probably have hypotheses that are very different from each other and your explorations might be further apart.

As you continue to run more experiments, your explorations will naturally become more focused and narrow. This happens both at the macroscopic as well as at the microscopic level of your experiments. As you learn more about what works for your customers, you may not need to explore as many "problem areas" simultaneously (as shown in Figure 5-23) *or* you may start to focus on changing only specific variables.

A key question that gets asked often is "How do you know when to stop experimenting?" It's perhaps better to answer this by saying you shouldn't ever think about "stopping" experiments, but rather changing the nature of the experiments you are running if you don't see more gains in the area you are pursuing.

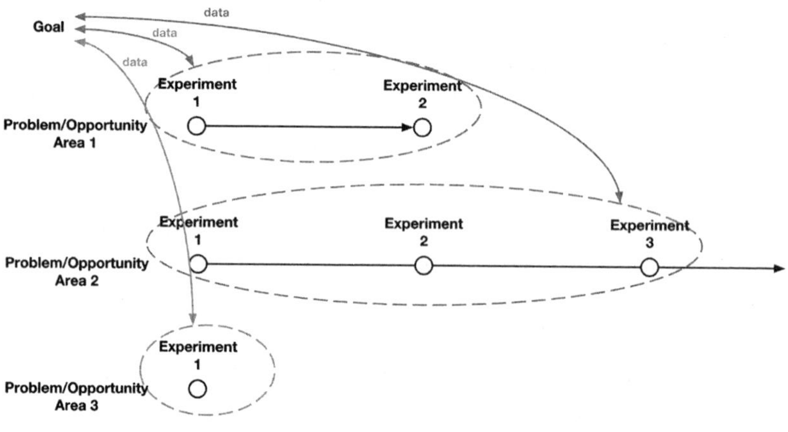

FIGURE 5-23.
You may explore multiple problem area/opportunities simultaneously.

You'll remember that we talked about this as the difference between global and local experiments and we'll revisit the return on investment in the following chapter as well when we look at results. Generally speaking, though, you will develop an understanding over time of how much effort it takes to run an experiment and the "cost" of different kinds of experiments. As you start to see how much improvement in your metrics these experiments result in, you'll become adept at making decisions around whether it's worth your efforts to continue down a single line of experimentation or to instead break out and look for a new direction.

Summary

As most designers know, there are many different ways to craft a design. In this chapter, we talked about the importance of creating multiple expressions of your hypothesis and understanding if your designs were going to be good expressions of your hypothesis.

With A/B testing, remember that each test cell is a proposed solution to a problem. It is your hope that each of the new test experiences you design will perform better in the metric that you are measuring than your control. To vet whether you're testing the right things or enough things or too many things, for each version you must keep asking yourself "What did I learn with this test cell or this design that I wouldn't have learned with the others?" If the answer to your question feels like it's premature (e.g., are you answering an evaluation question when you should be exploring?) or if it feels redundant (e.g., you already have another test cell that tells you the same thing) then consider eliminating that solution.

It's always a shame when you get to the end of the test and you realize that you've drawn yourself into a tangent during the design phase because you've somehow lost sight of the core metrics that you're trying to move or you've gotten caught up in the details. Part of data-aware design is having the ability to hold yourself accountable to producing design that is in service of delivering a great experience but also learning more about how you can make that experience as good as possible in the short and long term.

We encourage you to think as much about designing with the purpose of maximizing learning as you might think about solving the problem itself. This is a slightly different mindset than when you are "designing to ship." When you design with just shipping in mind, you sometimes don't think of the act of designing as an ongoing and iterative process. You might spend more time polishing every aspect of your design rather than focusing on the ones that are most critical to helping express your hypothesis. When you "design to learn," you're generally not designing just one experience but designing several experiences—use each of those opportunities to design as differently as you can and to learn as much as you can from the results you gather.

As a designer, you are defining and inspiring the changes in your product experience. You're in an ongoing dialogue with your customers to find out what is the best experience that you can craft for them. Your design will express the different possibilities and solutions that you can provide to your customers, and the data that you collect along the way will help you tune that experience and measure whether you've succeeded.

Finally, we want to end with a quick reminder that you can always ask your colleagues for feedback at this stage to see if they think that your designs capture the essence of the hypothesis that you are trying to represent. It's a simple way to get some feedback: think of it as "internal user testing" with your coworkers who may not have worked on the product or design. (And as you know, we always encourage leveraging methods other than A/B testing along the way to understand the impact of your designs.) Analysts who have worked with A/B testing analysis and results and user researchers who have countless hours of seeing how users respond to different designs are often very insightful at helping to recognize the effectiveness of your design and can be very good at predicting what outcomes you might expect.

Questions to Ask Yourself

We covered a lot of ground in this chapter, but wanted to highlight a few key questions that you might consider asking yourself along the way:

- How can you create a design or an experience which best expresses your hypothesis?
- How are the key components of your hypothesis represented in your design?
- How does the design you've made help you gather the right kind of data that will provide evidence in favor of or against your hypothesis?

- What are the elements that are key to your design *at this stage* in the process? What are the things you can afford to focus on later?
- What "Experiment 0" would you want to have run before running your current experiment? Should you run that "Experiment 0" first?
- Are there edge cases that could fail your design? Can you exclude them from the first iteration of your experiment to get feedback on the majority group earlier?
- For each test cell, what is the unique thing that you will learn from that cell compared to the others? (If you don't feel like you will learn something new or different, then you should question if you are really putting your effort into something that will give you measurable impact.)
- What is the minimum number of test cells (independent designs) that you need to create in order to get the learning that you are looking for?
- Can you articulate the differences between each of your test cells and also identify what it is that you will learn from them?
- Are you making the right kinds of experiments for the phase of exploration or evaluation that you are in? (Have you gone too narrow too quickly with your line of testing?) Have you aligned on that with your team?
- Are you properly scoped into a global problem or a local one? Have you aligned on that with your team?

[6]

The Analysis Phase (Getting Answers From Your Experiments)

LAUNCHING YOUR A/B TEST out "in the wild" is exciting—it's the first time you'll get to have a conversation with your users at scale about how your designs will serve them and meet their needs! This process of launching and learning from your test will be our focus in this chapter. One of the principles behind A/B testing is that it's a good idea to always test first with a very small portion of your user base. The data you get back from your experiments will give you a sense of how well your design is performing with respect to your goals, before you invest the time to launch a design to all of your users. Did the design(s) lead to the behaviors you were expecting to see? Did you see that people acted in ways which map more to your business metrics? Were you able to successfully improve the metrics that you were targeting? For example, if your goal is that your users watch more movies they like, did you see an uptick in movies selected and watched all the way through? This would indicate that your recommendation algorithms and/or your presentation of selections are more effective than in your previous design.

Once you get back data from your initial tests, you then need to decide what you'll do next. Do you take that experience and then roll it out to a larger part of your user base? Did the results suggest you are on the wrong track, that you should abandon the idea entirely? Or do you keep working on your hypothesis to improve it before testing it again? We will also tackle these types of questions in this chapter. Referring back to the framework we introduced in Chapter 3, this chapter focuses on the activities shown in Figure 6-1 (outlined in the dotted line).

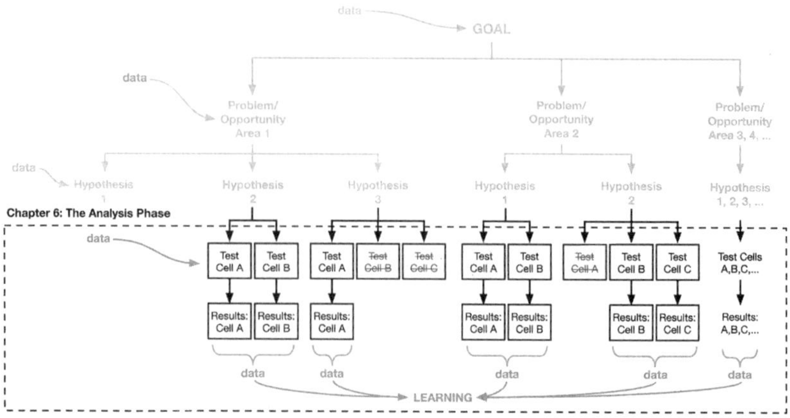

FIGURE 6-1.

"The Analysis Phase" of our experimentation framework is where you launch your test to your users, collect, and then analyze the resulting data.

Throughout this book we have been championing a data-aware strategy; part of that strategy is not reacting instantly to partial results but instead being considered and reflective about what your results mean within the context of your overall company and product goals.

In Chapters 4 and 5, we've highlighted the importance of thinking about how you'll launch your A/B test, and how that impacts the types of results you'll get and the things you can learn, right from the beginning. In this chapter, we'll have a more in-depth conversation about launching your A/B test, analyzing your results, and deciding what your next steps should be. We hope that you're excited to see everything come together as we introduce how to make actionable and data-aware decisions based on A/B testing.

Vetting Your Designs Ahead of Launch

Although we are focusing on A/B testing in this book, remember that throughout your design process you might use other forms of data to inform how you craft your experience. You can also use these methods and tools to evaluate your designs well ahead of launching them in an A/B test; you might find that you are able to eliminate a test cell or two before launch. We'll give you a quick survey (no pun intended!) of a few of the tools you might consider using. Many of the tools that we'll list here are equally useful for answering broader questions that you might be asking when first working to define your hypothesis, as well as later on in the process when you might be looking to fine-tune different elements of your experience (e.g., specific variables).

LAB STUDIES: INTERVIEWS AND USABILITY TESTING

Throughout the process leading up to launching your A/B test, there are many places where it will make sense to use lab-based user research methodologies like interviews and usability testing to refine your thinking. What we'd like to emphasize here is that speaking directly with your users throughout both the analytical and execution phases is a great way to ensure that you're ultimately designing and building something that has the potential to impact your user behavior (and therefore your metrics). And, of equal importance, doing so will ensure that the designs you launch and test at scale are a fair representation of the hypothesis and concept you're hoping to understand, not one that is doomed to fail due to implementation details.

Remember that speaking directly to users can give us insight into their motivations and the "why" behind the data we might be capturing. Here's where you can actually observe if certain design decisions resulted in the behavior you were hoping it would. Did making the image larger have the intended effect of making that feature more noticeable? Do your users describe their experience in terms that reflect your hypothesis? Are you confident that the differences between your test cells are strong enough that you can measure their differences in the data you get back? Do the designs that you've crafted feel like they address some of the problems that users identified in your analysis stage?

Many companies leverage different methods to vet designs that later get A/B tested. In a process called "Soundcheck," for example, the user research team at Spotify brings real users into the office every two or three weeks to collect user feedback on projects from across the company. Teams can sign up for a slot to get their projects Soundchecked, and because the cadence and dates of these sessions are known in advance, teams can plan to get feedback on their work in a way that aligns with their timeline and needs. Every time Spotify runs a Soundcheck, the product teams learn actionable things about their users to inspire copy and design changes that evolve the test cells before they are launched in an A/B test at scale, or encourage teams to go back to the drawing board on ideas that didn't succeed in small sample research. This helps those teams put forth the best possible designs when they deploy their A/B test to experiment at scale.

SURVEYS

Surveys are also useful ways to vet designs ahead of a launch. There are certain kinds of experiments that lend themselves well to surveys as a tool to get data back on your designs ahead of launch. We have seen this be very effective especially when testing changes that are more focused on the visual layer and don't necessarily require the user to step through a sequence of actions. Examples here might be logo or icon changes, or different visual and UI treatments. We've found surveys to be useful for measuring and understanding the emotional impact that a design might have, and identify reasons why different groups of users might have different responses to a design.

Surveys are a good complement to A/B tests because while surveys can give you a quantifiable signal about how users will perceive or react to something, they can't tell you how the design will actually perform in the wild. People are notoriously bad at predicting their own behaviors. However, surveys help provide nuance and context to the behaviors you might see in an A/B test by explaining the "why"—the emotions, attitudes, and need states that led to or correlate with those behaviors.

WORKING WITH YOUR PEERS IN DATA

Finally, we'll return to one of the themes we've been emphasizing throughout the book, which is that if you happen to work with people who are focused on doing the analysis of data or gathering the research, we have often found that they have even better tuned instincts around how customers will react than product managers or designers. Analysts and user researchers get exposed to a wide range of data from many different sources and are often quite strong at being able to guess the outcome of what testing your designs will have.

This is another point where we'd like to highlight that if you are working with data analysts who will be responsible for doing the analysis on your tests after they are launched, then bringing them in early into the process to help you "design" your test cell structure can be really useful. Data analysts can often help you to understand which variables will be most useful to test, whether you have test cells that seem redundant with each other, and ultimately how many test cells you might want to test or not. As we've discussed before, analysts and user researchers can help you to determine how to sequence your tests based on what it is that you hope to learn and what is most important to learn first, second, third, and so on.

Launching Your Design

By this point you've designed several test cells that you want to put in front of the world. You might have used complementary methods to vet the design ahead of launch, but now it's time to deploy your experiment at scale. The mechanics of launching your A/B test will depend a lot on things that might be particular to your business as well as your product and the technology it leverages. However, we will cover some of the things to consider when deploying your A/B test regardless of exactly how you do it.

As a reminder of where we are in the overall process, this is the first time that a group of your users at scale will be exposed to your design/experiment. After your test launches, there will be a period of time which you will have designated in your test design where your users are interacting with your design, you'll need to wait to see the behavioral impact of your design. Only after you get sufficient data can you decide what to do next; please check back to our discussion on the relationship between effect size and sample size.

Also remember that you'll only be launching this experience to a subset of your users, and therefore you'll want to take the necessary precautions so that you can be sure that the results that you get from your A/B test will be applicable to your broader user base (this includes thinking about cohorts, segments, and representativeness as discussed in Chapter 2, and making sure that there are no confounding variables such as seasonal variations or edge case conditions that might obviate what you can learn from your test). This is also where concepts that we first introduced in earlier chapters around minimum detectable effect, power, and sample size become important. We'll spend a little time in this section revisiting those concepts in service of helping you prepare to launch your test.

First, you should define the *minimum detectable effect* (MDE), or the minimum change that you want to detect in order to call your test a success. You should be partnering with your data friends in the business functions at your company to model the long-term impact of the MDE to your business. Remember that making any change to your experience isn't free—your business will have to pay for the time it takes to design, test, and implement those changes and roll them out to your entire user base. And, of equal or superior importance, your consumers will "pay" through the friction it takes them to relearn an existing experience, where bigger changes result in greater friction. Essentially, when you define an MDE you're saying observing *x* increase/decrease in your metrics will justify those business and experiential costs. Any difference below that MDE means for your test that it's probably not worth launching that experience right now.

BALANCING TRADE OFFS TO POWER YOUR TEST

Recall from Chapter 2 that you'll need a powerful enough and properly designed test to detect a difference at least as big as your MDE. Power in particular depends on a few things, including your sample size and how confident you want to be. And in turn, defining your sample size will force you to trade off between the percentage of users you roll out to and the time you leave your test running. As you can see from Figure 6-2, then, the different considerations for rollout that we've already introduced throughout the book so far constrain each other. In practice, this means that as you decide to roll out an A/B test, you'll be weighing different decisions against each other. We'll walk you through some of these tensions to help you think about how to make those types of decisions.

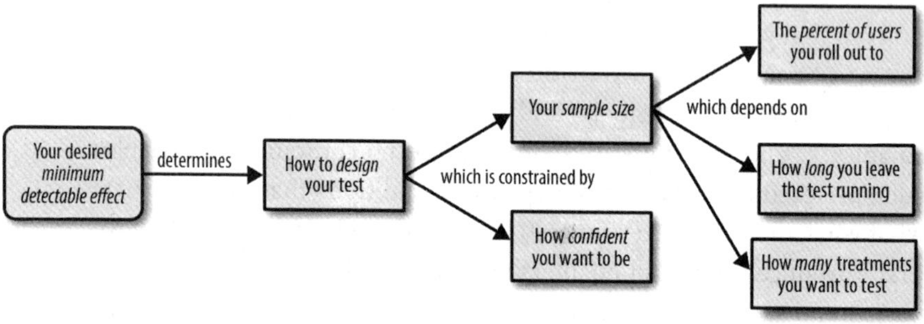

FIGURE 6-2.

Considerations you should take into account when rolling out your A/B test.

Weighing sample size and significance level

In Chapter 2, we told you that the power of your test depends on the sample size you have and the significance level you are comfortable with. In practice, you'll probably use a standard significance level for all experiments, usually 0.05, but there are scenarios when you may consider changing this, and we'll explore them here.

Let's say that you're thinking about rolling out a really substantial change to your experience, and now you want to evaluate whether this global change is worthwhile. In this specific case, your goal in making the proposed changes is to improve your overall user experience, which you hope leads to a measurable increase in your metric of interest, for instance, by increasing retention rates. Because the change is so huge, you won't roll the test or the change to everyone out unless you observe a measurable increase in retention in a well-crafted experiment. If the experiment indicates no or negative change, then the roll out to the entire user base should be blocked. In the scenario we just described, you'll notice that we kept emphasizing how important it was to observe a meaningful and measurable change. In other words, this is a scenario in which you and your coworkers would likely be relatively risk averse: you're looking for high confidence that the changes have the desired impact (since they change your product in a way it would be hard to turn back from), otherwise you won't roll out. In cases like this you'll want to have high confidence in your result to minimize the risk of being wrong. As you might recall from Chapter 2, this means that you'll need a relatively large sample size in order to power a test at such a significance level, let's say 0.01. For you, the added cost of a large sample size is worthwhile to have a higher degree of confidence in your result.

Compare the scenario we just described against a very early stage exploration of a concept—an exploratory learning test. In the latter case, you're looking for directional feedback about a new idea you're thinking about. Recall our discussion in Chapter 5 about designing and testing for the appropriate level of polish, and our earlier discussions of balancing speed and learning. In these exploratory tests, you should have already determined with your team that you aren't rolling out this first iteration of the concept. Instead, you are simply looking for a signal to understand whether you've identified a promising area to further consider, or whether abandoning the idea and moving on to something else before investing too much time and resources will better serve you. There will be more opportunities to validate the idea and verify that your design delivers the intended results; this is just the first iteration of the idea. While replication like this is part of the plan, this is the only case you might consider reducing your significance level to something like 0.1 and therefore your sample size (which means your test can be faster and less costly to run).

So, as you can see, you'll have to balance your degree of confidence in the data with the amount of time you have to learn.

Getting the sample that you need (rollout % versus test time)

Let's say you've made the decision about how to trade off confidence and sample size. You know the MDE you are aiming for, and have determined the sample size you need and how many treatments you can test. The last key question you'll need to think about is how to get that sample: Will you deploy the experience to a greater percentage of your users, or run your test for a longer time?

As we already mentioned, when you roll out an A/B test, it is not launched to your entire population at once. In practice, this means that you'll allocate some of your users to the test cells, and keep the rest of your users out of the experiment. This is because you want to avoid constantly shifting experiences for your users—remember an experiment from your perspective will always feel like a *new experience*, and possibly a bewildering one, for your users.

In Chapter 4 we talked about the balance between learning and speed. Larger companies with many active users generally roll out an A/B test to 1% or less, because they can afford to keep the experimental group small while still collecting a large enough sample in a reasonable amount of time without underpowering their experiment. Imagine comparing a company with a million daily active users to a company with 10,000. The company with a million daily active users can allot 1% of their daily users to the test condition and get 10,000 users in a single day. It would take the smaller company 100 days to get that same sample size—far too long for most A/B tests. If they ramped up their rollout rate from 1% to 10%, though, they could cut that time down to 10 days, which is much more reasonable.

It's important to allocate enough users to a test so that you can measure small changes to your metric of interest. Tests where the size of your user base is limited, either because your user base is too small or because you don't have enough time to let your test run, can pose challenges. For example, let's say you have significantly more users on iOS than you do on Android. You might find that running tests on the Android platform that get you results you can be confident might be much harder for you as a result. This is why we introduced the concepts of sample size and power early on—knowing about these constraints early on will help you think big enough with the hypothesis and tests you're running.

Who are you including in your sample?

Finally, we want to remind you that it's important to be sensitive to *who* you allocate into your test group, and how. Remember that when you're rolling out an A/B test, you should select a group of users to act as the control group (no changes to their experience) and then allocate other users into each of your test cells. Both your control and your test groups should be representative of the portion of your user base that you hope to learn about.

Let's return to our camp metaphor. Imagine if you allocated your campers to the experimental conditions for your race to the campsite based on when they arrived at camp. Let's say you had 20 people that you needed to put into four groups. One way to do this is to take the first 5 people and put them into one group, the next 5 people in the next group, and so on. The earliest campers might be the most eager because they've come to camp before, which would introduce bias because you're comparing a group of experienced campers to a group of new campers, who may never have gone hiking before. You would have inadvertently created a selection process where team 1 is stronger than team 2, which is stronger than team 3, and so on. So to counter this, you might instead have people count off in order—1, 2, 3, 4—and then ask all the 1s to form a team, all the 2s to form another team, and so on. This might be a better strategy for creating a more random sampling.

Recall from our conversation in Chapter 2 that the portion of your audience that you test with will constrain who the data *represents*. For instance, if your hypothesis targets a specific audience, you might want to experiment specifically on that audience first. In other cases, it might make sense to test with new or existing users. Another important reminder is that in order to meaningfully compare your test and control conditions, you'll need to be sure that there are no hidden differences between the users in your control condition and your test conditions that might lead to confounds: differences in your groups that did not result from the change you made, but instead from other differences that you did not anticipate and control for. We encourage you to revisit Chapter 2 as you're thinking about allocating your users to tests.

In line with this point, Eric Colson shared a story with us about how important it was for the team at Stitch Fix to be especially disciplined about how they selected users to be in the test and control cells for their A/B tests:

> A rookie mistake in A/B testing is not properly randomizing your test and control groups. Suppose you have a particular treatment you wanted to test—it could be a new offer, a new UI, whatever. It's intuitive to draw a sample of new users—say, 100,000 of them—and then give them a test treatment and then compare their behaviors to 'everybody else.' A naive team may draw the sample by exposing the next 100,000 users that come along to the experimental treatment and then resuming the default experience for everybody else after. But this is an arbitrary sample—not a random one! The naive team may push back. "What are you talking about? There was nothing special about those users. I just took the *next* 100,000 that came along." But there was a difference: time. The users that received the test treatment were selected at a different point in time from everyone else. The difference may have been just few days—or even just a few hours or minutes. It may seem like a subtle distinction, but this can result in biasing the sample.

> We found that the difference between our test & control groups and "everyone else" can be quite pronounced. We do properly sample a set of users and then randomly assign them to test and control. The sample may have been taken over a particular time period. But the test and control groups were randomly assigned from *within* this sample so any nuance as a result of the time period will apply equally to both groups. Often, we observe no difference in behavior between test and control groups. This can be disappointing as the treatment often represents someone's clever idea to improve the user experience. Inevitably—perhaps in desperation—someone will compare the test group to 'everybody else.' And alas, there is a difference—sometimes a striking one! Metrics for the test cell can be materially higher and statistically significant when compared to 'everybody else.' Perhaps the idea was a winner after all? Of course, this is a specious comparison! The samples were inherently different and can not be compared. The difference observed in metrics is due to sampling—not the treatment.
>
> We found that the day-of-week and time-of-day that a new user visits the site can really matter. For example, busy professionals may be less likely to visit the site on a weekday or during business hours. Even the inner workings of our internal systems can behave differently depending on the time-of-day or day-of-week. It's important to control for these idiosyncrasies by drawing a sample and then dividing it randomly into test and control groups.

We may not all have a user base that shifts based on day of the week in the way that the customers at Stitch Fix do. But we thought this was a great example of how you, as a designer, need to consider some of the ways in which the environment that you launch your test in might affect the outcome and results that you get. Recall that in our discussion about balancing learning and speed, running tests for at least a whole business cycle can help remediate some of these variations based on day of the week or hour. Being aware of these different conditions, both technical and behavioral (in your users), can help you understand how to design your test and how to interpret the results.

One way to help identify whether you've made mistakes in how you do your sampling is to run "A/A" tests every once and a while. In other words, you allocate users to the same experience, and see whether there are any differences in the metrics you observe. Since there is no change between the test cell and control, if you get false positives (that is, significant differences between these two groups) more than 5% of the time, it's likely that there's an issue with how you are allocating that would cause bias in your results. You should re-evaluate your methodologies to address these concerns, and be skeptical of any results run under these imperfect conditions.

We don't mean to overcomplicate the process of allocating your users into different test cells, but it is worth thinking about all the factors that might bias the results you get for your test, and to try to address them. However, you will also weigh these factors with some rational thinking around whether they actually *would* have major impact on your results. Some of the factors that may or may not influence what kinds of users you get are:

- Are these users that are familiar with your product or are they completely new to your product or service?
- What devices/platforms are they using? Does your product look or perform differently on different platforms? (Android, iOS, browser, etc.)
- How much technical expertise do your users have? Will your future users have similar technical expertise?

For users that are completely new to your experience:

- When did they sign up? (Time of day? Day of week?)
- Where did they sign up for it? (From an ad, from search result, etc.?)
- What country are they from? There are cultural differences as well as national standards and legal requirements that may affect the user experience and therefore users' behaviors.
- Will different types of users use your product in different ways, or with different frequency?

This list of questions will likely differ based on the kind of test that you are running, but also based on what kind of product you have. And for each of these kinds of questions that you might ask yourself, you should also ask "Does it really matter?"

As a very obvious example, suppose you were running an A/B test on a newly designed sign up process on mobile. You wouldn't bother to allocate any users who are signing up on the web to your test cells, you would *only* be putting users into your sample that were signing up on mobile, as this is the thing you are trying to test. Let's say that for your particular product, you know that people who shop during the day tend to be students (who have time to sign up for things during the day) but that people who sign up for your service in the evenings and weekends tend to be working professionals. Again, depending on the nature of what you are testing, you might want to make sure that you are thoughtfully getting both kinds of users. If you were *only* allocating users into your test cells on Saturday and Sunday, you might have inadvertently biased for getting more professionals into your test cells and it would have been worthwhile to make sure you were allocating users into your test cells over the course of a full week. Similarly, if you started your experiment on Saturday and ran it for eight days, you may have inadvertently biased for weekend behavior (because you have two Saturdays in your sample). A good rule of thumb is to run your experiment for multiples of seven days (or whatever the length of your business cycle is) to avoid these biases creeping into your data.

All of these variations can be challenging to keep straight. If you can, we encourage you to lean on the data-savvy folks within your company to help you think through these considerations. However, we believe that having a solid grasp on these concepts will let you participate in (and possibly even drive) those discussions. As a designer, your well-honed intuition about your users provides a valuable and unique perspective in identifying other possible confounds in allocation. What have you learned about your users and how they engage with your product? Have you seen systematic variation in how your users engage with your product? How might they affect sampling? As you get data back on your designs and make decisions on next steps, it's really important for you to be aware and thoughtful about how something like the sample that is being allocated to your test cells might have an impact on the results you get. Throughout the analysis portion of the chapter, we'll give you some practical tips to minimize the risk of bias in your results.

PRACTICAL IMPLEMENTATION DETAILS

So far in this book we talked about the implementation of your experiment, such as which users to run your experiment with, which countries to run your hypothesis in, and which platform to use for testing. These are important considerations for launching your test.

In many cases, the implementation details of your hypothesis are flexible, and you can choose them wisely to give your hypothesis the best chance of providing valuable insights. For instance, companies that have large international user bases like Facebook will run a test experience on an entire country. Since Facebook is a social network, it's important for their testing that the people in their test cells are actually connected to each other. By testing on an entire country that is somewhat isolated (e.g., by language and/or culture) from the rest of the world, you get a sample that will have good social connections, but is decoupled from the rest of the world so it allows for some testing to be done. Facebook uses New Zealand as one of its favorite testing grounds for exactly these reasons.[1] Localized testing can also help reduce or eliminate the risk that a single user is allocated to conflicting tests, since a user can't be both in China and in New Zealand at the same time. Again, because of cultural and other considerations, companies might choose countries that are either very similar to their key markets or countries that are very different from the market that they are most familiar with.

Other times, you can be flexible about choosing to test a hypothesis on just one platform, even if you want that hypothesis to eventually apply to all your platforms. You should ask yourself, which platform is going to be the best one for you to learn on? Is there a particular platform that will amplify the effects of what you are looking for? For instance, consider Netflix's hypothesis that automatically starting the next episode

1 *http://readwrite.com/2013/02/28/facebook-rolling-out-timeline-redesign-in-new-zealand-heres-what-it-looks-like*

of a TV show after the previous one finished would increase hours streamed, one of their main metrics of interest (because of its ability to predict likelihood of renewing one's subscription). This hypothesis could have been tested on any platform. However, the designers at Netflix decided to first pursue the hypothesis on the TV, since it's a lean-back experience that often occurs during longer sessions.

These two examples are cases where the details of how to launch the A/B test weren't fixed—the teams behind those tests could *choose* which platforms and countries that were most ideal for testing. In other cases, however, details of your test will be determined by the hypothesis itself. For instance, say you are working on a web application that lets individuals log their workouts to track progress toward their fitness goals. You've noticed that although your retention is high with people whose primary activity is weight lifting, retention is relatively low in runners. As a result, you formulate the following hypothesis:

> For runners, by using GPS to automatically import the details about a run, we will lower the friction for runners to use our app because they don't have to remember to track and log their details manually, which we will measure by an increase in retention for this population.

Runners don't run with their laptops or desktop computers: they run with their phones. Therefore, this hypothesis implicitly suggests that it must be tested on a mobile device, which may or may not be possible due to the limitations of your product (perhaps you don't have A/B testing capabilities on mobile just yet, or you don't have a mobile app at all).

Another case in which you might run into implementation limitations is when you're targeting a particular audience—for instance, users in an international market such as Japan. If you are an international company, only a subset of your users will be in Japan. You'll have to be cognizant of whether you can still get a large enough sample size in a reasonable amount of time to appropriately power your test.

Finally, we just want to remind you to make sure that you are set up to collect the data necessary to make a good and informed decision when you do get your results. Again, before you set off to launch your experience to your users, take the time to think about what data you will need to collect and if there are any other parts of your experience that you will want to make sure are tracked so that you can learn from them.

Instrumentation refers to the types of data that your company is able to collect. You'll need appropriate instrumentation for your metric of interest, and all of the secondary metrics you care to observe. Once you launch your test, it is often much harder to retroactively put things into place to measure the data and get the information that you want to get. We have seen many people have to rerun or relaunch A/B tests because they didn't take the time to take into consideration some of these basics before they launched. Remember that if your metric of interest is how you will evaluate the success or failure of your test, you'll need to have that measurable at a minimum in order to know what you've learned.

Is your experience "normal" right now?

If you recall our conversation in Chapter 2, one of the major strengths of A/B testing is that it is "in the wild." That is, you're not in a lab setting where users' attention and distractions might be different than in the real world; instead, you have all the messy considerations of life accounted for.

However, sometimes the nature of contextual research can be a pitfall, too. Major events in the world, or changing components of your experience, can confound your experiment. For instance, the Google home page is known for using a Google Doodle in place of its logo. Jon Wiley shared a story about a Google search page redesign, where the experience was made cleaner by removing everything except the Google doodle and the search bar.

The problem Jon shared with us was that they originally ran this experiment on the same day as when the Google Doodle was a barcode (Figure 6-3). So he shared with us that a lot of the users who were in the experiment landed on a home page that had a barcode and a search box, but nothing else, which created an unusual experience that confounded the test results. This story is a good reminder that in many of your products there are other things that might be going on at the same time as you are running your experiment that you didn't account for when you were crafting the design you want to test. When this happens, your best course of action to avoid being misled is to throw away the data and restart the experience under normal conditions. Though it can feel unfortunate, this is the best way to avoid making decisions with biased and misleading data, which could come out to be more costly in the end.

FIGURE 6-3.
This unusual Google doodle confounded an A/B test result that launched on the same day, by creating an unusually strange experience.

Sanity check: Questions to ask yourself

Before you launch, there are a few questions you will want to consider. Some of these are repeated from questions we've shared in the previous chapters; however, given that some time has probably transpired as you've been going through this process, asking them again might be a refreshing way to make sure you are still on track with your original goals:

- What am I trying to learn? Do I still believe that my design articulates what I'm trying to learn?
- What will I do if my experiment works or doesn't work? (Do you have a sense for what your next steps might be?)
- Does my test have a large enough sample size to be powerful at the significance level I want?
- Do you have an understanding of all the variables in your test? (So that when the results do come back you might have some ideas as to what things influenced which changes.)
- Do you have good secondary metrics or additional tracking built into your tests so that you can do deeper analysis if needed?
- Will this data be informative for developing new hypotheses or further experiments?

With these questions in mind, you'll be well prepared to launch an informative experiment to help you learn about your users and your product. In the next section, we'll give an in depth treatment of how to evaluate your results after your test has been completed.

Evaluating Your Results

Thus far in this chapter, we've focused on prelaunch considerations. Now, we'll imagine that you've paired closely with your engineering friends and managed to deploy your test to users. You've given the test the time it needs to acquire a sufficient sample size, and now you're ready to analyze the results.

If you've done everything right, then as you launch your test you should:

- Understand and know how different factors could influence or be reflected in your results (e.g., audience, platform, etc.)
- Have good secondary metrics or additional tracking built into your tests so that you can do deeper analysis if needed

After you launch a test, your work isn't over. In fact, some of the most important work comes with what you do after. A/B testing gives you huge potential to learn about your users and how your design affects them, but it's in the analysis part of your work that insights will crystalize and become concretely valuable for you, your team, and your product. During the analysis, focus on questions like the following:

- What impact did your changes have on your metrics of interest? Was this impact surprising, or did it align with your expectations?
- Did you observe impact to any other key, proxy, or secondary metrics? What was it?
- Are there any results that require further investigation using other techniques?
- What did these results show about your hypotheses?

It's useful at this point to revisit and reiterate some of the things you originally set out to learn and look for evidence of whether you were right or wrong in what actually happened. You should also be equally open to the possibility that the results you get are inconclusive—that you can't tell if you were either right or wrong. Getting an inconclusive result doesn't mean that you didn't learn anything. You might have learned that the behavior you were targeting is in fact not as impactful as you were hoping for.

REVISITING STATISTICAL SIGNIFICANCE

Recall that in Chapter 2, we told you that measures of *statistical significance* such as *p-values* help you quantify the probability that the difference you observed between your test cells and control group were due to random chance, rather than something true about the world. A *p*-value ranges between 0 and 1. When we see a very large *p*-value (that is, closer to 1 than to 0), this means that it is likely that the difference we observed was due to chance. In these cases, we conclude that the test did not have the intended effect. Smaller *p*-values observed suggest that observed difference was unlikely to be caused by random chance. You can't statistically *prove* a hypothesis to be true, but in a practical setting we often take smaller *p*-values as evidence that there is a causal relationship between the change we made and the metrics we observed. In many social science fields like psychology, and also in most A/B testing environments, we take a *p*-value of $p = 0.05$ or less to be statistically significant. This means we have 95% confidence in our result (computed as 1 – 0.05 = .95, or 95%). However, your team may work with larger *p*-values if you are willing to be wrong more often.

In quantifying the likelihood that your result was due to chance, *p*-values are a good indicator for the amount of *risk* you're taking on. Very small *p*-values can give you more confidence in your result, by minimizing the risk of *false positives*. A false positive is when you conclude that there is a difference between groups based on a test, when in fact there is no difference in the world. Recall that $p < 0.05$ means that if in reality there was no difference between our test and control group, we would see the difference we saw (or a bigger difference) less than 5% of the time (Figure 6-4).

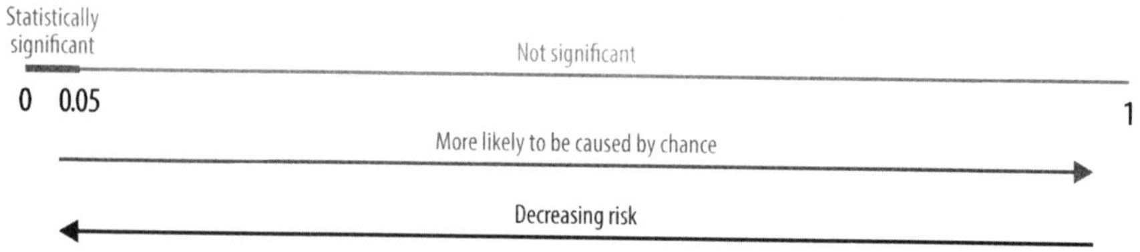

FIGURE 6-4.
P-values range from 0 to 1. The larger the p-value, the more likely the result was to be caused by chance. We often take p-values below 0.05 to be statistically significant in product design, but smaller significance levels can further reduce risk.

This means that 5% of the time, we will have a false positive. That's 1 in every 20 statistically significant results—which, if you're a company that runs a lot of A/B tests, can be quite a lot! If you set a lower threshold for statistical significance, say, 1%, then you reduce your risk: you'll only be wrong 1 in 100 times. However, to be confident at that level requires a larger sample size and more statistical power, so as we discussed before there are trade offs.

Fortunately, although false positives are a reality, there are methods you can use to reduce your risk of falling into that trap. Later in the chapter, we'll talk a little bit more about how you can use some of these methods to better understand whether you're observing a false positive. First, though, we'll talk a little bit about evaluating your results.

What Does the Data Say?

Remember that when you defined your hypothesis, you should have specified the metric you wanted to change and the expected direction of the change (e.g., *increase* retention, or *decrease* churn). Knowing this, you could see three types of results: an *expected* result, an *unexpected* result, or a *flat* result. An expected result is when you observe a statistically significant result in the direction you expected. An unexpected result is when your result is statistically significant but in the opposite direction. And finally, a flat result is when the difference you observed is not statistically significant at all.

In the next few pages, we'll talk about each of these results in turn.

EXPECTED ("POSITIVE") RESULTS

It's always great to see the results you hoped to see! You've probably found evidence that your hypothesis has merit, which is an exciting learning to share with your team. But remember that your goal in A/B testing is not to *ship* the tested design(s) as soon as you see the results you wanted, but to understand the *learning* behind that result, and what it means for your users and your product. From a practical and ethical standpoint, too, a positive result doesn't mean you should make your new default experience the test cell that won just yet. Remember that every change you make to your experience is a change that your users will have to live with. Constantly altering experiences for them can cause friction and frustration. We encourage you to ask yourself the following questions:

- How large of an effect will your changes have on users? Will this new experience require any new training or support? Will the new experience slow down the workflow for anyone who has become accustomed to how your current experience is?
- How much work will it take to maintain?
- Did you take any "shortcuts" in the process of running the test that you need to go back and address before your roll it out to a larger audience (e.g., edge cases or fine-tuning details)?
- Are you planning on doing additional testing and if so, what is the time frame you've established for that? If you have other large changes that are planned for the future, then you may not want to roll your first positive tests out to users right away.

As you can see from these questions, if the change that you're rolling out is substantially different from what your users are accustomed to and disruptive to the user, then you'll want to think carefully about how you roll out those changes, even if your metrics show that the result will be positive. As with any new feature rollout, you will want to think about how those changes are communicated to your customers, if you need to educate other people in your company about the changes to come, and what other steps you might need to take to ensure that your work is ready for a broader audience.

Sometimes, you'll decide that the results from a positive test aren't worth rolling out. Dan McKinley, formerly of the peer-to-peer independent marketplace Etsy, shared an example of a test that had expected results but never got rolled out. He said:

> In the seller backend we had people who are very heavily invested in specific workflows. Our best sellers were very important to us. We could design a listing process, the way to get an item for sale on Etsy, that's objectively better for any visitor. However, it could totally be the wrong thing to release because it's a different thing that thousands of people have to learn. So you could get a positive A/B testing result there and the decision would be "We're not going to release it" or "We're going to slowly evolve our way to that" to reduce the friction.

McKinley is speaking to the point that a rollout decision involves more than seeing positive results—it's also doing the "right" thing by your user base, which might be to leave the experience the same so they don't have to learn something new, or finding ways to slowly onboard them to the new experience so it doesn't feel so jarring.

One final consideration to keep in mind: Don't follow statistically significant results blindly. A statistically significant difference does not always mean a *significant* difference. Just because a result is statistically significant doesn't guarantee it will be practically important (or what statisticians would call "substantive"). Your data friends can help, and we link to a relevant paper in the Resources appendix.

UNEXPECTED AND UNDESIRABLE ("NEGATIVE") RESULTS

Sometimes, you see results that are unexpected or undesirable. A design change that you hoped would make a positive impact for your users caused the opposite: those test cells perform worse according to your metric of interest than the existing experience. Even though it can feel disappointing to have an A/B test that went differently than you were hoping, we want to remind you that these failures can sometimes be the greatest opportunity for learning. Unexpected results challenge your and your team's assumptions, and being challenged in this way forces you to reevaluate and hone your instinct about your users.

Seeing a negative result might mean that something was wrong with your hypothesis and your hypothesis is a reflection of your own instinct as to what would cause a positive reaction in your users. Always reflect on what led you to devise a hypothesis that didn't resonate with your users. Here are a few questions to get you started:

- Are they using the feature the way you think they do?
- Do they care about different things than you think they do?
- Are you focusing on something that only appeals to a small segment of the base but not the majority?

Spend a lot of time with the data to see if you can understand why your test had a negative result. Exploring secondary metrics here can help you gather a more holistic image of what happened that led to the result you observed. You may also consider supplementing your test with usability studies, surveys, or interviews to get a better understanding of why your test showed the results you got.

Understanding the context of why the experiment failed can also help you decide what to do next. Dan McKinley reminds us with this example that the result of an A/B test is one piece of information that should be weighed among many other considerations.

> There would be cases where you'd have negative results that you'd still want to release. You do A/B tests so you have data when you're discussing whether or not to release the experience. You're not acting out an algorithm and taking human judgment, out of the process. This is only one of the inputs, but we still talk about it. And we decide, "OK, this affects us negatively but we're going to release it anyway," or "This is positive but we think it might be an evil change that we shouldn't do." Both of those things are possible. Human judgments are very much part of the decision to release a thing or not.
>
> The best example of negative results that we released anyway was switching Etsy from sorting search results by recency to sorting by relevance. Very early on, search results on Etsy were ordered so the most recent item was first. That made sense when there were a thousand items on the site.

> Then a few years later, there were 20 million items on the site and it made less sense. At that time, listing an item cost 20 cents, so Etsy was getting a decent amount of its revenue from people renewing items [so that they would get pushed to the top of search results]. We realized this was a horrible user experience. We thought we could improve conversion somewhat by releasing search relevance. In the test, we improved conversion very slightly. But nowhere near enough to pay us back for the loss in revenue. We ultimately released an ad product that was a better use of sellers' marketing budget than just pressing the 20 cent button over and over again. But there was a discussion of "Here's how much money we're going to lose when we release this—we're just going to do it." So we could have made the globally optimal decision [for revenue] and not released that at the time. My instinct is that the company wouldn't exist now if we did.

As we've discussed, deciding whether or not to release a specific experience isn't always as simple as just looking to see if the results of your experiment are positive or negative relative to your metric of interest. As you can see, sometimes unexpected results can still lead to a rollout of an idea, because it's the learning that's more important than the outcome of the test. Making such decisions should involve thinking about the broader decisions you are making to ensure the best possible experience for your customers.

In other contexts, however, all of the evidence you receive will point to your test cell being unfavorable. This is true when both your key and secondary metrics tell the same story: the test cell had an unexpected and unwanted consequence for user behavior. When this happens, you should stop running the test, consider putting the users in that test cell back into the control experience, and decide whether or not there is any value in further exploring that hypothesis.

At the design level, you should resist the urge to revisit it and polish the "failed" design. In tests like this, incremental tweaks to language and execution rarely overcome a negative result. Thinking you can turn an unwanted result into a positive outcome can often be too costly and is unlikely to work. In these cases, it's often better to go back to the drawing board and see if you can't refine or revise your hypothesis in a way that will create a more favorable result. Or perhaps consider abandoning that hypothesis for the meantime in favor of better-performing hypotheses.

WHEN THE WORLD IS FLAT

So far, we've focused on two cases where you find a statistically significant difference between your two groups, whether it was the one you intended or not. In practice, many A/B tests are inconclusive, where there doesn't seem to be any measurable difference between the test experience and the control. Null or flat results are common and occur even when you feel that there are huge differences between your test cells. For instance, in his book *Uncontrolled*, Jim Manzi reports that only 10% of experiments lead to business changes at Google,[2] and at Skyscanner,[3] roughly 80% of tests fail to improve predicted metrics in a statistically significant way.

There are two ways you can interpret these kinds of results:

- Your hypothesis may have merit, but you haven't found the right expression of it yet (you haven't gone *big* enough yet). More formally, it could be that your experiment was under-powered, a true effect exists but you need more power since it's smaller than you designed the experiment for.
- The hypothesis that you were testing won't affect the behavior of your users in a large enough way that it changes metrics.

The "art" of A/B testing becomes apparent when you hit impasses such as this. Because you don't know whether your hypothesis has the potential to cause a meaningful impact to the user behavior you want to alter, you'll have to trust your instincts on whether this line of thinking is worth investing in further. If you have other evidence to support the hypothesis (for instance, a strong signal from in-lab user research), it might be worth investing additional time making some refinements to your explorations. However, if you've investigated this hypothesis unsuccessfully several times, or you don't have other evidence to support it, it might be that you've exhausted your options and should abandon the idea. A lot of A/B testing is an iterative process where each test

2 Manzi, Jim. *Uncontrolled: The Surprising Payoff of Trial-and-Error for Business, Politics and Society*. New York, NY: Basic Books, 2012.

3 *http://codevoyagers.com/2015/11/26/common-pitfalls-in-experimentation/*

helps to further develop your thinking. So if you're considering retesting, think about what your specific concerns are and why you didn't get stronger results. If we revisit some of the factors listed earlier in this chapter, you might ask yourself the following:

- Did you select the right sample?
- Do you need more users to be able to measure the effect of this change?
- Did you keep your test running for long enough? (Remember that depending on the metrics you are measuring you might need to run longer tests to see the effects—retention is a good example of this.) Remember also that you should always run your tests for *X* business cycles.
- Were there other external factors that might have affected your test?

Think also about the execution of the test:

- Were the changes between the test cells pronounced enough? Were they substantially differentiated? (Did you jump too quickly into testing details before you had established the basic concept?)
- Is there something upstream in the user flow that might have affected your results?
- Can you dig into your secondary metrics to see if there are any clues or differences in these metrics that might give you a hint as to what is going on?

Address these concerns, decide whether you have other evidence to support your hypothesis or not, and then consider retesting. Secondary metrics can be of huge value here to help you tease out whether there were any meaningful behavioral changes for your users that may not have ultimately caused a change in your metric of interest. Remember that you *shouldn't* base rollout decisions solely on secondary metrics, but they can be a good indicator to help you gain a more complete picture of *why* your result was flat: were there behaviors that counteracted the metric you were interested in? Did your test have no effect on any behavior at all?

If you didn't see an impact from your changes, there is no clear benefit to forcing your users through the friction of adopting a new workflow or experience. Remember, any change you make to the experience will have an effect on your existing users. They've become accustomed to using your product in a certain way. If there isn't a clear benefit to the changes you've made, it might still cause some confusion and frustration.

There are, of course, times where it makes sense to roll out your changes even if you come to the conclusion that you didn't affect any of your key metrics. For example, if you believe that your feature adds value because it's something that users have been requesting, it is a simplification (or improvement) to the UI, or it has strategic value, then you might decide to roll it out. In these situations, the changes you are making have value beyond what you might be able to measure in metrics. (You might, of course, find other ways to capture the impact in data—for example, usability studies, surveys, and other methods could be employed to better understand this.) For instance, you might be able to make an announcement that you've addressed the most requested feature from users, you might be able to make a change that is more in line with your brand or your design principles, or you can set the stage for being able to do something more strategic in the future. In these situations, you can make the decision with confidence that your change won't have a negative impact on your key metrics.

One example of this is when Spotify rolled out their new and unified dark interface. The new redesign did not affect retention. However, the design team at Spotify got to examine the holistic experience of Spotify as a brand and an app, which "cleaned up" a lot of the issues with the UI. Survey results also showed positive user sentiment toward the redesign, which gave the team additional confidence that they should roll out the new interface.

Another example comes from a conversation with Dan McKinley, where he shared some interesting insights as to how the nature of the work that you are testing influences the kind of results you are expecting to see. Specifically, Dan talked about the series of tests that they were doing to ensure that their site worked as well on mobile as it did on the web. At that time, many of their experiments were run with the goal of creating a coherent design and a responsive site on mobile rather than directly impacting the bottom line.

> Flat tests are the normal experience. Most experiments were run to make sure that we're not inadvertently impacting users in a way we're not meaning to. We always hope for improvements but a lot of work wasn't to get a direct monetary response. You know, it's more like "All

> right, this is a site that's been on the internet since 2006 and we're accidentally using 20 slightly different shades of grey." We're gradually making a more coherent design and making a responsive site. This is a massive undertaking; there's a certain amount of work you have to do just to keep up with the state of the internet, right? It was rare that any of those changes affected the bottom line.
>
> But that's still work that we want to be doing. It's strategically important even though we don't expect massive windfalls from single tests.

The caution with rolling out changes in any scenario is that you should be thoughtful about the inconvenience to users and cost in the form of resources at your company that rolling out those changes will incur. For example, if you're adding a completely new feature (you're not improving an existing one)—then how much additional work does that feature represent for the future? Will it somehow constrain future innovation?

In summary, you generally won't roll out changes if you don't see the impact you were hoping for. When you make changes to your experience, it has costs. This cost might be as small as causing a little friction for your users who have become accustomed to a specific experience, or it might be as large as adding a new part to your experience that you now need to maintain and change as you go forward.

ERRORS

Errors are inevitable in experiments. With industry standard significance *p*-values of 0.05%, around 1 in 20 A/B experiments will result in a false positive, and therefore a false learning! Worse yet, with every new treatment you add, your error rate will increase by another 5%—so with 4 additional treatments, your error rate could be as high as 25%. Keeping this at the top of your mind will help you keep an eye out for these errors so that you can spot them before you make decisions on "bad" data. The best way to limit errors is to run fewer treatments, or speak to your data friends about correction for multiple comparisons.

There are two kinds of errors. In a *false positive*, we conclude that there was a change when in fact there wasn't. In a *false negative*, we declare that there was no effect when an effect was there—our experiment just didn't find it. It's impossible to reduce both types entirely. Instead, our goal as good experimenters should be to limit them as much as possible. More importantly, we should keep in mind that we are not dealing with certainty, only data with a specified level of confidence, and therefore the potential to be wrong.

Replication

The idea of *replication*, or repeating an experiment to see whether it has the same findings, is borrowed from academic science. Replicating an experiment helps increase our confidence that we aren't observing a false positive. Remember that for a *p*-value of .05, we would expect to be wrong 1 out of every 20 times. But getting a *p*-value below that *twice* due to chance has a probability of much less than 1%—about 1 in every 400 times. As you can see, then, repeating an experiment can vastly increase your confidence in your result.

If an uplift or negative seems highly unusual or particularly surprising, your best course of action is to validate with a new experiment to see whether your finding replicates. This will help you have increasing confidence in your results, and therefore reduce the risk of error.

Using secondary metrics

Another way to help spot errors is by leveraging your secondary metrics. We introduced the concept of a secondary metric in Chapter 4. These can help you in two ways:

- As a gut check on your key metrics
- To gather other insights or learning that build your knowledge base

If you see that your secondary metrics align with your primary metrics, then you have even greater confidence in your results. This is because if multiple metrics point to the same underlying user behavior, then you'll feel more comfortable that you've correctly identified the cause of the change in metrics. This helps reduce the probability of a false positive.

Recall our earlier example from Etsy. If you see that there is something unexpected or even counterintuitive, secondary metrics can help you understand what's going on to paint a more complete picture of how your users are behaving. There might be a flag that the results you are seeing aren't sustainable. For instance, that your primary metric of interest did change, but other metrics that should vary with that metric did not change (or changed in the wrong direction). This might indicate that your test falsely increased a key metric without building the right behavior in your user base.

You can also use the secondary metrics you are gathering to build up your existing knowledge about how your users interact with your experience. How much time do your users generally spend on the site? Where are they going? Use this information to help feed into future hypotheses or to further refine your tests.

Secondary metrics and digging deeper with other data that you have can also help dispel false narratives that arise from the human desire to "explain" things. Eric Colson from Stitch Fix talked about how they are able to use data to understand what is really happening with their customers and how having access to rich data can give you insights that you might not have had otherwise:

> Our model affords us rich data that can be used to understand the variation in business metrics. This prevents us from falling victim to narrative fallacies—the plausible but unsupported explanations for the variation. Traditional retail models lack the data and therefore are often prone to latch on to easy-to-grasp narratives. I am told that it is common for store managers at department stores to blame the weather for a bad day of sales. Other times they blame the merchandise ("how can you expect me to sell this stuff?"). Other times still they blame the customers ("Customers these days are so promotion-driven. How do you expect me to sell this stuff at our prices?"). Of course, when sales are good the store manager accepts the credit ("it's due to the service level we provide in this store"). Each narrative is plausible. And, indeed we gravitate to any explanation that seems satisfying—it's not in human nature to let things go unexplained. We'll even accept them in the absence of evidence. The response, "I don't know," just isn't a tenable answer to the question of 'why did sales go up or down?'
>
> At Stitch Fix we have so much rich data that we not only have the ability to explain phenomenon, but also the obligation. We can statistically tease apart the effects owing to the client, the merchandise, even seasonality. Narratives still surface, however, they are offered up as hypotheses until validated. By studying the data with proper statistical rigor we can either accept or reject them. For example, a few Halloweens ago we had this weird drop in metrics. A tempting

narrative circulated that the drop was due to the fact that Halloween fell on a Friday this year, distracting our clients from their typical shopping behaviors. It was a reasonable and relatable explanation. Yet, the narrative was stopped from spreading in the office because it had no evidence to support it. Instead it was recast as a hypothesis. We framed it up as such and looked for evidence. Customer behavior was not consistent with the hypothesis, causing us to reject the hypothesis. Eventually it was revealed that it had nothing to do with Friday Halloween. It was a bug in some recently released code!

While the amount of data that a company like Stitch Fix has is perhaps a lot more than your average company, we think this story helps to give a good overview of the approach you can use as you learn to leverage your data to understand your users' behaviors in a more granular way. As humans, we can be quick to jump onto stories that resonate with us, but data (and especially data triangulation) can help us to either back up those stories or debunk them.

Using multiple test cells

When you're designing to learn, your goal is to understand how your hypothesis "holds up" in the world. Although it's important to get the design execution right, understanding how your hypothesis performs is a generalizable learning that you can apply to tweaking your design in the future. Remember that in Chapter 5 we talked about different test cells. Sometimes, each test cell will express a different hypothesis. However, in other cases you may have multiple treatments of a single hypothesis, which you can use to help you learn more.

When you have different test cells expressing the same hypothesis, you'll want to evaluate your results both by looking at individual test cells as well as looking at your test as a group of test cells. You might find that all of the test cells in your experiment changed your metrics of interest in the way you intended compared to the control. If each of the test cells changed in the same direction relative to the control, your confidence about the underlying hypothesis should increase because each of those treatments led to the user behavior you expected. If all of the test cells caused unwanted changes to your metrics compared to the control, then you've probably disproven your hypothesis. Assuming that there was no issue with how you allocated users into your test conditions, it's unlikely that every treatment would have failed if your hypothesis was true of the world.

Sometimes, you'll see a mix within the test cells, where some are expected and desired results, and others are unexpected and undesirable. In those cases, you'll want to look further at what might have caused these differences. You should dig deeply in these cases to understand why your test cells were performing differently. Is it possible that you might be observing a false positive in some of your test cells? Or, can you use secondary metrics to learn about what the difference was in user behavior that caused only some test cells to exhibit the intended behavior? This will help you tease out the cause of these discrepancies and help you be more confident in the results you're observing, and what they mean for your hypothesis.

Rolling out to more users

One of the best ways to reduce the risk of false positives is to roll out an experience to users in increments, allowing you to gain additional confidence in your results before you launch to 100% of your user base. This helps you understand how the data you observed in an A/B test scales to the larger population, and increases the probability that you "catch" an unexpected impact.

Sometimes you might still get a surprising result even if all of your data turned out positive, so ramping up is a way to see whether an effect you observed in an initial A/B test scales to the larger user base. This story from Jon Wiley at Google is a great example of how even when you get positive results from an experiment, you might find that the response is different when you launch your winning experience to your full user base. The Google home page is very iconic and poses an interesting design problem because of its simplicity. One exploration that Jon did was to clean up the home page by removing all of the navigation, all of the links, anything in the footer and header, sign-in, and so on. However, many of those links are quite useful and he also wanted to make sure that they didn't lose utility from the home page. The team came up with the idea to initially hide the links and then to fade them in if the user moved their mouse (which they believed showed intent). The team believed that this way the links would become available to the user at the moment they needed them:

> After running the experiment, all of the metrics that we had tracked told us that it was a good experience for users. We just said, "Oh, OK, we'll launch this. The numbers say it's good."

> Then, we got a wall of user wrath. I just started getting tons and tons of email from people who were furious. We had done the opposite of what we had intended to do. Rather than making those things on the page go away unless you needed them, it turns out that everybody used their mouse even when they had no intention to click. We were actually calling attention to these things on the page. We were giving them more prominence than they deserved. This was one of those occasions where our metrics told us one thing, but the reality was that it drove everybody nuts.
>
> Now, we had other methods of trying to elucidate this reaction. We have user research. We do qualitative research. In our qualitative research, people didn't really notice it because it's one of those cases where we tested it with 8 people or 16 people. People weren't really paying attention to it. However, in aggregate, over a much larger number of people, it actually struck a nerve and really bothered people. This is a place where we were just very surprised that all of the signals that we saw weren't true.

This story is a good illustration of some of the limitations of using data in the design process, and how sometimes the data that you observe in an A/B test might not scale in the larger population. It also points to the constant "conversation" that continually happens between your designs and your customers that we discussed in Chapter 4. That "conversation" might evolve over time. At each stage of your experiment, from running usability tests in-house, to an initial A/B testing test, to an additional roll out test, and finally to launching to your full customer base, the conditions in which your customers are evaluating your design might be different. The response you get could be different if it's in a lab setting in your offices, on a small segment of your customer base, or launched to the full population. This was also a great example of recognizing how we need to consider both the emotional response to our designs as well as the impact on metrics. We will discuss the idea of "ramping up" later in the chapter.

Revisiting "thick" data

Finally, remember that data triangulation can be a great way to improve confidence in your results. Tricia Wang, global tech ethnographer, draws a distinction between "big data" (the type of data collected at scale, such as that which comes from an A/B test) and "thick data" (for instance, that which is collected from ethnography.) Thick data is drawn from a small sample, but its depth can give you good insights into the very human reasons why you might have seen a behavior emerge through numbers (Figure 6-5).[4]

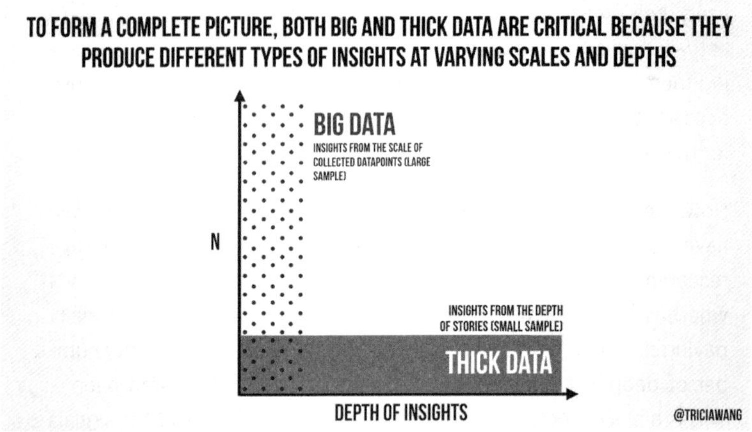

FIGURE 6-5.
An illustration of the difference between big data and "thick data' by Tricia Wang.

At the end of an A/B test, we encourage you to be thoughtful about using other sources of data to supplement what you've learned, and make sure you haven't made any mistakes in your measurements along the way. Arianna McClain shared an IDEO project to explain why collecting "thick data" is so important to catch errors in "big data." By triangulating different research methodologies, the IDEO team learned that one of their client's metrics—churn—wasn't actually measuring what they thought it was measuring:

> One of our clients sought to deepen their customer relationships, from new to current to churned customers. They were concerned about their churn rate, which was measured as days since last purchase. In addition to working with a team that ran quantitative analyses, IDEO conducted qualitative interviews with multiple customers who churned-some after one purchase, others after dozens of purchases.

4 *https://medium.com/ethnography-matters/why-big-data-needs-thick-data-b4b3e75e3d7#.506enoxex*

What IDEO learned was that many of our client's customers were continuing to engage with the product, they just weren't purchasing. There was no way for our client to know this because customers weren't signed in. When we asked customers why they never signed in, they simply said that there was no reason to—signing in still showed them the same content. This insight was a relief to our client. First, they realized they were not losing as many customers as they originally believed. Second, they learned they needed to measure churn differently. Finally, they saw an opportunity for how they could personalize their product by addressing churned customers: give them new content that incentivized those customers to sign in.

This example from Arianna shows how sometimes our assumptions about how to measure something (e.g., churn) can be wrong. Additionally, the measurements we get back are dependent on the design and experience that we're offering. Because their client's product did not offer an incentive to sign in, users weren't signing in, and this reflected back into their churn metrics—but not in the way that they had expected.

We encourage you to think about how to apply this to your own work. Should you double-check your big data with thick data? How can you apply other methodologies to help you reduce the risk of an error in your data? Doing so can help you increase your confidence that you've measured the right thing—and help you avoid mistakes along the way.

GETTING TRUSTWORTHY DATA

"Getting data is easy, getting data you can trust is hard."

—RONNY KOHAVI

The worst situation (which happens even with teams that have a lot of experience with A/B testing) is that you go through all this effort to plan, design, and then build and launch an A/B test, but you aren't able to get good takeaways due to poor data quality. This is why it's really important to feel that the data you get back is significant and that you are basing your decisions on the right representative sample.

It's always very tempting to look at your results as soon as they start to come back and to immediately want to take some kind of action based on what you are seeing. As we've articulated in several chapters, it's an important exercise in discipline to wait until your test is complete (that is, has run as long as you intended and has obtained the predetermined sample size) before checking for statistical significance and taking action as a result. There are a number of examples where a team decided to act prematurely on some data, only to find that the results changed after they had a sufficiently large sample size (and therefore a powerful enough test). If you have data analysts on your team, they're experts in knowing and communicating how clean your data is, and what the limitations of it might be.

So, let's assume that you feel confident in beginning to evaluate the results that you're getting from your test. This means that you feel good about the quality of the data that you're getting back, and that the test has run for a long enough time and with enough people in each test cell that you are responding to significant data. However, even if you've been hygienic about your data up until this point, we want to review a few pitfalls you'll need to be careful to avoid so that you can make sure you have the most trustworthy data possible.

Novelty effect

In previous chapters we talked a lot about the differences between new and existing users. In practice, this difference is important not only when you're planning your test, but also as you're analyzing your results.

When teams see a flat or negative result, they sometimes attribute it to users needing to "get used to" the new experience. Looking at new users can be a good way to understand whether something like this is happening. New users don't have habits or assumptions that have developed based on your control condition—they're not familiar with your product at all. If the experiment is flat or negative compared to your metrics of interest, it shows that needing to get used to the new experience is not the cause of the undesirable results.

On the flip side, if an experiment is a win for new users only, it suggests that you could be observing a novelty effect. The *novelty effect* is when people "perform better" (in this context, use your product better) because of excitement about the new product rather than a true improvement in behavior or achievement. You'll want to make sure you run your experiment for long enough to let this novelty effect wear off—after some time when the feature is no longer novel, you would expect to see a leveling off of performance.

Seasonality bias

One of the strengths of A/B testing is that it occurs in context, allowing you to measure how your products perform in the wild. This lets you take into account the practical factors that will impact how your product gets used and adopted. However, this can become a weakness for factors that are hard to control. *Seasonality bias* is bias introduced due to seasonal patterns in the world—for instance, due to weather or holidays. Imagine that you were running an ecommerce website. A/B tests run during the month of December might be subjected to seasonality bias because of last-minute holiday shopping.

As you are thinking about your A/B tests, be thoughtful about whether seasonal effects might confound your results. Remember that such effects are often specific to your product. If so, consider waiting until the season has passed to test your ideas at a time where you can be clear on what you are getting in terms of results.

Rolling Out Your Experience, or Not

By now, you should know what the impact of your experiment was: was it flat and inconclusive? Did it make a measurable improvement to your existing solution? Or did it make the behavior worse? Remember that your goal in A/B testing is to learn something, and take that learning to decide what to do next for your users.

We'll spend the next part of this section talking in a little more detail about how you will go about making the decision on what to do. Part of what you will factor into your decision is the result from your test and whether it performed as you expected. You will also be influenced by how mature your testing is, how refined the work has been up until this point, how many more iterations you expect to do, and how large the changes will feel to your existing user base.

You might decide on any of the following paths:

Roll out to 100%
: Take one of your test experiences and give it to your entire user base; this experience now becomes your new default and new control for all future tests. You do this when your test is successful, but also when you feel like your testing is mature enough. For example, you don't want to roll out a change to 100% of your audience if you feel like you'll be making another large change just a few weeks later, or if you haven't done the due diligence to polish your experience and satisfy your 100% rollout plan (see Chapter 5).

Roll out to a larger audience
: You have a good feeling about where you're going but you don't yet want to commit all the way. Recall that this is one way to reduce the risk of errors. Additionally, you might still have some questions about the data that you've gotten back from your current experience and want to gather data from a broader audience. You might have observed interesting changes while segmenting that data that you want to validate with a new experiment. You may have learned you didn't have the power you needed to measure a change and need a bigger sample to obtain significance.

Keep your existing experience
: No changes for the majority of your user base. This is usually the situation when you find that your test didn't have the results or impact that you were expecting, or if you plan on doing further iterations or refinements on the experience you are testing (even if the results were positive).

We'll talk a little bit about each of these decisions in the coming pages to help you decide what makes most sense based on what you've learned, and where you are in your product process.

WHAT'S NEXT FOR YOUR DESIGNS?

A few times throughout this book, we've used the framework of global versus local problems and exploration versus evaluation. This was partly to encourage focusing your design and A/B testing on solving the right type of problem. Now that you're deciding what to do with your results, revisiting what you set out to do will help you make decisions on how to apply your data and new learning.

Were you exploring or evaluating?

Recall that exploration and evaluation exist on a spectrum that helps you and your team focus on establishing the goal(s) of your A/B test In more exploratory problems, A/B tests allow you to understand the problem space and explore possible solutions; to that end, you can seek directional feedback about what to keep pursuing. Comparatively, in evaluatory contexts, your goal is to see whether the design changes made have the causal impact expected in real users. These types of problems are probably closer to being "complete" and therefore closer to rolling out.

Our point in introducing this part of the framework was to help you and your teams align on how close you are to a "finished" product. Intuitively, this is an essential component in deciding what to do with your insights now that you've finished your test. Figure 6-6 helps summarize what you'll probably be thinking about after different types of tests along this spectrum.

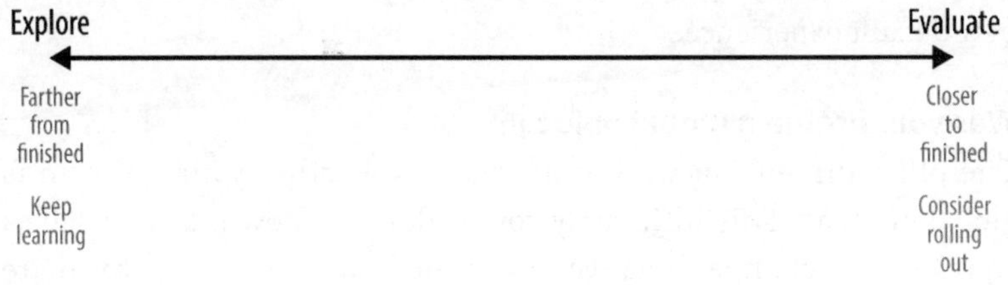

FIGURE 6-6.

The spectrum of exploration to evaluation.

If you were *exploring* the space of possible designs and hypotheses, it's unlikely that you've found the best solution on your first or second try. Doing exploratory A/B tests is in service of helping you eventually narrow down a design to evaluate. The results you got from this test can help you with directional feedback on which of your hypotheses (if any) makes the most sense to pursue further. This might lead you to explore at a smaller scale, looking at different treatments of a single hypothesis to tweak smaller details. Or you could feel confident enough to begin evaluating whether a treatment of that hypothesis is a good candidate to roll out more broadly. You might also decide that you haven't learned enough to narrow down just yet. Perhaps your test was inconclusive or you haven't yet collected enough data to rally behind a hypothesis. In this case, you might find yourself running additional broad exploratory tests to complement the learnings from this one. In either case, you probably won't be rolling out any designs from an exploratory test. Instead, you'll be taking the insights back to your team to keep working toward the right solution.

Comparatively, tests for the purposes of *evaluation* are close to being released: you were probably looking for major blockers or issues such as unexpected negative impact to your metrics (such as in Dan McKinley's example from before—they anticipated "flat" results, since the goal was to create a more coherent design experience rather than to improve metrics), and to confirm whether your design caused the desired user behavior. In other words, the test cells you put forth in an evaluation test were probably candidates for rollout already, and you and your team were seeking confirmation on the best cell. If you've found evidence in favor of one of your test cells, you might consider rolling it out to a larger part of your audience to gain increasing confidence, until you eventually feel strongly enough to roll out to 100% and make it your new default experience.

Was your problem global or local?

The other dimension we introduced was whether your problem is global or local. This ultimately comes down to how many variables your test cell changed relative to your default experience. If you are changing just one or two variables, or pieces of your experience (e.g., color, language, placement), your problem is probably on the local end of the spectrum. However, if your change is impacting more than a few variables (closer to a "redesign" than a "tweak") you're probably thinking about a more global problem. Several recent examples of "global" changes are the brand redesigns of companies like Uber and Instagram, which completely altered the look and feel of their products.

Remember that our goal in running an A/B test is to causally attribute a change in the experience to a change in user behavior. One of the things that can be challenging about the difference between a global and local A/B test is that it can be hard to know *what part* of the change caused an impact when you're changing many variables at once (global test). Arianna McClain articulated this well, when talking about the differences between testing new user flows and testing button colors:

> Say we're testing a three-step user flow versus a one-step flow. User flows can contain dozens of features and confounders, so it's difficult to take the results of an A/B test at face value. If the three-step flow performs significantly better than the one-step flow, designers and analysts really need to dig in to understand why they are seeing these statistical differences. Knowing the reasons why the three-step flow worked so well may let them design even more effective products in the future. However, if a designer is simply trying to determine if a red or blue button gets more people to sign up, then they're more able to just trust the data directly.

She reminds us that for these global tests, you might want to triangulate with other sources of data to understand which parts of the change might be leading to the difference in behavior that you observed.

Once you've triangulated with other sources of data for your global test, it's time to think about rollout. Unlike the distinction between exploration and evaluation A/B tests, both global and local test cells are potential candidates for rollout. However, *how* you go about rolling out a global and a local test that performs well in an A/B test can be quite different. We summarize this in Figure 6-7.

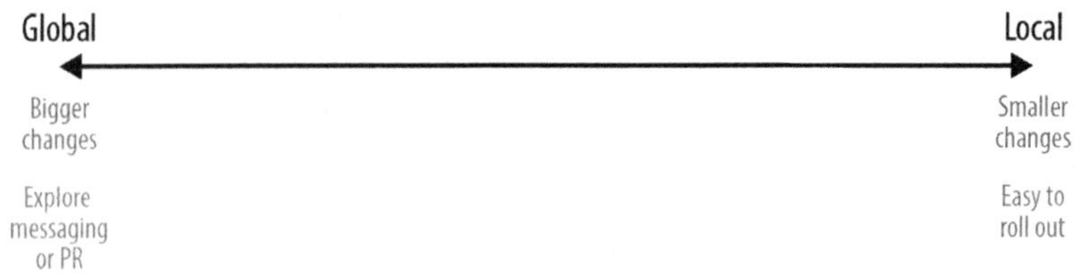

FIGURE 6-7.
The spectrum of global to local.

Local changes are only small tweaks to your existing experience. The result of this from your user's perspective is that nothing much has changed, and therefore there's little friction to adoption. In many cases, local changes get rolled out without anybody noticing. If you decide to move forward with a local change, you can just slowly ramp up the percentage of users with that new change until you've hit 100%.

Comparatively, global changes to your experience will generally draw attention. If you pursue a global change, you have to know that your users will not only *notice* the change, but they may have strong emotions about or face significant friction when using the new look and feel or flow of your product. In addition to rolling out the change, global changes require communications and PR to your users to help them understand the change and help them with the transition. For instance, when Instagram rebranded in May 2016, they posted a video and write-up on their blog to reintroduce the new iconography and color scheme, and motivate why the change was important.[5] This helped loyal Instagram users understand the change, and feel supported rather than abandoned by the Instagram team during the change. In these cases, a team might also want to notify or staff up their Customer Support team to accommodate the potential increase in support outreach as the result of a large change.

Knowing when to stop

Finally, one additional consideration is that if you're doing optimization tests, you'll have to decide when to stop. Make sure you don't get so focused on fine-tuning a test that you come to a point of diminishing returns. After all, there is only so much time that you really want to spend on tweaking

5 *http://blog.instagram.com/post/144198429587/160511-a-new-look*

button colors or layout. By keeping an eye on how much your changes are reflected in the metrics, you can determine whether you want to keep investing in optimizing your design. If you feel like you are making big changes but not a big impact on your metrics, then it's probably not worth it for you to continue investing time in these changes.

RAMP UP

One of the choices we offered you when deciding what to do next is to "roll out to 100%." However, it's rare to do this straight after a small experiment. Even if you have positive results, it's best practice in the industry to slowly increase the percentage of users who get the new experience over a period of time until you eventually reach 100%. How fast or slow you ramp up your user base onto the new experience depends somewhat on your company's engineering resources and/or the engineering release schedule, which might be out of your control. This is one of many reasons why designers and engineers should maintain open communication and collaboration channels. However, you might also consider the speed at which you roll out the new experience to be a factor of how complicated or large the change is to the experience.

Assuming that you had a large enough user base to start A/B testing with 1% of your population, the first ramp-up stage will be within a 5% range of users aiming to identify large negative changes that indicate something is wrong with the experiment. Ramping up to a percentage that is still small limits the potential risk of changing your users' experience frequently until you feel more confident in the design and hypothesis underlying the test cell that you ramp up. The second stage gives you even more confidence—you might look to start expanding to 10% or even 25% of your population. A third and final stage, with 50% test cell/50% control, gives you the most power to detect the impact of your test cell and may be used to learn more about segments and impact to your overall user base. See Figure 6-8 for an illustration of this. Colin McFarland talks about the importance of having an effective ramp-up strategy with clear requirements that you need to meet before moving to the next stage of testing.[6] He says, "It's crucial your ramp-up strategy doesn't slow you down unnecessarily. An effective ramp-up strategy should have clear goals against each

6 *http://codevoyagers.com/2015/11/26/common-pitfalls-in-experimentation*

stage, and move forward to the next stage unless results are unsatisfactory. For example, stage 1 may look to validate there is no significant detrimental impact while ensuring engineering and platform resources are performing reliably in less than 24 hours."

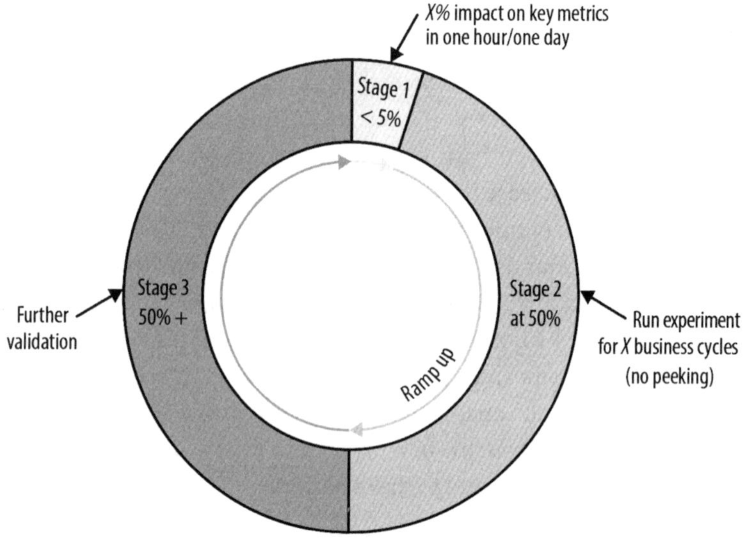

FIGURE 6-8.
Ramp-up in phases: by first launching to a very small group of users (< 5%), then to 50%, and then finally rolling out to a majority group.

As you roll out your experience to an increasingly larger audience, you'll want to continuously keep an eye on the impact of that new experience on your metrics. Remember that if you have statistically significant results, then you have a fair amount of confidence that as you expose this feature to a broader group, those results will continue to hold. However, there might be things that you didn't predict would happen, so monitoring the data along the way is a bit of insurance to make sure that you are indeed having the impact that you expect to have. Another way to look for unexpected results is to use holdback groups, which we will discuss next.

HOLDBACK GROUPS

Note that even when we say that you are going to roll out your results to your full user base, the common and best practice is to release a new experience to the vast majority of your user base and "hold back," keeping just a small percentage of users (usually 1% or 5%) on the old experience (the former control). This practice can be helpful to keep measuring the long-term impact of your design change. Some tests might have a prolonged effect, where you could see interesting results a few months after you launch and you want to have a way to monitor these changes over a much longer period of time (but where that period of time might be too long to run as a prolonged A/B test). Additionally, some metrics, called "lagging metrics," can take a long time to impact. You want a way to measure causally how your design change affected these lagging metrics, which you can only do using a holdback group.

You can think of holdback groups as a safety measure to ensure that you didn't make any mistakes in the analysis of your experiment. You can never predict if you might have missed something that could get amplified or change the results of your test as you expose your new design to a much larger population. If you roll out your new experiment directly to a full 100% of your user population, you'll no longer have an old experience to compare to, and therefore no way to confirm that at scale, your experiment had the intended effect. Keeping a small percentage of your population on the original experience will allow you to make that comparison. Then, when you are certain that your experience is sound and that it indeed has the positive effect you were hoping for, you can move the last percentage of users to the new experience.

One more reason to care about holdback groups is that they let you continue to evaluate whether your proxy metrics eventually have impact on your company's key metrics. Remember that sometimes the metrics your company cares about can take a very long time to measure. Letting these experiments run in the background is one strategy to reassess the casual relationships between proxy and key metrics. There are some pitfalls associated with long-running experiments. We'll note some additional resources at the end of the book. John Ciancutti described this well to us when he said:

> You run that test, you improve your proxy metric on the first day. You're like, "Great, we're going to act as if this drives the key metric, and we're going to move on," but occasionally you have to reassess that.
>
> You leave it running and you confirm that in fact there's still a causal relationship between the key and proxy metrics. In other words, in this A/B test, we raised that proxy metric. And later, it did raise that hard-to-move key metric that we actually care about. It can take a very long time to get some of the data.
>
> So you leave these things running in the background, and act as if it's true, but then you validate it. Also, you try all of these other metrics and see what else correlates. Lots of things correlate, so you gotta find those causal effects. Lots of metrics move together, so you find the ones that are intuitively strongest and have the clearest relationship.

By continually looking for ways to evaluate these relationships between your company's metrics, you can strengthen your data toolkit in the long term. A single experiment may be important, but it is the cumulative impact of multiple experiments that address one metric in depth or many metrics over time will allow you and your data friends to develop an impactful data practice for your entire company.

We hope that this chapter so far has helped give you a high-level view of the decisions that come after an A/B test. To close out our discussion about analyzing a test, we want to share the decision tree shown in Figure 6-9. We believe that structuring your thinking when deciding to roll out, abandon a hypothesis, or keep iterating can help you be systematic about applying A/B testing insights in the best possible way.

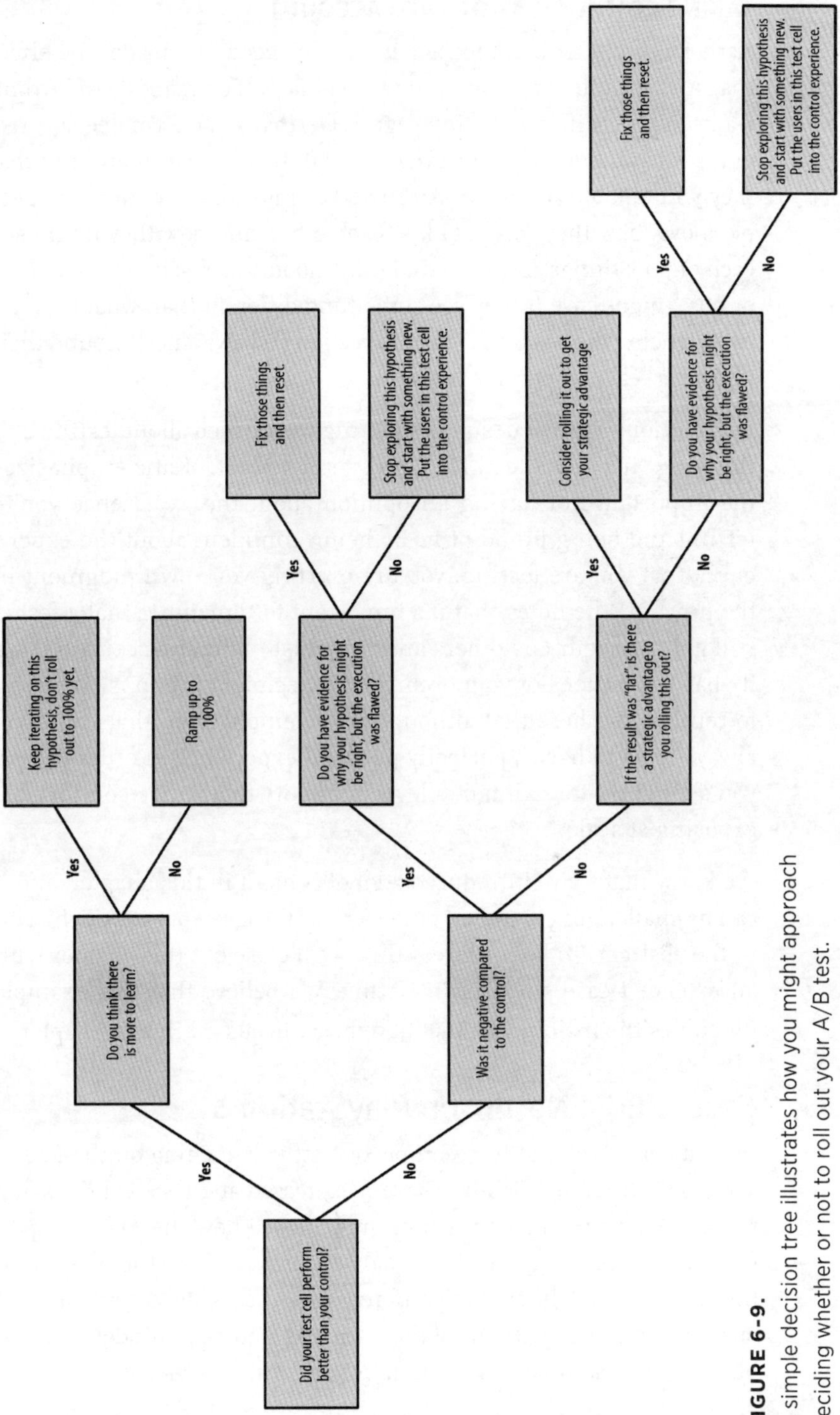

FIGURE 6-9.
A simple decision tree illustrates how you might approach deciding whether or not to roll out your A/B test.

TAKING COMMUNICATION INTO ACCOUNT

Katie Dill from Airbnb reminds us that we need to consider the effect that A/B testing can have on our customers. For example, if Airbnb wants to test a different listing page in Germany, the team needs to recognize that there are Americans who will travel to Germany and that they will talk to each other. Airbnb takes into consideration how people move, how they might talk to each other, and how they might see each other's things. They need to think about the reaction that a guest or host might have if they see something different than what they are experiencing themselves. Communication and awareness around their testing is really important to them.

She cautions against designers getting too relaxed about testing and thinking "it's just a test, it's OK if it's not great." Katie emphasizes the importance of having an opinion about the experience you're testing and being proud of it. By being confident about the experiences that you are testing, you are exerting your own judgment in the process. She notes that it's important to remember that a test is still going to your customers and you must maintain a certain quality bar no matter how big or small the recipient group is. We want to remind you here that although we've emphasized that you don't always need to have a perfectly polished experience in order to test, you should try to maintain a level of quality that you're comfortable exposing at scale.

We know that we've introduced a lot of content in this chapter, and it can be challenging to understand some of the concepts we touched on in the abstract. To help address this, we'll close out this chapter with an extended case study from Netflix. We believe that this example illustrates the major ideas that have been discussed in this chapter.

Case Study: Netflix on PlayStation 3

In Chapter 5, we used the example of Netflix launching on the PS3 to show how different hypotheses were expressed and tested at the same time. We'll return now to that example to see how they actually performed. Before we get to the actual results, we wanted to ask you to think first about which of the different hypotheses you would have bet on winning if you were part of the team. (As a quick reminder, remember that the main success criteria for the test was viewing hours or "consumption." Which experience would result in Netflix users watching the most TV and movies?) Examples of the four hypotheses the team tested are shown in Figure 6-10.

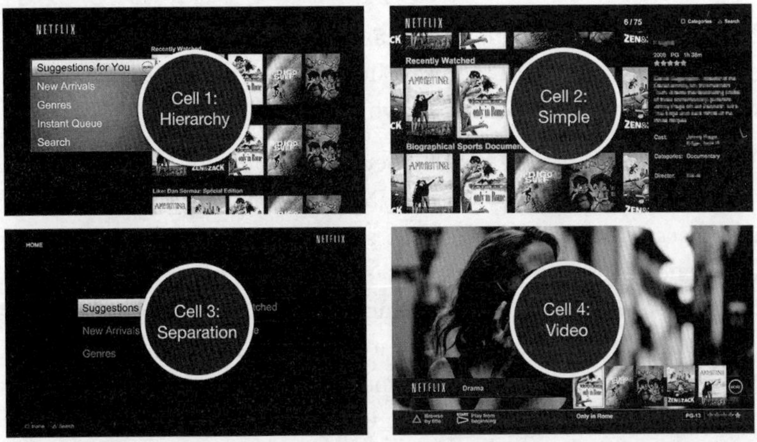

FIGURE 6-10.
As a reminder, these four designs represent the four main hypotheses that the Netflix team was exploring.

Whenever we share this example, most people assume that Cell 2 or Cell 4 was most successful. About a quarter select Cell 1, and usually about 5% of people select Cell 3. We love this exercise because it demonstrates how even in a room filled with designers and product managers—all of whom should have great consumer instinct—there can be disagreement. Using data can help address these disagreements and make everyone's consumer instinct works better the next time around.

Within Netflix, the team was pretty split about which cell would perform best. The designers tended to favor Cell 1. This was probably because in many ways it was the most robust design, and it allowed for the most scalability. They felt like it did the best job at addressing the majority of the user complaints about the original UI. It also performed well in usability testing during the prototyping phase. On the other hand, the product managers and engineers tended to favor Cell 4. They were passionate about using video as a way to evaluate content (as opposed to having to read through a long paragraph that described what you were going to see). Why read when you can watch? The engineers also did an amazing job on the technical backend of making the video load and playback extremely quickly, so there was some development pride in the performance of this cell as well. However, Cell 4 got really polarizing feedback when it was user tested. Some people loved the immersive experience, but others found it distracting.

This example illustrates how the biases of the people that are working on the experience might manifest in what they believe to be the best experience for the customers. So which group was "right"? Neither.

One interesting note here is that because the team was using a completely new platform, they weren't able to use the original PlayStation experience as a "control." For the sake of testing, the team had to assign one of the four new hypotheses to be the control. They chose Cell 1 because it was the experience that had been under development the longest. Consequently, it was the more thoroughly user tested and therefore best understood. In some ways, by declaring Cell 1 as the control, it was as though the team overall was betting that it would be the "winning" cell.

So we mentioned that neither the designers nor the engineers and product managers accurately predicted which experience would fare the best with real users. We illustrate the outcomes in Figure 6-11.

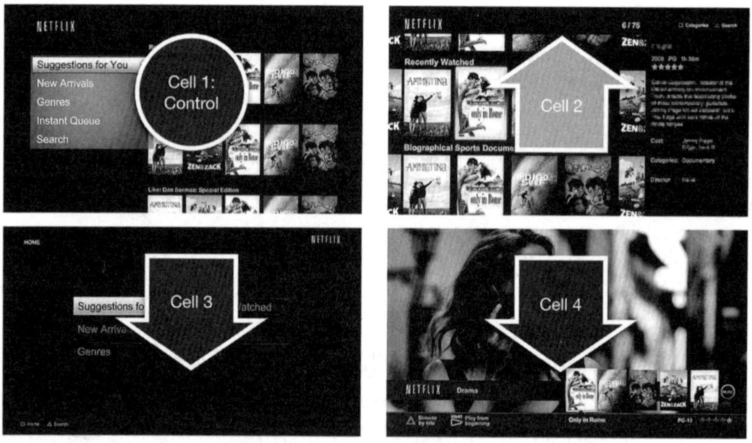

FIGURE 6-11.
When compared to Cell 1, which was deemed the "control" cell, only Cell 2 led to a statistically significant increase in consumption metrics.

Compared to Cell 1 (the control group), both Cell 3 and Cell 4 had a negative impact on consumption. But compared to Cell 1, Cell 2 increased consumption. This caused the collective teams to swallow their pride a bit and examine what we thought worked well on a TV. Looking back on this initiative, without A/B testing, there probably would have been a huge disagreement between design, product, and development before we launched about which version we should release. Without data, both sides would have ultimately been wrong and in the end lost viewing hours rather than increasing them.

Based on what we discussed earlier in this chapter, you would probably expect test Cells 1, 3, and 4 to be scrapped, and all users moved to Cell 2. While that *is* what eventually happened, it's worth going into a few more details about this test and how it evolved over time. Remember that this is just the first iteration of testing on the PS3 platform, essentially the first experiment ever run for the TV experience. This made it a more exploratory test than an evaluatory test, so the team used what they learned to keep iterating on the experience to make it as good as possible.

MANY TREATMENTS OF THE FOUR HYPOTHESES

For the sake of simplicity, we only shared one test cell for each of the four hypotheses tested when we walked through the preceding example. However, that's not quite accurate. In this test, the team didn't actually just test four different cells, but actually had close to 20 cells overall. Each test cell had a "sub-hypothesis" on exactly how to treat the overarching hypothesis at hand. So, for example, with Cell 3, there was a version that had box art at the top level. It had only four pieces of box art (so thematically it stayed more "true" to the original concept). And in fact, the test cell that had the box art at the top level actually performed better than the version that didn't have any box art at all—that is to say, it had the most positive impact on the metric of interest for the team (consumption). The positive performance of Cell 2 and the improved performance of this small variation helped solidify the team's conviction that having some visual representation of the content at the top level was extremely important. This example illustrates the importance of evaluating the results of your test both holistically and at the level of individual cells. Doing so can help you spot high-level trends across your data that could serve as potential design principles for your product or service moving forward. As a principle, the importance of visual content helped justify why Cell 3 didn't perform well.

When analyzing and interpreting your results, remember that A/B testing shows you behaviors but not why they occurred. To do great design and really understand your users, you'll also need to understand the psychology behind what influenced your users to behave in the way that they did. For this test, the team tried to tease apart some of the reasons why they got these results using surveys and qualitative user research. This helped the team understand why they saw the results they did, and gave them a clear directive on what pieces of each design they should move forward into future testing. For instance, this helped show the team that focusing on simplicity was more important than giving users full control.

EVOLVING THE DESIGN THROUGH ITERATIVE TESTS

It's very unlikely that you'll land on the optimal experience from a single test. Therefore, you'll want to continue to iterate and see if you can improve your results even more. In this stage, a team might borrow features or variables from some of the other hypotheses to "beef up" the winners from a previous test, or continue to pursue an idea that they believed had potential (or that performed well in other forms of research). Figures 6-12 and 6-13 gives some examples of how the winning Cell 2 was iterated on.

In the design featured in Figure 6-12, the team borrowed a feature that performed well on the website version of Netflix and applied it to the TV UI. When you mouse over a piece of content on the website, a pop-over with information about the movie or TV show appears. This seemed like a good mechanism to use that might simplify this experience even further, and you could argue that the team was pushing even further on the theme or concept of simplicity. Internally at Netflix, this mechanism was called the "BOB" or "back of box" because it represented the kind of information you'd find on the back of a DVD box if you were looking for a movie in the video store.

FIGURE 6-12.
Removing the informational side area, and using the "BOB."

In the design shown in Figure 6-13, the "BOB" was reduced even further. Less information was included to see if the team could determine the bare-minimum information that users needed to make a decision about what to watch. If the team found that this cell performed well, they could consider applying what they learned to other platforms as well (website, mobile, etc.). This demonstrates the point we made earlier about how insights might generalize and apply beyond the specific context of testing, helping you and your team build a wealth of knowledge from your different tests.

FIGURE 6-13.
A design with a very minimal "BOB."

WHAT IF YOU STILL BELIEVE?

One downside of doing global A/B tests where multiple variables are changing at a time is that there is a higher chance that you might mask an interesting positive result from several of your changes with the negative effect of one poor choice. This occurs when one of the many variables that you changed in that cell was actually limiting its success. If you had changed all the variables except for that one, then you may have had a positive result.

If you believe that a failed or flat hypothesis has merit (especially when you have other evidence to support this belief), you should continue to do large-scale concept testing until you understand exactly what you've been missing. This is exactly what happened with Cell 4, the video cell. There was a strong belief within the company that finding what you want to watch through the act of watching is actually a very powerful proposition. So, why didn't we see that reflected in the results from the A/B test? There were several ideas as to what might have happened:

Performance
: Even though the engineering team had done a great job of making the video start up as fast as possible, it may still not have felt quick enough to users. Or they may not have had an especially fast internet connection at home, so it just felt too slow and then they lost patience.

Limited choices
: They learned from Cell 2 winning that having a lot of box shots on the screen seemed to make a difference in getting people to play more. Perhaps the original video UI felt too limited in terms of the number of options.

Loss of content
: Perhaps the full-bleed video was not the right execution because it overtook the information that is normally conveyed in the "BOB." That information might still be valuable to users in a video preview context.

Outlining a few ideas like this is a great way to help refine your concept while keeping your ideas broad. For instance, were there ways to incorporate video into the winning Cell 2? By getting creative, the team found new ways to incorporate video into the previewing and movie selection process. Even after they released Cell 2 to the larger population, the team continued to explore video because they wanted to keep open the possibility of video in the interface. However, after two or three more rounds of testing different conceptual ideas around video, the team saw no uplift in metrics and decided to abandon the idea for the time being.

Once you have the data back on your first iteration, it's tempting to roll out the winning cell to the rest of the population right away. However, this is rarely what you want to do with a global test such as this example from Netflix on PS3. Why? If your concepts are wildly different, one round of testing probably isn't enough to settle on the best concept. Another reason you might not want to roll out after a single test is that there may be other big hypotheses that you want to test but didn't build out yet. Running those concepts first can give you more insights to work with as you begin to refine your own ideas.

When A/B testing smaller variables, it's easy to change those things without causing too much negative user feedback. However, in cases like this when you are about to fundamentally change the way that your service or product works, remember that your customers will have to live through (and often, struggle through) every change you make. Keeping your control running until you have a stable idea of what experience you want to settle on will limit the number of changed experiences you put your users through. This isn't to say that once you launch a design you can never change it, but keeping this in the back of your mind will ensure that you only roll out ideas that you feel good about to 100% of your user base.

We hope that this case study helped the concepts from this chapter come to life. As you can see, data can feed back into your design and product process in many ways—by challenging your preconceptions about your user, inspiring new designs, and helping you know when you're on the right track. A/B testing data can't make decisions for you, and is one of many factors that weigh into the choice of what to do next. But it can uncover valuable insights so that you can ask more thoughtful and well-informed questions to better understand your users in the future, and make the most informed choices possible to do right by your users when you launch design changes at scale.

One final quick example that demonstrates the value of iterating on your design further despite negative results comes from Katie Dill at Airbnb. Katie talks about ways that the team at Airbnb has reacted to negative or confounding results:

> Sometimes the data doesn't tell the whole story. For example, we made changes to our navigation on our website and the data showed that key metrics went down. The conclusion at first was that the core idea for the information hierarchy was wrong. But when the multidisciplinary team assembled to discuss the findings and next steps, one of the designers pushed to keep the original idea but make a few changes. Through review of the design work that was done, the team found that some of the design decisions were likely at fault for the poor performance. They made a few changes including adding a carrot to indicate a drop-down menu, and saw the key metrics go right back up. It was a simple change, but a good example that when something isn't working before throwing the whole thing out, it's best to identify potential spot fixes. It's just a matter of fighting for what you believe in and making sure that we're giving it its best chance to be successful.

What's important here is that they didn't just take the results at face value as a direct indication of what to do next; rather, they used their experience and intuition to understand that the design didn't perform to expectations because of bad execution on the part of design.

This chapter closes out our practical how-to guide to A/B testing as a designer. We hope that you feel empowered to get your hands dirty by being involved in A/B testing from the start. In the next chapter, we'll give you some tips on how to build a culture of data at your company. We hope that this book so far has gotten you excited about using data in your design process. But only by building a culture to support that data can it truly make maximal impact. This topic will be the focus of Chapter 7.

Summary

We started this chapter by reviewing the things to take into consideration when launching your test and exposing your "experiment" to your users for the first time at scale. We echoed a constant theme in this book—that good planning ahead of time and thinking about how your current experiment might fit into your holistic framework around testing to learn (and grow your knowledge base) is really important.

Core to this is understanding that to gather data that is meaningful to your business and that allows you to make good decisions, you will need data that is representative of your user base. So how you decide to allocate users to the test cells in your experiment and thinking about what biases you might encounter in that process is important. Having "good data," data that is gathered programmatically and that can be generalized from a small population to a broader population will help to ensure that what you learn from the data you collect on a smaller population can be broadly applied to your customer base.

Once your test is launched and has been running long enough to achieve the necessary sample size and statistical power, you can better evaluate your hypothesis—that is, see if the changes you made are having the effect on their behavior that you were hoping for. You'll gather the results, analyze, and then evaluate the impact of the experiment. As you work more with experimentation and data analysis, you will understand that design explorations may not have clear "winners" and that a number of the solutions you propose may not have the intended effect on your users' behavior that you were hoping for. Planning and articulating your work upfront can help to ensure that you will always learn something no matter what the outcome. The results you get from your test will help you get a sense of whether you did a good job of designing your test cells to maximize learning, the key concept we articulated in Chapter 5.

Finally, deciding the next steps for your experiment and the experiences you designed isn't always as straightforward as "was our experiment successful or not?" If your results support your hypothesis, you will want to consider if you should continue to evolve and test your thinking before slowly rolling the design(s) out to a larger audience. If your results were negative or inconclusive (flat), you might want to consider if there was more you could have done to make the experiment positive or if there was a flaw in your hypothesis. So, many of the decisions you make at this stage cannot be put into a simple chart or diagram, but will require you to draw on your experience as a designer, your understanding of what has worked well for customers in your past experience, and an understanding of where you and the team you are working with are in the larger cycle of experimenting and learning. Hopefully, seeing how complex some of these decisions might be will give you an appreciation for how leveraging experimentation and data in the design process is *not* just a simple matter of "doing what the data says." Instead, it's a blend of art and science.

We believe that by being more involved in the process of experimentation, and by participating within each of the phases in the process, designers can help to shape the future of their products for the better.

Because the practice of data and design is still at such an early stage, it is of paramount importance that you, as a user-centered designer, be part of the conversation.

Questions to Ask Yourself

As you go through this last stage in the process of A/B testing and experimentation, there are a number of questions that you can ask yourself that can help you to reflect on how experimentation and experimental data analysis can help you and how well you are learning to maximize your ability to learn through the use of data. Each experiment that you run is an opportunity to hone your instincts around what will or will not work with your customers.

Good ideation processes stand up to scrutiny and collecting data on your design and vetting them with users is a great way to measure the value and impact of your work.

Here are some questions you can ask yourself:

- Did you correctly identify the behavior you wanted to change? Was that behavior appropriately reflected in your metrics?
- Was your team (and your stakeholders) in agreement with what you were measuring and the success metrics that you selected?
- Did you craft a clear hypothesis that accurately reflected what you wanted to learn and what you predicted would happen?
- Were the experiences you designed differentiated enough to provide you with good learning? Were they impactful enough that you could measure and observe a change in behavior from your users?
- Were you too focused in your tests? Were you too broad?

- What was the impact of your designs on your user behavior? What did you do as a result, and why did you make that decision?
- On reviewing your data, is there something different you would do next time in designing your experiment?

Remember, there is no negative consequence of being "wrong." In the end, asking these questions will help you will learn from "failed" tests as well as from the "successes." Applying a "learning" mindset to the overall process of designing with data, is about engaging your customers in an ongoing conversation about your experience. Beyond the design itself, you'll also be creating the deeper skills you need to continually respond and react to changes in your customer behavior as it evolves over time.

[7]

Creating the Right Environment for Data-Aware Design

WE ALL KNOW THAT the environment in which we work has a huge impact on our behavior, the expectations we have of ourselves and of others, and our ability to produce great work. If you're planning to adopt a data-aware approach to your design work, then taking the steps to create a healthy environment to support that effort is going to be as important as the tactical work we've outlined in the previous chapters. Although we've been focusing primarily on A/B testing methodology, many of the things that we outline in this chapter are applicable to creating an environment that supports all forms of data collection and analysis: "big" data and "small data," qualitative data and quantitative data.

The strategic and programmatic capture, management, and analysis of user data has not always been considered integral to design practice. However, as we have argued in earlier chapters, we believe that designers have a strategic role to play in the design of data capture and analysis, and we also believe that designers can play a key strategic role in the design of data culture and communication strategies and practices. Carefully collected and analyzed data allows you to bring your users' voice into the conversation in a grounded way. In some sense, the data is a representation of some facet of your users, of what they need and don't need, of what they care about and when.

Creating a shared data-aware culture and developing a common vocabulary around data capture and analysis, and around insights derived from experimentation, *will* lead to a more successful business. It is important to actively work toward the creation of a culture of questioning, learning, and innovation around user-centered evaluation methods, plus a culture of discussion and common goal setting where *user-focused* metrics are emphasized.

Companies that prioritize communication and collaborative learning provide a more fertile environment for sharing design perspectives and advocating for a user-centered viewpoint. In this chapter, we address how you can structure an environment that enables you and your team to be successful at integrating data into your design process. We share how you can communicate a data-aware mindset, showcasing where product excellence is derived from strategic, systematic, and programmatic engagement with data. We advocate that you work through three principles:

- A data-aware practice needs to be supported by a shared company culture that values understanding their users and continuous learning.
- Hiring and growing the right people is essential to supporting data-aware processes and culture.
- Clear processes that help educate and align employees are needed to support a data-aware culture and values.

We'll walk through each of these to help you consider which ideas make sense to adopt for your organization and which may not be as relevant for you or your team.

Principle 1: Shared Company Culture and Values

A data-aware practice needs to be supported by a shared company culture that values understanding users and continuous learning.

For a data-informed approach to be successful in any organization, it must be both universally embraced and understood. By "universal" we mean both in terms of *depth* (that it is accepted from senior executives to individual contributors) and *breadth* (that it is accepted throughout the company, beyond the organization that builds the product experience).

This means that people at all levels in the company and across a broad set of functions within the company recognize that all kinds of data are used to inform product decisions, and that everyone can have a part to play in designing, understanding, and taking action on data. It also means that they have at least a basic understanding of what this process looks like, as well as the pros and cons of using data. This means that there is a good "support net" for data-aware design to happen—having transparency in the process and a common understanding can help to hold the design and product teams accountable to good practices.

DEPTH: COMMUNICATING ACROSS LEVELS

One of the goals of designing with data is to avoid or diminish the necessity of "gut" decision making. Consequently,, it can break hierarchical decision-making structures. The stereotype of management-led, top-down decision making based on hunches cannot flourish in a data-literate environment. Rather, company-wide data literacy that includes addressing well-formulated, carefully investigated questions, invites discussion, challenge, and most importantly the potential to be wrong.

This data is best when collected using any number of techniques (not just A/B testing, but also ethnographic field research, field deployments of prototypes, surveys, lab studies, usability research, etc.). Such grounded and carefully gathered user data can drive your decisions, and is a less risky prospect than relying on hunches from individual executives working from a "gut feeling." An early paper that focused on A/B testing published in 2007 by Ron Kohavi, Randal Henne, and Dan Sommerfield entitled "Practical Guide to Controlled Experiments on the Web: Listen to Your Customers not to the HIPPO,"[1] addressed this issue:

> Many organizations have strong managers who have strong opinions, but lack data, so we started to use the term HiPPO, which stands for Highest Paid Person's Opinion, as a way to remind everyone that success really depends on the users' perceptions.

1 *http://www.exp-platform.com/Documents/GuideControlledExperiments.pdf*

The underlying principle in this quotation from Ronny Kohavi is how data is an effective way to resolve conflicts in decision making without relying on rank, hierarchy, or company politics. John Ciancutti also shared some thoughts with us about how data can resolve conflicts in decision making within a company. He worked at Netflix for a number of years, eventually as VP of Product Engineering, and illustrates how data literacy across all roles at Netflix became a source of freedom and innovation within the company. He said:

> Everybody needs a source of truth, right? In a company, what's your source of truth? How are you going to resolve debate? Sometimes this becomes about, "oh, you were at the company before me," or title, or "I work for you," or "I scream louder than you do." There's always some model for deciding these debates when people disagree. It could be explicit or implicit, but it's there, and people figure out very quickly what it is. If you can make the decision maker data, then that's really your customers' voice making the decisions.
>
> Data literacy was the greatest key to freedom at Netflix early on. That is a culture where there was a lot of freedom. You had to build a successful track record. It didn't matter if you were a designer, an engineer, or a product manager. The skillset that gave you creative freedom at that company was data literacy. You had to have good consumer instincts to take advantage of that freedom to leverage your way in the organization.

Within the tech industry, Netflix has a reputation for being particularly effective at leveraging data. Throughout this chapter, we share a number of stories from Patty McCord who for over 12 years was the Chief Talent Officer at Netflix, where she oversaw talent acquisition and HR. She currently runs her own consulting business and has a great way of showing how an environment that embraces data can help its employees. Patty points out how having a mechanism to measure whether you are doing the right thing for your customers allows for more people to have a voice in the development of the product.

One of the things that made the data-driven approach so successful at Netflix was that the practice of leveraging data was well established and universally accepted throughout the company. It may have started at the top with Reed Hastings and Neil Hunt (Netflix CEO and CPO) driving and believing in the value of leveraging data, but it was also embraced by everyone through management to the individual contributors on the team.

While at some companies the CEO might get to do whatever he wants, at Netflix Patty says it's different:

> At Netflix, Reed gets any *test* he wants. He can move it to the front of the line because he's the CEO, but he's not always right. When he's wrong, people don't gloat necessarily. We do a little ... but the important part is that he learns so much from being wrong. Particularly in consumer-facing products, it's easy for employees to get so into the product that you think, "Who else is a better expert of what our customers want than me? I spend my whole life paying attention to them." Well, that's not the same as being a customer.

Patty highlights a common tendency, that any employee, including executives, can get caught up in thinking they know the answer. One of the reasons that embracing A/B testing can help to mitigate a top-down approach to problem solving is that everyone can learn from experimentation. For example, when Reed would engage in product testing and had a strong idea for what he wanted to see in the product, he would submit his ideas to the same rigor of A/B testing as everyone else in the product team. On rare occasions, Reed might dictate the exact way that a product idea would work, but he would do this on "his test cell"; that is, on the experimental group in the test that he was backing. This cell would be tested against other cells that were proposed by the product team. If it didn't win, then it didn't get launched. Having the upper-level management hold themselves accountable to the same process as the individual teams therefore reinforced the practice of subjecting ideas, prototypes, features, and flows to grounded review through experimentation, and to the possibility of "failing" as a positive outcome. This value was central to a view of how the company should work.

If you are trying to shift into a data-aware framework, it will be critical to look at the way product and design decisions have been made to date. If these decisions were largely in the hands of one or two individuals, then it's worth taking the time to make sure that those people can understand and recognize the value of bringing in user/customer data into the decision-making process because in the end, they may find that their weight is diminished (as is the "weight" of any individual opinion). This is a good point to check with yourself as well—are *you* also comfortable and willing to see how incorporating data will change the weight of your own opinion within the design and product development process?

BREADTH: BEYOND DESIGN AND PRODUCT

In addition to getting all levels of an organization onboard with a data-informed approach, it is just as important for teams beyond those directly involved in building the product experience to have a basic understanding of a data-aware framework and how it's being employed. All teams that exist should be incented to communicate with each other around the data. Company cultures that embrace data sharing and open discussion both vertically and horizontally will encourage participation and engagement from their staff.

Sharing well-summarized data will engage parts of the organization that are not normally part of the design and product development process and make them feel like they have a closer affinity with how the product is shaped. If people in teams beyond your own organization feel like they can empathize with your users, then they can also feel empowered as part of this process. By being more transparent with the rest of the company about how product and design decisions are made (especially in product-driven companies), you can build broader support within the company for the decisions that you make.

It may initially seem superfluous to have teams like recruiting, HR, sales, or finance fundamentally understand your data-aware approach to product design. However, it is always helpful to have any team that you work with in any capacity understand how you do your work.

For example, when recruiting and HR teams understand the company's engagement with data it helps to attract and retain top talent. (We'll be touching more on the people side of this in the next section.) Business teams also benefit when they understand how product experience questions are being posed, prioritized, and then answered through data. They become more empowered in the idea generation stage and both sides become better aligned around product and business success. Imagine the sales executive who feels she knows exactly what you need to build into your product but may be overly swayed by a key vocal client. If that sales executive understands that you build products by looking at the data, then she may realize that she needs to articulate her arguments into the same framework—and it helps to get you and her aligned with what you are building, why you are building it, and what impact you think it will have on your overall user base.

Netflix has a very strong culture around data; it wouldn't be surprising at all to find a finance or HR person asking a member of the product organization about the original hypothesis and what the test cells were when a new product launched. To illustrate this culture, Patty McCord shared another story around how she brought that mindset to the HR team at an ecommerce company she consulted with.

With every person that she met on the HR team, she opened with a story about how a small business owner she frequently visited used the company's products, and how the products transformed their business. She would then prompt the HR person with whom she was talking to share their own personal story about somebody who uses the product, and, in doing so, reinforced her expectation that all company employees should be curious and outward facing, concerned with gathering data about the user experience.

There is a difference between using data to make and inform decisions in one part of an organization versus having it be universally embraced by the entire organization. To get this level of understanding throughout the company, using data has to be something that you actively share as a value and belief within all parts of the company and it has to be something that is talked about and participated in broadly (e.g., in company all-hands meetings and other public forums).

THE IMPORTANCE OF A LEARNING CULTURE

Data-aware design environments work best when they are seen as part of an overall company culture that encourages learning, one which ensures that you are perennially growing your knowledge base. Many companies are focusing on creating "learning environments" where there is a focus on both building individual skills and encouraging development as a company. Data-aware design lends itself to this kind of environment because it relies on you to constantly build up and expand your knowledge around your customer's behavior. Using a data-aware approach is fundamentally about "honing your customer instinct." This is an ongoing activity and every project is an opportunity to get better at developing that instinct through learning, information, and data.

There are some practical habits and best practices that can help to support this culture. Some things that we've seen be especially effective are:

- Keeping sharp on both theory and practice (especially as "best practices" around leveraging data evolve)
- Encouraging employees to be self-aware and evaluating their capabilities often
- Sharing results and information broadly

We'll be touching on all three of these points throughout the chapter as we talk more about how people and processes can help to support the larger culture. In this section, we'll focus for now on education:

Lectures

We've seen a number of teams use lectures as a way to introduce relevant data topics to a broad audience. This can be an effective way to plant some of the seeds of data-aware design. Lectures can be given by external or internal speakers. When you are introducing a new concept to an organization it is often useful for both leaders and individuals alike to hear about how other companies are using data to their advantage. Lectures can be good to:

- Provide an overview of data and design best practices
- Give an overview of different methods and techniques and when to use them
- Introduce systems like company-wide metrics and present how they are measured
- Share insights from research studies, and explain how they've informed product decisions to a larger audience than the immediate product team

In our experience, monthly lecture series or "lunch and learns" have been especially helpful for teams that are trying to establish new habits and are looking to bring people to a common level of understanding. Some larger companies have periodic events where all those interested in user-centered design, from user experience researchers to data scientists to designers, are invited to come together for mini-conferences of talks to share ideas and findings.

Online courses

There are a number of courses and formal training available online with respect to using data and A/B testing. Companies which are large enough to have internal training platforms and programs sometimes opt to establish their own program or class. We've seen teams that are new to data, or hoping to sharpen their skillset, sign up for a course together or book a room in their office and make a virtual "classroom." As it's become more and more common for conferences to post their talks online, sometimes teams will cobble together their own "course" by bringing together a number of good representative talks from across the internet. We've included a few suggestions in the Additional References appendix.

The rewards of taking risks: Redefining "failure"

One of the pitfalls mentioned earlier in this book is when people are driven to *only* pursue incremental and "safe" results because they fear running experiments that don't yield "successful" results. As we mentioned in Chapter 6, rather than focusing on whether tests succeed or fail, we try to instead focus on whether the outcomes were what we expected. Most people will find that they'll have their assumptions and hypotheses challenged when they don't accurately predict the outcome of an experiment.

A culture that supports a data-aware approach to design should also be an environment where you feel more comfortable taking risks in the design of your product experience, with the goal of pursuing big rewards. Taking risks will mean that you won't always "win" (otherwise there is no "risk"). Sometimes the results will not be what you expected, but that doesn't mean that the experiment was a failure. Failure without learning is truly a failure. But so long as you can take your results and apply that information to future experiments, you're contributing to a larger environment of learning. Chris Maliwat articulated this well when he defined what failure means to him:

> I think failure within the context of an A/B test is finding no signal. Meaning you design three different cells against a control and you can't differentiate the results between any of those cells and the control. You didn't push it hard enough.

> Here are some examples of what failure is not. Failure is not seeing a metric tank as a result of a test cell. That's a signal. I think any signal is actually not a failure at all. I think it's a failure to not run a test obviously. It's a failure to not define what metrics are important. It's also a failure when you don't design your test well or adhere to the right procedures for a test.
>
> For example, when people say "Well, we've let it run long enough so we're just going to choose A." Actually, that's cheating, right? Stats are stats and you can massage them if that's what you're in the business of wanting to do, but I think it's also a failure to test things that you think you know are the winner and then don't allow the other answer to be true when that's what the results show. You should do a test because you don't know, and then accept the answer when it comes.

Here, Chris is arguing that the only real way to fail is to not learn anything, whether that means because you didn't go "big enough" to detect a signal, or you weren't willing to let data challenge your existing beliefs.

Some organizations find ways to "celebrate failure" as a way to encourage employees to ask big questions with the intent of sometimes being wrong, and find insights that they can apply to future work. At Skyscanner, they speak about "failing forward."[2] Their goal is to have a successful experiment, *or* fail forward with it. Mary Porter writes in the Skyscanner blog:

> We needed to force ourselves to become more comfortable with sharing our failures, not just our successes. If we didn't, we risked repeating each other's mistakes, which would slow any progress we could make.... We didn't have time to do that. We needed to share our learnings as quickly as possible so that we could start "failing forward."

Teams at Skyscanner receive "fail-forward" cakes for speed in applying learnings from "failed" experiments (Figure 7-1). In this way, the company culture supports failure that is thoughtfully applied to improving their user instinct as a valuable piece of the learning process.

2 *https://medium.com/@Skyscanner/we-need-to-fail-forward-if-we-want-to-succeed-137836db7eb4/*

FIGURE 7-1. A Skyscanner "fail-forward" cake, ready to be served and celebrated

The value of developing your customer instinct

As we've mentioned before, one of the biggest benefits of a data-informed approach to design is that it gives you a great tool to hone your customer instinct over time. It's essential to encourage an environment where people are comfortable with transparency around their experimental results. This allows for an objective evaluation of not just your work, but everyone else's as well, allowing you to hold everyone accountable to the same standard. When you're motivated to understand the user rather than "be right" or build your ego, then it only makes sense to share what you are learning about your customers with each other.

John Ciancutti of 60dB shares his view on the role data plays in shaping your instinct:

> If I was giving advice, I'd say that the only math class everyone in the world needs is a statistics class. Just understand statistics. Today, everybody's talking about "consumer science." It's easy to get started, because people have written about it. As an entrepreneur, you can

> imagine that you're flying a plane and you don't have a pilot's license. So you better have a compass, and you'd better have good instrumentation on your aircraft, because it's already really hard. Having that stuff is the data. And you need to understand how to read the instrumentation, or have a manual to fly the plane. That is your statistics class.
>
> All data does is it informs your product intuition. It doesn't tell you what to build, so don't lose confidence in yourself, just because you need data. I have a point of view about the way my market is going to develop. I have a point of view about what's going to work. I just haven't validated it yet. Then I'm going to learn, and adapt, and adjust.
>
> When I come up with insight, it is data-driven insight. So for me, it's not some bolt from the blue. It is steady, relentless, meticulous study with open eyes in a data-driven way about a market, about a product, about a space that leads me to conclusions that countervail prevailing wisdom. And that's how I get any genius I have. I grind it out. And you can do that, too.

Another story from Patty McCord is about recognizing that your customers change over time, that their needs might change over time, and that your company's business also changes over time:

> The other deep cultural effect of a data-driven company is you realize with data-driven companies that finding out you're wrong is as valuable as finding out you're right. It's a great elephant in the room, where somebody would say, "Well, we tried that and customers don't like that." The smart person in the room would respond, "Well, we did test that when most of our customers were customers on DVD, or we did test that when our customers were all early adopters and now they're my grandmother."
>
> People would always come back to the obvious ideas, because obvious ideas usually are right. But they also have to line up with the customer being in the right place for the obvious idea. Seeing ideas like that that originally failed be then working was wonderful. It was like, "Get out!" What we absolutely believe to be true is just not.
>
> Netflix certainly learned that when we first started doing international. It was like, "Oh, yeah. Nobody knows more about how streaming customers behave than us." But that statement wasn't true worldwide and outside the US.

When we talked about "keeping your old hypotheses in your back pocket" in Chapter 4, this is what we meant. An idea that failed for a previous user group (for instance, when the demographic of the users was very different than it is now) may perform differently as the product and users evolve. One way to make sure that you are truly improving and building your customer instinct over time is to "keep track of track records." Being self-aware of, and knowing when your instinct has differed from what was reflected in the data, is one of the fastest ways to improve your understanding of customer behavior.

There are risks to not recognizing the value of experimentation in building instinct. For example, running too many tests, or "overtesting," is often a side effect of not having a strong enough instinct for the right things to test. Developing a good instinct for what will give you the best return on your resource investment (your "ROI") comes from constant questioning and evaluation as to how well your team is operating and how well your instincts are validated by data. Not only should this be applied at an individual level, but also to the organization overall. You and those you work with should explicitly think about fine-tuning and improving your collective understanding about your customers over time and with every experiment that you are running.

Some teams actually make a game of seeing how these instincts have developed over time. These companies have people place bets on how they think different tests will perform. This healthy dose of competition can be a small incentive to focus on honing those instincts. For instance, Chris Maliwat says:

> We had a Google spreadsheet that captured what metrics and which direction people thought they would go. It's just fun and it makes you think. One of the responsibilities of a product team is to make sure that people understand why you're doing the project, to have a vested interest in the results, and to be comfortable with the idea that we don't always know the outcome.
>
> One could believe that a designer or product person who doesn't know the right answer must not have enough experience. Actually it's almost inversely true. Because I have some experience, I know that we don't know the right answer until we test. Now, based on my intuition that I've built over years of solid examples, I can go from 40 test cell possibilities

> to three or four and I feel really confident that we're going to find something in this realm. I can generally pick out the things that feel big or not big. Sometimes I get it right, but sometimes I'm totally surprised.

These betting games often serve as a reminder that despite all the work that's been done, there's always more to learn. Even the most experienced designers and product people will often have their assumptions challenged when using data, which Chris admits to in his preceding quotation. But, as Chris says, over time your instincts will become sharper, helping you focus your experiments on projects that have great potential. This is one of the long-term benefits to A/B testing.

Principle 2: Hiring and Growing the Right People

Hiring and growing the right people is essential to supporting data-aware processes and culture.

The people in your organization are the key to creating a culture of grounded, data-aware, user-focused design. As our first principle noted, you will want to locate and establish allies and copartners and develop "data friends" with whom you create alignment across company functions. Now, depending on the size of your organization, you may also want to build a team through strategic hiring to reflect, amplify, and grow a data-aware design practice. We'll talk about how to do both of these things in this section.

ESTABLISHING A DATA-AWARE ENVIRONMENT THROUGH YOUR PEERS

If a process isn't already established in a company, there will always be some level of skepticism around trying something new. You might find that there are people who will say "Yes! We should definitely start to take a data-aware approach to design, but we shouldn't do *X*, *Y*, and *Z*." Sometimes, those folks might think being data aware is something very specific (like *only* A/B testing) and aren't considering the bigger picture where different kinds of data collection and analysis fit together to answer strategically important questions.

If this is new, then it's also important to think about how you introduce the methodology and approach. We have found it's really useful to be selective about the first few experiments that you run and who you involve. In your first real foray into a data-aware approach to design, you might make a few mistakes and misstep, as you are generally still learning. By working with people who are empathetic to this and interested in supporting your efforts and learning alongside you, you will be more likely succeed and help cultivate your new culture of experimentation.

Look inside your company, seek out your "data friends" and other sympathetic or curious colleagues. Recruit allies through conversation, question asking, and engaging in their processes. Invite colleagues to be "pilots"—that is, early testers for studies and to comment on designs and plans—to get them actively involved in the process.

If your company or organization has not been data aware historically, and/or has not engaged in a design practice that leverages data before, you're likely to find that there are two groups of people. On the one hand, some people will be eager to try something new. On the other hand, there will be those who view the adoption of a new practice as a hassle. This is why finding a few "allies" who are willing to try something out with you and who are also going to be more forgiving in the initial stages when you are likely to make a lot of mistakes can be really helpful. This will give you a chance to work out any kinks in the process with a small group of supportive people and then have more confidence as you try to roll it out to other designers or teams.

To find a good "pilot" project, there are a couple of characteristics to consider. Find something small so that you can ideally get a "quick win," such as a local project that can demonstrate how data-aware decision making and learning can lead to surprisingly impactful results. This way you will be able to share the payoff of using data-aware design with others. If the first project you choose takes you a few months just to establish what data you're looking for or to do the analysis on the results, it's very unlikely that you'll get a lot of enthusiasm from others to adopt something new.

In addition, a project that has well defined success metrics will make the conclusions you can draw from your first test more clear. This will make it easier for you to explain what you have and haven't learned or not by applying a data-aware process. A project that allows you to do a couple of quick iterations can also be good because it can demonstrate a data-aware process over a couple of cycles. We encourage using data to do more than "just optimization," but when you're establishing the practice for the first time these kinds of projects are perfect for warming up the larger organization to the concept of data-aware design and to build confidence in adopting a new framework for design.

Finally, a note on "allies." As mentioned before, some people will be naturally drawn to a data-aware approach and others will not. The best allies exist in other teams. Having many different voices that can advocate for a process that integrates data is very powerful. Some of the best advocates are in analytics teams and in marketing. Seeking support from the broader organization helps to make this more than "just a design thing" and helps to elevate it to the level of a company-wide initiative. This also helps with the "universally accepted" aspect of culture we discussed earlier. Should you be in the enviable position of having many allies, think carefully about how to scale your program of activities to maintain a good rhythm of communication—small group meetings may become broader group presentations, or weekly bulletins emailed to collaborators.

HIRING FOR SUCCESS

In addition to gaining internal allies and collaborators, the people you hire play a huge role in the success of your team. If you have the option of hiring, building a team to work effectively with data-informed design requires hiring a certain kind of profile. If you are not able to hire, we recommend you still use the criteria listed here for seeking out allies and collaborators who are willing to be hands-on in helping you develop your program of activities. There are several qualities that are central to creating a strong data-aware design team and design practice in your organization:

Fundamental design skills

The best designers know how to interpret a difficult problem and create a solution that addresses it. They can also articulate and justify the reasoning behind their design decisions. It's no different working in a data-aware environment. The best designers in a data-aware environment will leverage these fundamental design skills to address and articulate user problems and needs that will often be identified and measured using data.

A passion for driving a successful business that is also consumer/user-centered

Ideally the people you hire will have a passion and curiosity about the business you're in. To build a data-aware design environment, it becomes even more important for people to have a certain level of business curiosity and the desire to contribute to strategic thinking about the business. This is because it all ties back to being able to create hypotheses that impact the metrics you care most about in your business. If the designers and product managers who are tasked with building the business solutions don't have a baseline level of passion for the business bottom-line measures and metrics, if they are happier being tasked and primarily motivated by delivery rather than by playing a role in the defining process—what has often been called "throwing designs over the wall"—then they will be unhappy in the environment you are creating.

An affinity for understanding, generalizing, and being able to replicate design success and drive consistent user-centered design and product excellence

Being programmatic and systematic through data is about understanding and being able to derive general principles and being able to replicate your results and to derive general principles. Even if results cannot be replicated for good data reasons, it is important that general principles are extracted that could be applicable to adjacent or downstream projects. This is essential to hone a long-term user and product intuition from many A/B tests.

A desire to engage with and learn about the scientific method and develop some skill or empathy for statistics and/or mathematics

It is true that having some basic understanding of statistics and analysis can make a big difference in whether an individual can succeed in a data-aware design environment. It is important to have some basic comfort with or curiosity about math so that conversations with those who are doing the analytic work are enjoyable and informative. This will also enable dialogue about the work and its actual and potential impact. Without some fundamental understanding of the theory behind many of the techniques in a data-aware environment, it is hard to engage in the more strategic conversations.

An ability to be open-minded, iterative, and engaged but not enslaved by initial design inspirations

For some designers, a healthy ego and a deep belief in the fundamental "rightness" of their designs is a necessary and positive characteristic as it can sometimes give designers the confidence and ability to convince others of their vision and to sell them on that. Ego is a necessary component for creativity to survive. That said, in an experimental, iterative design environment, ego-driven overattachment to designs can get in the way of success. This is because as part of a data-informed organization you often have to be willing to let the user and usage data make the decisions. Designers must recognize that letting go of their ideas can be hard but may sometimes be necessary.

An ability to be very focused on results as well as production

Especially in the A/B testing part of data-informed design, it can be easy to get distracted with different options for experimental designs. As we have shown through the examples we shared in Chapters 4, 5, and 6, by having a certain amount of focus and discipline, you will be better equipped to resist the urge to fall into the various pitfalls of A/B testing around making a decision too early or building out too many test cells.

We also talked to Patty McCord about hiring people with an appreciation for data. She actively talks to people in the interview process about using the scientific method on a daily basis, having a hypothesis, and an opinion about what the outcome of their work is going to be. She asks them variations on the question "What leads you to believe that something is true?", using it as a way to get a sense of an individual's tendency for data and facts to support their opinion. Example questions included:

- If you've been in a situation where you were confused, what did you do to correct that?
- Tell me about a situation where your team didn't accomplish what they wanted to accomplish. What do you think was missing? What would you have done differently? How have you learned from that?

You don't always need to hire people who have actually have experience using data in design, but you at least need to find people that seem to have an affinity for working within that framework and who are motivated toward developing deeper expertise around testing designs.

If the folks that you hire aren't fundamentally open to the concept of data-driven design, it can be very difficult for them to be successful on the team. This, of course, doesn't mean that they are "bad" designers; it just means that they would probably be more effective (and more appreciated by their peers) in a different environment. As we mention throughout the book, there are many ways to do design and to build products. What fundamentally determines the success of a design or product is finding the right fit between the individuals, organization, and the processes that you use to be successful.

Building the team with data involved from the start

We've emphasized throughout the book how important it is during the product development cycle for designers to work closely with the people in your organization who deal with data. Katie Dill shared how Airbnb ensures that data is integrated into their design process by starting with how they assemble the teams and where/how they work:

> Our teams are all cross-disciplinary. We have separate pillars within our org—folks that are focused on hosts and their homes, folks that are focused on the guests' marketplace, folks that are focused on growth, etc. These different pillars are teams made up of engineers, designers, product managers, content strategists, researchers and data scientists. We need to have the full set of disciplines before the team is really ready to go. It can be tough to manage resourcing and decision making, but we feel this is critical to build a thoughtful and balanced product.
>
> I appreciate that this multidisciplinary partnership is maintained at every level of our product org. We sometimes call it the triforce, with engineering (including data science), product management, and design (including content and research) in a tight-knit partnership from our executive level down to the most junior level. With each discipline having a seat at the table we know our business, our users, and our technology are all well represented throughout the product development process.
>
> In the beginning of the product development process, the question is "where is the opportunity?" Data science and user research play a huge role in answering this question. Our user research team is incredibly close to our community and they can help us see where there are unmet needs. Data science can help us identify positive and negative

> occurrences on our current product and understand the scale of opportunities. Data science can help us see when an anecdote is a trend and a valuable place to focus our efforts.
>
> For example, let's say we hear from hosts that they're frustrated their homes aren't getting booked as often as they'd like. By looking at the data we can see how they compare to other hosts like them and start to identify the issue. Perhaps their listing description is too bare and they lack quality images. Next, we can see how big this issue is globally by looking at the data. We might see that this is a problem that a lot of other hosts face and that this is something we should go after. The data [early on] helps us to actually size and understand the problem, making it concrete. It quantifies the opportunity and helps us understand how urgent the issue is and how many resources to dedicate to the solution.

Arianna McClain reiterated this point while explaining to us how she worked at IDEO:

> It's important for researchers, data scientists, and designers to consistently and collaboratively work together.
>
> Sometimes teams can debate over a design direction for days or weeks. However, on a transdisciplinary team, a researcher can quickly run a survey or test to see how people react; or talk to a few people to hear users' points of view. Transdisciplinary teams enable a flow that constantly shapes the product without formal and stagnating handoffs between researchers and designers.

When the "data folks" and the "design folks" are on the same team, there's very little friction to get data involved in the process. As Arianna said, it doesn't have to feel "formal" to get insights work involved and help resolve questions that the team might have in real time.

While you may not have a team of dedicated data scientists and researchers at the beginning of every project, it's easy to see the reasoning behind why a company like Airbnb or IDEO would include these disciplines from the start and how it was part of the expectations of the company at all levels (which points back to some of the ideas we discussed in Principle 1: Shared Company Culture and Values). Even if you don't have people who are responsible for data, you can find ways to actively represent data at the beginning of any project. This will help to set expectations that it's an integral part of the ideation, execution, and evaluation of your design process.

Principle 3: Processes to Support and Align

Clear processes that help to align and educate employees need to be put in place to support a data-aware culture and values.

As you embark on establishing a data-aware environment and culture, you'll want to create a dialogue, set expectations, and define a shared vocabulary for your work. This will help you to lay the foundations for the engaged and transparent conversations that should emerge when you work with data. Data ignorance fuels data reticence. To create a successful culture around data in your company, it is important to make sure that the people in your organization and those you work with understand, at least superficially, what's involved in capturing user data and analyzing it. This may include a range of data—whether that be in the form of A/B testing or user activity logs; as we've said before, data in all forms is essential to the process when it comes to leveraging it effectively.

If you are actively using a data-aware design framework, one of the best things that you can do for your company is to broadly share the results and to give everyone access to the data. Such sharing reinforces that most decisions are influenced by data, and that decisions are made based on evidence not anecdote or personal preference. It also helps folks to build up shared knowledge about what works and what doesn't work. As we've noted throughout the book, all this experimentation doesn't really get you far if you're only using it to make decisions on a microlevel. What you should be focusing on is adding up everything you learn from your experiments along the way and then using it to hone your instincts about your users over time. The best way to do this is to vet it with your peers and to subject your testing to debate and discussion.

Active sharing of data and debate around it allows us, as designers, to develop an understanding of how our designs are actually performing, and how they are being judged. While designers are often engaged with foundational qualitative and quantitative user research, there are many environments where once the design is done, the designer disengages from the product development process and doesn't or is not able to stay as engaged with the results of their designs on their users postlaunch. Designers being actively involved in the review and discussion of the results of their experiments changes this dynamic. Having access to data in this way is a key shift in skill development and in being able to become more strategic.

ESTABLISHING A KNOWLEDGE BASELINE

Having decided you want to create shared understanding of the value of data capture, analysis, and consumption in your company, you will need to create a dialogue. Find out what people really do know and don't know about taking a data-aware approach to design, perhaps by setting up informal meetings with key people in your organization. Treat these like information-gathering interviews.

You will find that some people may understand some methodologies like interviews, but have much less experience with A/B testing (or vice versa). Find out what the biases and assumptions are about leveraging data in design and do this at all levels of the organization (from CEO to individual designer or product manager). Having all of this understanding upfront about what people think and know can save a lot of time in the long run: you'll be able to assess where you might want to focus initially in terms of establishing best practices and you'll also become aware of any challenges you might face as you try to get a data-aware design process established.

Once you've established what the knowledge level is, where there is deep knowledge, and where there are opportunities for teaching, learning, and sharing, then explicitly talk about what practices you want to establish and why. Getting your team and others that you work with to agree to try out some of these things will be important if they're not familiar with some of these tactics.

Patty McCord talks about how creating a culture of data is as much about the people having the right mindset as it is about methodology or having the concrete skills:

> I think you can teach the culture of data by just learning how to ask questions about people's thinking ... I would teach people how to have those conversations all of the time. "How do you think that should work?" "If you were in charge of that, what would your hypothesis be?" "How would you test it?"

> The idea of data-driven thinking, there's a mindset and a methodology. The question that I use a lot is, "What leads you to believe that's true?" Which is fundamentally asking, "What's your data?" Asking over and over again, "How do you know? How do you know? How do you know?"
>
> There are a lot of ways to have day-to-day human interaction that sets people up to have those conversations and to test people. I don't think it comes naturally to people. I think it's learned behavior.

Although we've focused on A/B testing in this book, let's talk a little more broadly about leveraging all kinds of data into your work. As you work to incorporate all kinds of data, it's always good to set expectations for what you will do and what you expect to see as a result; for example, "I'd like to take an extra few days on this to make sure we have time for user feedback on how usable this flow is." Make it clear that the cost will be a little more time to introduce something new and *what level of results you hope to get from it.*

When running any kind of exercise where you will be capturing data from your users, be clear about what method you will be using to answer which questions and why; as we've cautioned throughout the book, too often A/B tests are used to answer questions that would have been more effectively addressed in a usability lab with a few participants or usability lab tests are employed to answer questions that would have been better addressed with surveys or field observations. Literacy in data collection and analysis methods of all kinds matters; being literate about methods means you can create a clear rationale for why you are proposing studies. You can set appropriate expectations, and you can help others understand the power of asking the right questions and addressing those questions with the right method for the deepest user understanding. In practice, we know that it's a specialist's job to understand what the best methodologies are. However, one way to help remediate the pitfall of jumping too soon into the wrong kind of data collection is to always start with a *question* rather than a *method.* For instance, rather than having conversations about how "the team wants a survey," the discussion should start with something method-agnostic: "What do we want to learn?" This can help refocus the conversation around learning rather than around methodologies.

Sharing results from ongoing work means that you're sharing knowledge and insights along the way, which helps people develop a better understanding when it comes to your particular product or project, helps them feel more involved, and also allows people who have less experience with data in the design practice have the opportunity to build a good foundation about the practice itself.

Discussions and debate around more general topics and "theory" of data-informed design can be very helpful to make sure that everyone has a common foundation. Topics might include everything from how to select the right technique for different kinds of projects, the pros and cons of different methodologies, or even details such as what a *p*-value is. The number and level of discussions that you have on these best practices will be determined by how mature the organization is with respect to data-aware design. If everyone can have a common baseline of knowledge on the theory behind the practice of data and design, you'll find that your discussions on actual projects will be much richer and more efficient. You'll also hopefully avoid some of the pitfalls of not using the data properly (and therefore being more likely to subjective bias or misinterpretation).

ESTABLISHING A COMMON VOCABULARY

A key part of establishing a shared set of values is the language that you use. Think about the words that you most often hear at your company. What are the words and phrases that are unique to your company? Which acronyms have you created and embraced? When you first joined, what were the things that stood out to you as unique? To make sure a data-aware decision-making framework that is universally embraced, it's important to establish a common vocabulary and way of speaking about it.

You'll find that a common vocabulary will help in a number of ways, from making brainstorms more effective to making debate over product and design decisions even more rich because you'll have a shorthand for the things that are most important to the discussion. Seemingly simple questions that can get asked over and over again—"How do we know *X*?", "How are we going to measure *Y*?", "How do you expect the majority of users will react?", "What is the learning curve for this?", "What user errors or stumbling blocks do we think are reasonable or not?", "What do you expect to learn about user behavior from this design?", "What does design success look like?", and "What does design failure look like?"—can quickly help to train people and set expectations about the role that data can play in decision making and in strategic, grounded design iteration.

Remember though, this should be as much about having common definitions as it is about having a common vocabulary. Since a data-aware environment requires a certain amount of discipline and rigor to the practice, you can't ensure consistent application of this framework if you don't also have alignment on your definitions as well as your vocabulary. Key phrases and vocabulary for a data-aware approach have been defined throughout the book, especially in Chapters 2, 3, and 4. Words and phrases like *hypothesis, test cell, segment, sample, population,* and *statistically significant* are all good examples that can become the foundation of your own data-aware vocabulary.

The consistent usage of vocabulary helps to reinforce a specific mind-set and a way of thinking. Like working in any company, the vocabulary can help to shape the culture. And like any other language, it's important to have people speak it and to have the people who are leaders also speak it. Patty McCord talks about how, as head of HR, she used A/B testing language in conversations with people about their behavior:

> Part of the other reason I did it was it got me respect with people who were data driven. I wasn't talking to them about their feelings, which made them feel weird and uncomfortable. I was saying, "Well, I know you said that you believe this person doesn't like you or you believe that this is an interdepartmental issue. Here's the evidence I find from observing you." Observation is data, too.
>
> I would often say, "What's your hypothesis on that?" "Begin with the end in mind, know what you're trying to achieve." The data of what success looks like is the starting point, not the end point.

We have found that when you can steer people away from using phrases like "my idea is ..." and toward saying "my hypothesis is..." instead, they become less attached to what they are proposing. The implied scientific nature of vetting a hypothesis places an individual's idea within the context of everyone else's idea and also makes people more open to testing their ideas and more accepting if their assumptions prove false. It helps them see the bigger picture beyond their specific ideas.

A great example of this comes from Leisa Reichelt. While she was at GOV.UK she instituted a program where everyone was required to sit in on at least two hours of user research every six weeks, and it became common practice to ask people "Have you done your two hours?"[3,4] They kept track of how many tests the team had run and what percentage of the team had attended a user session in the past six weeks on a simple (but public) dashboard. Think about how you can use workshops, presentations, and shared resources like short research reports to create a set of terms and concepts that everyone understands that reflects the value of a data-grounded and supported approach to user-centered design.

While we strongly emphasize creating a literacy and a common language around data, we also want to caution you to not get too caught up in acronyms (especially around metrics) such that you forget that the ultimate goal is to provide the best, most compelling experience for your users. Find ways to actively represent the user in your definitions so that everyone recognizes that data itself does not humanize; instead, it's how we interpret it and how it is applied and used to rationalize decisions about product design and product quality that can humanizes the data.

DEVELOPING A RHYTHM AROUND DATA COLLECTION AND SHARING

As you begin applying a data-aware framework, there's no way to just turn it "on"—it will take time. However, your goal should be to make data-grounded design an effective reflection of user needs, and a consistent part of product development. To do that, you will need discipline and vigilance. This is probably true of any decision-making platform.

There are also many long-term benefits to consistently leveraging a data-aware design process. Ideally, you find patterns in your work that lead you to larger insights that you can apply more broadly to your product experience and in identifying new opportunities to solve problems for your users. Therefore, one of the ways to create a shared culture around user-centered data is to be programmatic about your data

3 *https://userresearch.blog.gov.uk/2014/08/06/have-you-had-your-recommended-dose-of-research/*

4 *http://www.slideshare.net/leisa/changing-yourorgsproductmakingdna-leisareichelt*

collection and sharing. What does this mean? We have already talked about crafting a careful and consistent practice; however, beyond this you need to create a framework for sharing results.

The more you can create a set of data-sharing formats and practices the more people will sign up. For example, create a consistent structure to your reports and make those reports easily available in some form of report "library." Create events where data sharing is the point of the event, and make these regular events. If you work in a shared workspace, use that physical space to showcase results as they come in. Present your data in ways that help others to understand and interpret their significance, and collaborate with them to determine the next actionable steps. With careful management of results over time you can avoid ephemerality, the constant redoing of work, and the "reinventing the wheel." Systematic record keeping and sharing in common formats makes your message potential stronger, and makes the business stronger. We advocate putting considerable effort into your "data hygiene" practices; that is, the careful management, curation, and sharing of data.

You might find that there are some very easy ways to set up a rhythm around experimental design, data sharing, and results consolidation. For example, in Chapter 6 we mentioned that the team at Spotify runs user research sessions called "Soundcheck" every two weeks; they publish the schedule and invite people who are working on a product to come in and see how their work is being received by users. At Spotify, this has created a bit of a mini-culture around the rhythm of Soundcheck sessions, and it's common to hear throughout the product teams at Spotify statements like, "We should Soundcheck this" or "Has this been Soundchecked?" The rhythm and brand established by the team has thus extended to its own vocabulary as well.

There may be other things that you can look to piggyback on to set up an expectation within your team about good habits that you can make part of a recurring rhythm. You might also consider sending out a monthly update with insights from the various experiments and projects that you've been working on. By starting to set up expectations that data will be collected on a regular basis or creating dashboards that show how metrics might be changing over time given changes that you are making to the product, you can start to establish a working rhythm in your organization around data.

Project review meetings

One of the most effective ways to share knowledge is a recurring project review meeting. This might be an ongoing meeting between a broad set of product managers and designers to review a number of topics around ongoing work. The key is when you invite people who may not normally work with one another on a day-to-day basis. Such meetings provide an opportunity to share what they are learning in each of their areas to the broader organization and it helps generally with building up that shared knowledge base of what is working and what doesn't work when it comes to your users. You might break this meeting into two sections:

- Ongoing or upcoming work
- Results from launched projects

The meeting should encourage a lot of discussion and debate about the projects that are being shared and should feel more like a working meeting where everyone is vetting what is being presented. Presenters should leave the room feeling more confident about the approach that they are taking and perhaps have some new insights as well. To get you started, here are some of the kinds of things you might present and discuss.

On ongoing or upcoming projects your discussion might include the following (you should recognize a number of these questions from the previous chapters):

Hypothesis

- What is the hypothesis? Is it a valid hypothesis?
- What prior work/data/research influenced the hypothesis? Why was this hypothesis generated?
- Does it resonate and contribute to the overall product goals? More specifically, is the hypothesis valid?

Methodology

- What techniques are you using to collect data for this project (e.g., lab interviews, A/B testing, etc.)?
- What do you hope to learn?
- Are there other methods that could reveal better data? Would some form of data triangulation give you deeper insights?

- To what extent were methods chosen as a result of extraneous constraints (e.g., time constraints)?
- Given an infinite amount of time, what would the ideal method(s) be?

Design

- How effective is the design at reflecting the hypothesis or variations of that hypothesis?
- How does the design support what you want to learn from this project?

Note: This meeting will be different from a design review where you might be looking at consistency within your design language, and giving more pure design feedback. Those meetings are still useful, but probably a separate meeting from this one.

Success metrics

- What are the success metrics? How were they derived?
- Are the success metrics the right ones? Will these really measure the validity of the hypothesis?
- What other things might you measure or use to measure success?

For projects that have launched and where you are reviewing results, discussion might revolve around the following:

Summary of methodology

- What methods were used and why? What other methods were considered? Why were they not selected?
- How effective were the methods used at getting the insights that were sought?

Results and analysis

- Was the hypothesis proven? Why or why not?
- What did the team learn and what can be applied to other work that is going on?
- Did the results support any other larger trends that you might have seen before?

- How do these results compare to prior work?
- What are the next steps?

Concerns

- Did we see anomalies or surprises?
- Did we test the right things?
- Could or should we have tested other things at the same time?
- Could there have been any confounds?

By reviewing the work that is done in this manner on a regular basis, people can actively learn about what works and doesn't work for users. It also encourages people to ask questions and discuss, thereby actively learning while doing. When the organization is newer to data-aware design, having a meeting like this is a good way for the few who might be more comfortable with the concepts to teach those who are less familiar. When the organization is more mature at using data-informed methodologies, then the discussion can stimulate further learning and perhaps even innovation in methods and analyses.

We also advocate subscribing to user-testing and design-related newsletters and services, and doing regular searches for slide decks and white papers online. Although results from other companies may not always be transferrable to your company, garnering an understanding of what other companies have learned can be a good way to stimulate creative ways to look at your own product(s) and your own practices. Looking to what may already be written or shared can be a great way to preinform or to accelerate acceptance for adopting a data-informed design process in your company. For example, you might be considering creating a side-navigation system, but an article from Next Web suggests side-drawer navigation reduces user engagement.[5] Sharing this data with your team could motivate running a test on your own navigational system. You can definitely learn a lot by looking externally at what other companies are sharing about their findings, and thinking rigorously and critically about what external learnings do or don't apply to your own business and product.

---

5 *http://thenextweb.com/dd/2014/04/08/ux-designers-side-drawer-navigation-costing-half-user-engagement/*

Through these techniques, you can establish your own internal process of data-informed design and ultimately build up your own knowledge base of things that work best for your company and your product.

Spreading data across the organization

One of the most challenging components of disseminating data and insights across an organization is finding ways to communicate about data and data collection with various kinds of stakeholders from different departments and/or disciplinary backgrounds. Intuitively, you might expect that a data scientist would have very different questions about how an A/B test was run than someone from the marketing team. In practice, finding ways to share insights in a way that resonates with the many different "consumers" of data at your company can be challenging, but it's really important to make sure that an A/B test has meaningful impact in a company. Arianna McClain shared the story of how she makes data compelling, a task that is particularly important when working in a consultancy like IDEO:

> At IDEO, we believe that numbers don't move people, stories do. So, if I'm trying to explain to a client why something is valuable and would like them to pay attention, I tell them a story rather than just show them the "data." For each major point, I connect the quantitative data with human stories and photos we've taken in the field. This helps illuminate the insight and elevate the data. This way, the client understands that the insight isn't just numbers; rather, it's grounded in human experience and connects to a larger system.

Chris Maliwat echoed this sentiment when he talked about the importance of data not just for data's sake, but in service of telling a compelling story about users to an often diverse and cross-functional group of people at a company. He said:

> Miscommunication often happens when people don't connect the two sides of the brain (qualitative with quantitative) to tell the complete story. Different people react to different communication methods so if you tell both, it makes it easier for people to have the conversation. As testers, as designers, as product people, more often than not it's our job to bridge that gap. You as a product builder have to figure out how to help everyone understand. You know, at the end of the day, the test

> results don't matter if people don't understand what you were testing and why, what your hypothesis is, how you're going to measure it, and what the analysis and data said.

Beyond communicating results clearly to stakeholders, how we talk about data can also influence how accessible it feels. This also serves as a great way to remind the folks we work with that, at its core, all data (including quantitative measures) are about people and giving them a voice in product and design decisions. Arianna McClain also shared some wisdom with us about how she speaks about using data in her organization:

> As a data person, I actually don't like the word "data" because it holds so much. There's automotive data, financial data, and then there is user data, also known as human data. I feel that calling human stories "data" makes you forget the differences between machines and humans.
>
> I've noticed that when it comes to digital products, services, and experiences, companies often forget that the data they're collecting (e.g., clicks, search terms, responses to surveys) represent people's attitudes and needs. They're traces of human behavior. And these data points represent people's stories.
>
> At IDEO, rather than "collecting data," we reframe it as trying to understand the feelings, needs, attitudes, and behaviors of significantly more people. It's great to talk to two people, but we can also quickly talk to 1,000 people through surveys and other forms of data collection.
>
> We take the "design" in survey and measurement design seriously. There's a tendency for people to be human-centered and conversational at a user interview, but then write a survey like a robot. We design surveys for real people at scale, in a way that feels more like a friendly conversation.

This advice from Arianna and Chris is fundamentally about making data feel human, rather than cold and emotionless as aggregate numbers sometimes feel. As you now know, all numerical data reflects real human needs and behaviors underneath. Always making an effort to speak about data in this way helps make data feel accessible, and gives it a more powerful voice in the decision-making process.

CREATING A PRESENCE IN THE OFFICE

One of the best ways to build a culture around data is to find ways to share your data within the company. It's fairly common for teams to display the metrics that they are most focused on large displays around the office. This is definitely a good tool, but two of the most clever and thoughtful things that we've seen in this space come from Airbnb.

Airbnb has a large storyboard (shown in Figure 7-2) that outlines the guest and host journey (essentially their user journeys). They've woven the data into the customer journey by adding colored boxes to the journey to say in which moments they're doing well and in which moments they're not. Airbnb is both humanizing the data and making it relevant to the people who work on the product by showing it at the right points in time relative to the customer journey.

FIGURE 7-2.
Airbnb storyboard showing the host and guest user journey; colors are used to indicate how well that part of the journey is working

The Airbnb team also put together a book for their "Growth" team whose focus is to increase the user base (Figure 7-3). This book outlines the principles that guide their work in addition to the metric that they look at to guide it. This well-designed book is both energizing for the designers as well as the larger team. It helps the team better describe what they do by showcasing both the experience principles and the data that they use.

FIGURE 7-3.
The Airbnb Product Growth book showing their principles

The book also includes clear definitions of their metrics so that everyone is working from the same page about what is being measured and what it represents. Understanding the language that is being used when it comes to data is often the first step in empowering the team to begin to participate in the conversation around data.

LEARNING FROM THE PAST

Another good practice as you establish a data-aware environment is to look at previous projects in your organization. We've found that one effective technique is to take relevant past projects and revisit both the methods you've used as well as insights that were originally drawn. It's a nice way of exercising the skills you're developing in thinking about data. This might be especially effective on projects where the outcome wasn't what you were expecting. If you do this as a team, you also have the benefit of learning together and bringing those different perspectives to this retrospective exercise. Many companies have online "libraries" of previous research studies in the form of reports.

As you've developed your skills in blending data and design, what might you have done differently now? Was there something that in hindsight might have changed the way you approached using data on that project?

For example, was there a project where you were hoping to see a big lift in user acquisition as a result of a change in the onboarding flow and it didn't happen? Going back to the data, was there anything you could have looked at prior to making those changes that might have given you a hint as to the fact that it wasn't going to be successful? How can you build that knowledge into future tests? Or perhaps your users reacted very badly to a new feature you launched thinking it was going to make them happy.... Applying some survey techniques or user research in these instances (even though the feature has already been launched) will give you insight into what your users might have been able to tell you ahead of time if you had done this work prelaunch.

When you can share these kinds of insights with the team (even if it does feel "too late") it makes people that much more enthusiastic to incorporate a data-informed approach earlier in the process the next time. This also leverages the power of triangulating methods, a topic we covered in earlier chapters.

Another good practice in A/B testing is to keep track of how different team members' hunches relate to outcomes. You can ask all the members of the team to write down what they think the results will be and why they think those results will happen. When you get the actual results and can compare the votes that were cast prior to the test being launched, you can see how well you and your team were actually able to predict the impact to users.

Over time, it's always interesting to keep track of who in the team has good user-product instincts. This need not be about being competitive—it is about team learning and improving not just individuals' but also the team's intuitions about user engagement with your product(s) and service(s) over time.

Having clear and consistent processes around data can help to not only establish a data aware design practice in your organization, but also help to make it evolve and flourish over time. Any process that you establish should be in support of and fit in with your larger culture, and it's unlikely that you'll find a single process that works in every organization without fail. To this end, finding and establishing the right process for your organization will also require an experimental approach in and of itself.

Summary

Ultimately, if you want to be effective at integrating any kind of new framework into your company, you'll want it woven into the DNA of your company culture. Even if your company has the mechanics in place to embrace data as part of the decision-making process, it will be hard to succeed without buy-in from the other folks at your company.

It's a hundred times easier to adopt something when the culture supports it ... and that's why the success of a data-aware framework is really going to depend on the culture at your company.

If you're interested enough in creating a lasting and deep culture around using a data-aware framework for design in your organization so you can make *grounded, user-centered product decisions,* you'll also invest some time in building up a culture that can support it with the right processes as well as the right people.

With respect to data, there are a handful of tactics that we've seen work really well at different companies. Some of these tactics may be about defining new or transforming existing individual roles and mindsets; some are more directed at establishing collaborations and support from the team or larger organization.

As we mentioned when we started this chapter, culture is unique to every organization and we would never dictate what the right solution is for you and your organization. You may want to take some of the practical things we've suggested and put them in place right away. You will find that some of them will work well and endure, whereas others will not get traction or will require considerable perseverance to establish.

In keeping with our theme of data-aware design, we've always taken an experimental approach to organizational processes too. We advise you to do the same. Find different ways to introduce data into your company and then get feedback from "users" (in this case, it might be teams or individuals in your own company). Ask them which activities they found valuable and effective and which they found less so. Find out the underlying reasons behind their feedback and then modify what you are doing to address them. See if you can create ways to measure your success, to measure what works and why. Ask yourself: How well has your "common vocabulary" taken hold? Are people using the terms you have introduced in meetings and in company correspondence in email, messaging, and announcements? Are people actively asking to bring data into the design and product development cycle? Has your time spent "selling" the idea reduced? Are your outreach activities meeting with more positive responses? How much does data-informed design get credited when product successes are observed?

Throughout this book, we have emphasized patience, persistence, resilience, and tenacity. It will take a while to see the fruits of your labor paying off (or not). It can take anywhere upwards of six months to really see a change in the mindset of an organization. The length of time depends on the size of your organization and the business you are in. Aim for some small successes to start and build from those. Establish, share, and monitor your success metrics. With time, iteration, and allies, you'll find that data-aware design really does have a positive effect not just on how you build your products, but on your culture as well.

Questions to Ask Yourself

As you set this up, we also suggest that you ask yourself the following questions:

- What challenges will you individually face if your company adopts a data-aware culture?
- What are some of the things that will be challenging for your organization or team as you move to a more data-aware approach to design?
- How does your organization currently communicate? Do you talk about data already? In what capacity?
- Who initiates user testing? Who owns the results?
- Who do you already have in your organization that might prove helpful for you to pair with as you try to establish these practices?
- What resources and skills do you and your team currently have in place and what do you need to acquire, create, and/or develop?
- What existing habits and cultural aspects are already in place that might make a good foundation upon which to build a culture of data-informed design and decision making?
- What platforms could you use to share ideas and research reports? How could you create a browsable repository of past test results and study reports?

[8]

Conclusion

We have covered a lot of ground in this book. We hope you have enjoyed reading it as much as we have enjoyed writing it.

Throughout the book we have been arguing that designers will gain value from, and will also add immense value to, the design of A/B tests. Hopefully, you now understand the basics of A/B testing, how A/B testing enables you to compare one or more versions of a designed service experience, and how A/B testing can help you understand more about your users' needs. The benefits of conducting A/B experiments are being able to get access to a large number of users at one time in their real-world context, and the ability to compare many different versions of your design(s) simultaneously. A/B tests can improve product performance for different cohorts of users, and can help you figure out how to attract and retain new users. As the purpose of A/B testing is to evaluate which experiences perform better for users and for your business according to previously defined, relevant metrics (such as which links or buttons are clicked or how long someone stays on a site), we hope that you are now also intrigued by understanding what metrics work best for your business context.

Beyond specific features, products, or business models, though, A/B tests can help you develop an understanding of human behavior more generally; they can help you to hone your skills regarding what works best for your users in your interfaces and in your information and service design. This is the power of A/B testing, and as we pointed out at the beginning of this book with our analog and digital photography example, it is only since the advent of the internet that we have been able to conduct this kind of research.

But, as the old phrase goes, with great power comes great responsibility. In this chapter, we will review some critical concepts from the book, and introduce some reflections on the ethics of experimentation.

A key point we have emphasized is that experimentation and data analysis should always be in service of helping you understand your users more deeply and helping you to become more aware of your users' needs and the motivations for their actions; it should never dehumanize people, and should never "reduce them to numbers."

To help you keep focused on a holistic view of your users, we stressed that one of the most important aspects of experimental work is triangulating with other sources and types of data—that is, making sure you draw on results from surveys, interviews, lab experiments, and other methodologies. Experimentation cannot answer all your questions. You need to always be contextualizing the data you collect from individual experiments into a program of design evaluation and user understanding, based on collation of results from other experiments. You should also take inspiration for interpretation from, and cross-check, your results, with other data you have in the company. This kind of back-and-forth will also provide inspiration for more experiments.

Picking up from the idea of triangulation, as we pointed out in the Preface and Chapter 1, a company benefits greatly when user experience researchers, designers, data scientists, market analysts, frontend developers, systems engineers, and business strategists are in dialogue, when they come together to work on the design of data collection and the sharing of insights. For designers who are interested in this bigger picture, their work remit can extend beyond the design of specific features of a technology or service. We emphasized the value of these conversations and collaborations by pointing out that alliances at the grass roots level of a company that can truly facilitate a more holistic and user-centric focus and make your company more successful. We talked about making "data friends" to further develop your data but also your business literacy; this is a means of sharing your insights and educating others about the user-centric aspects of the product(s) you are designing. Through data sharing, you and your work can have a broader impact on the company values as well as a specific feature's success or failure in moving a single business metric. Making such data friends can transform a company from the bottom up, giving voice to your users. Experimental data can be a boundary-crossing asset within a business.

To ground these grand beliefs and claims and get you on your way to engaging more fully with experimentation and experimental data, in the early chapters of the book we introduced you to central concepts that underpin the basics of all experimental design, not just A/B testing.

In Chapters 2 and 3 we reviewed some basic concepts from experimental science, including statistical ways of establishing reliable and replicable causality, hypothesis generation, sample and test group determination (ways of dividing up all your users into different groups), significance testing, and so on. We laid the foundations for a framework we ourselves use to turn questions into hypotheses, to prioritize hypotheses, and to design experiments to test those hypotheses. We introduced some methods and shared some examples to show you how to think about the results you get from your experiments.

In Chapters 4, 5, and 6 we got even more concrete, covering the basics of designing and running A/B tests. We illustrated all these concepts using examples: first our summer camp metaphor, and then specific examples from our work and from the work of our associates and colleagues.

Finally, in Chapter 7 we discussed the importance of summarizing, sharing, and collating results and sharing those across your company. If you are in a small company, go and talk to people in person. You can also set up regular meetings, create a regular newsletter, and create physical posters to adorn your workspace with results if you share physical office space. Of course, the larger your company, the more planned-out and formal the processes, procedures, and platforms for such sharing may need to be. Many large companies invest a great deal of resources into insights-sharing platforms and portals, and host regularly calendared meetings to facilitate cross-functional as well as cross-team and within-team communication. Communication and collaboration are key to a successful experimentation strategy that foregrounds the value of good, user-centered design.

As we close out this book, we want to remind you that our philosophy about data isn't that quantitative data experimentally collected has all the answers all the time; we believe the process of data gathering, analysis, and interpretation needs to be conducted judiciously. In the next section we will remind you of some of the pitfalls people have fallen into with A/B testing in the past and also to introduce you to some high-level considerations in the area of research ethics. In raising research and data ethics as an important topic, we don't want to scare you; we just want to point to some of the conversations around data ethics, to note that the areas of research and data ethics are constantly shifting as we learn more about the power of what can be done with data at scale, and to invite you to the conversation if you are interested.

Ethical Considerations

As we have discussed examples in this book, we have alerted you to be cautious about your experimental design(s), about how many and what kinds of tests to run, and about how you interpret your results. We pointed out that experimental testing and data analysis cannot answer all research and business questions. We also pointed to occasions where running too many experiments can cause problems—"over testing." We noted that users can become confused if interfaces and interactions shift constantly, and if features that they value are moved or removed. And, if you run too many experiments concurrently, you risk having users exposed to multiple variables at the same time, creating experimental confounds such that you will not be able to tell which one is having an impact on behavior, ultimately muddying your results.

Beyond these cautions though, there is one potential risk we haven't yet discussed about experimentation at scale. Poorly constructed research with human participants can have deleterious effects on your users' wellbeing.

The area of research and data ethics focuses on understanding and remediating these concerns. While we are strong advocates for designing through data collection and experimentation, we also believe that ethical issues around data collection and experimentation should always be foregrounded when designing experiments. We believe that as advocates for a human-centered approach to crafting great experiences, designers are well equipped to play an important role in driving the ethics of experimentation. To whet your appetite for these considerations, we will briefly introduce some high-level thoughts on the topic of ethics in the next section.

Ethics in Online Experimentation

Ethics in philosophy addresses the moral principles that govern a person's behavior. Research Ethics refers to the correct rules of conduct necessary for carrying out research, including experimentation at scale, as with A/B tests. Of course, moral issues rarely involve unambiguous right or wrong answers; they involve judgment.

The area of research ethics is always in flux, responding to unexpected ramifications and unforeseen consequences of research engagements. Indeed, there is a long history of concern about experimentation with human participants in modern science, dating back at least as far as the 1930s. Examples include: the Tuskegee Syphilis Study, which ran from 1932 until 1972, where researchers sponsored by the US Department of Health withheld treatment from 400 African American men, even when penicillin became widely available; the CIA's studies throughout the 1950s and 1960s on mind control research that included administering LSD to research participants who were not informed as to what they were being given; and Stanley Milgram's now very famous 1960s "electric shock" experiments that showed many people are willing to do morally questionable things when ordered to do so by an authority figure. In 1974 Congress passed the National Research Act and in 1979, the National Commission released The Belmont Report, a report that lays out guidelines for ethical research on human subjects.

As authors of this book, we personally advocate that anyone whose work touches people's lives should take time to be aware of legal and ethical concerns and engage in company discussions around the ethics of data collection and use. As much as we have focused in this book on designing rigorous experiments to understand the impact of your work on human behavior, it is equally important to consider whether your users are inconvenienced or exposed to potential harm as a result of these endeavors. As you think through potential issues, you will need to make a judgment call as to whether the research is justified or not.

We aren't suggesting you become an expert in research ethics, unless you wish to investigate the area further for your own interest and satisfaction. Yet the internet industry is gaining better insight as to potential hazards to users of poor experimentation, poor data management practices, and flawed data analysis. As an industry, we are becoming more aware of the importance of exploring and addressing ethical questions up-front. Our aim here is neither to scare you away from this type of research, nor to undermine its many benefits. Rather, we hope to empower you with a nuanced view of both the benefits and potential detriments of A/B testing so that you can be an active participant in the discourse around experimenting at scale with human participants, driving discussions about how to design research that is fair and ethical for participants.

Design Experimentation Versus Social Experimentation

An important thing to keep in mind when you are designing experiments is to think carefully about how your experimental tests may affect what information people have available to them and how your changes may affect people's behavior.

For example, there are important differences between what have been called "deception experiments" and the ones we have been advocating for. In our discussion of A/B tests, we have been advocating for the testing of interface and interaction specific design characteristics such as flows, layouts, informational features, call-to-action buttons, or explanatory text. We have advocated for and have shared illustrative examples where variants of a design are tested alongside one another in different test conditions in order to compare their effects. We have also introduced a few algorithmic examples with the intention of surfacing the best, most relevant search results in order to help users most successfully find what they are looking for.

In contrast to "surface-level testing," "power of suggestion" or "deception" examples involve what Raquel Benbunan-Fich calls Code/Deception or C/D experimentation.[1] In this kind of experimentation,

1 *https://www.baruch.cuny.edu/facultyhandbook/documents/RaquelBenbunan-Fitch-EthicsOnlineExperimentation_Final.pdf*

"the programming code of an algorithm is altered to induce deception"; these are examples of "behavioral experimentation" and the experimental engineering of social relationships and relationship structures. These experiments carry a significantly higher risk of having an impact on people's lives beyond the interface, beyond the service encounter. To be clear on the distinction, C/D experimentation differs from the kind of feature and flow focused A/B testing we have been discussing in this book in that in the former case, socially relevant information is being deliberately manipulated, and what is presented is misleading or inaccurate. Further, in these instances, the social functioning of individuals within their existing or emerging social relationships are affected. By contrast, the manipulation of features and flows in the interface focuses on the performance of the site itself, through evaluation of call-to-action button design, icon and image salience, the effectiveness of different color schemes, the comprehensibility of descriptive text, and so on.

In our experience though, the distinction between surface-level feature testing and social manipulation may not always be crystal clear. So, if a study involves any potential effects that reach far beyond the service interaction you are designing for, caution must be taken.

TWO "POWER OF SUGGESTION" EXPERIMENTS

In 2012, the social networking site Facebook conducted a mood manipulation study[2] in collaboration with some university academics. For one week in January 2012, data scientists altered what 700,000 Facebook users saw in their newsfeed when they logged in. The emotional valence of the newsfeed was skewed such that some people were shown content with a lot of happy, upbeat words, while others were shown content that contained more sad, downbeat words. Analysis of user behavior after a week of being exposed to these differentially loaded newsfeeds revealed that users who were in the emotional manipulation conditions were affected: there was a kind of emotional "contagion," such that they were more likely to post content in accord with the emotional valence they'd experienced–happy to happy and sad to sad.

2 *https://www.theguardian.com/technology/2014/jun/29/facebook-users-emotions-news-feeds*

Shortly after the Facebook study became a news sensation, OKCupid, an online dating site, revealed it had conducted experiments on users that had similarly manipulated the user experience.[3] For background, OKCupid has very compelling user engagement and onboarding methods in which users fill out extensive surveys about their hopes, fears, and desires, their likes and dislikes, and their values and concerns around possible partners, around dates, and around dating. The results of these surveys are used to estimate degrees of compatibility between users of the site, fueling the recommendations that are made. In the experimental test(s), OKCupid adjusted the compatibility scores on a small test group without notifying participants. Users received altered compatibility scores that suggested they were more or less compatible with others on the site. Some changes were significant—for example, driving compatibility ratings up from 30% to 90% compatible. After the experiment was over, the affected users who were the unwitting participants in the study, were emailed with details of the accurate compatibility scores. While people may have experienced awful dates or had their hopes raised based on false information, OKCupid was matter-of-fact in their response, publicly stating that they did not know of the relationship outcomes, but that there was a statistically significant increase in communications between (false) positive matches–presumably because people were trying to figure out why the matches were positive.

The Facebook and OKCupid "power of suggestion" experiments both involve instances of deception, whether about compatibility matches, or the emotional valence of content. This type of deception is a major topic of focus for ethics researchers.

Toward Ethical A/B Testing

These experiments and the surrounding controversy underscores that as designers, researchers and product teams who engage in scientific inquiry through experimentation, we should always be careful to ask questions and to act in the best interests of our users, and to be ethically, scientifically, and legally critical in our practice.

3 *https://www.theguardian.com/technology/2014/jul/29/okcupid-experiment-human-beings-dating*

One important consequence designers becoming involved in the design of experiments is that it reduces the distance between the disciplines of design and research; this means that the area of research ethics will become part of your design practice. Many well-trained user experience researchers and data scientists are required to take ethics classes so they can develop a sensibility for user safety and protection. In our promise to equip you to participate in the conversations around user protection in experimentation, we wanted to provide you with a brief introduction to the best practices established by more mature fields (including psychology and medicine) for the protection of research participants. As online internet experimentation grows as a discipline, we would encourage you to take some of these best practices and look for opportunities to apply them to your own A/B testing culture and practice.

Key Concepts

One essential concept in research with human participants is *informed consent*. This is the process in which a study participant consents to participate in a research project after being informed of its procedures, as well as the potential risks and benefits. Of course, people cannot be truly informed if they don't understand or can't decipher the terms and conditions of the services they use. Most online services roll consent to be studied into their "Terms of Service." However it is well known that most people don't read the terms of service, and even if they do, they don't understand what the terms really mean. The creation of terms of service that are easier to understand is itself an interesting design opportunity. In practice, however, it is not always possible to gain informed consent. This concern may be addressed by asking a smaller but representative group of people how they would feel about taking part in a particular study. If they find the study permissible, it can usually be assumed that the real participants will also find it acceptable. This is known as presumptive consent.

In fields such as medicine and psychology, most researchers offer *debriefs* after studies. The goal of a debrief is to share the overall purpose of the experiment and what will happen with the results to participants. Often participants are also given the opportunity to give feedback on their experience of the experiment. Finding opportunities to scale the practice of debriefs to online, large-scale experiments is another exciting way to mature the practice of A/B testing. Consider, for instance, connecting with your users through blogs and "trusted tester" programs; you'd be surprised how many people are eager to be part of co-designing the services they use by being active participants in studies.

Central to all research is *confidentiality*. This means all participant data that is personally identifying should remain confidential. It should not be shared with anyone not directly involved in the experimental logistics, and all experimental data should be cleaned—or "scrubbed"—of anything that would allow a participant to be personally identified. All user data, especially personally identifiable information (PII) needs to be carefully managed following legal guidelines. For A/B testing, this means finding ways to anonymize user data and avoid designing experiments or logging information that requires storing, measuring, or tracking personally identifiable information. Also note, if your company operates in multiple countries, you should be aware that legal restrictions and cultural norms around data collection vary significantly; check out the restrictions and regulations about the collection, management, and storage of user data, which can include data from large scale experiments.

The ability to *withdraw* from an experiment is also usually offered. All participants are given the opportunity to withdraw from an experiment at any time, even if it is in the middle of the experiment. How this best practice would scale to an online A/B test remains an open question—how can we effectively allow users to know they are being observed without substantially changing their behavior is, again, a design challenge.

Finally, there is the issue of *deception*, which we mentioned earlier. Here, participants are intentionally misled in order to test their behavior under certain conditions. Deception can include withholding information, deliberately distorting information, misrepresentation of the value of information, and so on. Deception is a tricky ethical issue, especially where it may have an impact on the user's life beyond the immediate interactions with your service. Understanding and avoiding deception will have increasingly far-reaching effects, as many online businesses begin sitting more at the intersection of different groups of people (such as hosts and guests, buyers and sellers, or creators and consumers of art, music, culture, etc.), whose relationships and livelihood depend on their online experiences.

Not all of these have been effectively translated into the context of A/B testing—for example, the issue of debriefing and the ability to withdraw—but we thought we would give you some ideas as to how issues of the ethical protection of participants have unfolded in the social sciences, medicine, and in some cases user research. As A/B testing matures as a discipline, scaling many of these practices will become increasingly pressing. We hope you are excited and empowered to apply your expertise in human-centered design to participate in these discussions going forward.

Asking Questions, Thinking Ethically

As an advocate for users, providing them with the best possible experience as they interact with your design—your designed device, application, or service—can feel a bit lofty. We've posed and introduced many broad and challenging questions which will take the collaboration of many folks in the industry to address. However, the implications of these ethical considerations can also have immediate and close-to-home impact on how your business runs online experiments.

Taking the time to ask yourself and your colleagues questions about the ethics of your studies can make ethics a piece of your A/B testing routine. When designing an experiment, we encourage you to think through whether the research has any potential for causing your users any kind of harm. In general, the bottom line is that test participants should not be exposed to any risk greater than those encountered in their normal daily life.

We want to get you into thinking this way, thinking ethically, right from the get-go. Here are a few questions to get you started:

- Are we acting in our users' best interest?
- Could this research cause any distress to the research participants?
- Could they be exposed to any physical harm by taking part in the research? Will the experimental tests we are planning on running cause psychological distress or harm to those who are exposed to our treatments? Does the experimental test have risk of impeding anyone's ability to form meaningful relationships or make a living?
- Could they be shamed, socially embarrassed, offended, or will the test condition frighten them?

- Could the experiment possibly be implemented as, experienced as, or construed as an algorithmic, deceptive, behavioral experiment?
- Are you releasing the experiment to vulnerable populations such as the elderly, disabled, or children? If so, you may need to make some special accommodations.
- Carefully consider what, if any, spill-overs there are of your experiment to other online actions and interactions, and to offline behaviors. Ask yourself, could your study have a negative effect on a person's everyday life circumstances?

We also note that, as a designer–researcher, often you cannot accurately predict the risks of taking part in an A/B study. Over time, however, you will develop a keener sensibility around potential hazards so will be able to predict and preempt them in your experimental design phase, in the same way that your intuition for human behavior will become honed through repeated exposure to A/B testing and experimental outcomes.

We discussed triangulation in the context of making sense of different sources of data together to further your intuition about your users and your product. More broadly, considering different sources of feedback is another way to look for potential ethical concerns. One good source of insight as you hone your sensibilities around experimental design ethics is the feedback that may come in to the company through other channels in tandem with the launch of your study. Did your customer service helpline or community managers get an unexpected influx of complaints? As you are learning how to design successful experiments it may be worth making friends with some customer service experts in your company. Talking with them and reviewing incoming comments from users who may be in an experimental treatment group is another form of data triangulation. In this instance, though, the data triangulation is for the protection of your users as much as for the interpretation of your results.

As mentioned, another area in which you can get involved with your design skills is in the area of the terms of service for the product experiences you are designing. This dovetails with the area of informed consent. Terms of service for many online services legally cover companies for carrying out user testing. Check your company's terms of service, and review how your users experience their "permissioning" of different kinds of user data collection.

Another area you can get involved in is participation on review boards and committees. Most governmental and educational institutions that engage with human participant research have Institutional Review Boards, commonly shortened to "IRBs." Committees review proposals to assess if the potential benefits of the research are justifiable in the light of possible risk of harm to participants. These committees may request researchers make changes to the study's design or procedure, or in extreme cases deny approval of the study altogether. Many large organizations have review boards consisting of experts from research and legal departments who can review, raise questions about potential risks, and suggest alternatives. In smaller companies, we would encourage you to make reviewing your work with your peers and coworkers—for both research methodology as well as ethical considerations—a necessary component of your workflow.

We hope that you have found this discussion about ethics engaging and empowering. As stated, our goal is certainly not to make you nervous about the risks of experimentation. When executed ethically, it is a powerful tool to deliver great experiences to your users, increase the health of your business, and hone your intuitions as a designer. We believe that adding ethical considerations to your A/B testing practice will make you a better and more effective designer of research and data collection, and let you continue to push toward the goal of making all product development fundamentally human-centered.

Last Words

Throughout this book we have stressed that in the online world of digital services, applications, and devices, design is centrally focused on users, the consumers who use our products. We have shared our belief that successful businesses need to engage with their users, with the people who use their services—a business with no users is not a successful business. We wrote this book because we believe that designers should have a stronger role in user data gathering and user-focused product strategy, and that designers can have an impact on business metric evaluation. Industry-based design practice is focused on designing the best possible experience for users.

Why do we feel these beliefs needed to be explicitly stated?

In the Preface to the book we laid out several concerns we have encountered in our own practice as user-centered design advocates, concerns that led us to write this book. These concerns include worries that experimentation takes the creativity out of design practice. Or that experimentation denies the skill set and authority of the designer. Or that experimentation is too limited to truly offer insights into what is meaningful for users.

Our experience suggests that our perspective is somewhat different from that of many designers, many product managers, and many business strategists. Therefore, we wanted to share it more clearly.

We believe:

- *Design always advocates for users and is accountable to users,* and that good design brings with it a responsibility toward reflecting and addressing user needs through well-designed products and experiences.
- *Design practice needs to be invested in representing users accurately and appropriately* and that new methods are always needed to develop an understanding of users and user behaviors. Data is the new currency for business, and a new creative "mulch," a fertile ground for design insights to be tested, inspired, developed, and extended. Experimentation and experimental data analysis can be an integral part of the design process. We believe that designers are, or should be, fundamentally interested in being disciplined about data and its collection, analysis, and use.
- *A design perspective is needed to ensure that optimal user experiences are appropriately represented in business goals, measures, and metrics.* Designers, user experience researchers, and data scientists are the perfect people to call out when metrics that concern users and usage do not make sense, when there is a gap between company vision and mission, and how that lands with everyday users. Understanding the gaps, verifying hunches and informal observations with data, can help you have influence on business metrics and business strategy.

Throughout the book we have shared examples to demonstrate how gathering data about different design options can furnish evidence for deciding between different features but also for making more strategic decisions about the technology or service, and thus business directions. We have illustrated how experimental investigation through data collection has helped us decisions about *local* elements such as selecting between different features and also help with *global* decisions such as business strategy. We consider experimental investigations to be *conversational engagements* with users.

We also offered three ways of thinking about data: data driven, data informed, and data aware:

- *Data-driven* design implies that the data drives all design decisions. As we have shown through the chapters in this book, sometimes collecting experimental data through A/B tests delivers critical design insight. Sometimes, collecting data can help you decide between different versions of a similar feature, at other times you can decide between whole user flows and or services options. This is not always the case, however. Being data driven in this way only works if you've done the prior work to establish the questions that need to be addressed as well as the overall goals.
- Being *data informed* means that you may not be as targeted and directed in what you are trying to understand. Instead, what you're trying to do is actually inform the way you think about a problem.
- Finally, we introduced a term we use every day to be inclusive of all kinds of data gathering, from experimental A/B testing to interview studies—"data aware." In a *data-aware* mindset, you are aware of the fact that there are many types of data to answer many questions. Our use of "aware" rather than "driven" or "informed" is intended to underscore the fact that not only is design a creative process but that designing ways in to collect data to understand the user experience is also fundamentally a creative process.

As you continue to develop your skills, think about these different levels of engagement of experimentation and data: how data can answer clearly stated questions, how data can inform the way you think about a problem, and how a rich philosophy around and fascination with different kinds of data can enrich your design practice.

As we conclude this book, we'd like to acknowledge that this is not the last word on the topic of A/B testing, and certainly not the last word on the ways in which data and design are intimately related and intertwined, or how they are excellent partners in the creation of services, of products, and of user experiences. We hope that this book has given you foundational knowledge for exploring further, both in practice but also in your reading and learning.

[*Appendix*]

Resources

THIS APPENDIX LISTS SOME additional resources that you may find useful and/or interesting as you dive deeper into experimentation, or into user experience research around your designs.

Keywords

We all know one of the best ways to learn about an area is to start with some keyword searches online. Here are some keywords to get you started, listed chapter by chapter:

CHAPTER 1

Keywords: data analytics, data science, data visualization, design thinking, experimental design, introduction to statistics, mixed methods, reasoning biases, user experience research

CHAPTER 2

Keywords: acquiescence bias, attitudinal data, correlation, causality, cohorts, data triangulation, demographics, dependent variable, detectable difference, independent variable, local versus global effects, metric, Philosophy of Science, population, qualitative data, quantitative data, research methods, samples, segments, social desirability bias, statistical significance, test users

CHAPTER 3

Keywords: design opportunity, experimentation framework, hypothesis statement

CHAPTERS 4, 5, AND 6

Keywords: A/B testing, big data, daily active users, errors, experimentation, lab studies, metric of interest, metric sensitivity, metrics, minimal detectable effect (MDE), multiple hypotheses, negative results, novelty effect, pilot studies, positive results, proxy metrics, sample, seasonal bias, secondary metrics, surveys, test cells, thick data, thin data, usability testing

CHAPTER 7

Keywords: collaborative teams, common language, company culture, distributed teams, hiring, learning culture, organizational learning, project reviews, shared vocabulary

CHAPTER 8

Keywords: ethics, institutional review board (IRB), legal, social media experiments

Books

Following are some books we have regularly referred to over the years:

- Abelson, Robert P. *Statistics as Principled Argument.* New York: Psychology Press, 1995.
- Gauch, Hugh G. *Scientific Method in Practice.* Cambridge: Cambridge University Press, 2002.
- Hubbard, Douglas W. *How to Measure Anything: Finding the Value of Intangibles in Business.* 3rd ed. Hoboken: John Wiley & Sons, 2014.
- Levy, Jaime. *UX Strategy: How to Devise Innovative Digital Products That People Want.* Sebastopol: O'Reilly, 2015.
- Pearl, Judea. *Causality.* Cambridge: Cambridge University Press, 2009.
- Rubin, Jeffrey, Dana Chisnell, and Jared Spool. "How to Plan, Design, and Conduct Effective Tests." *Handbook of Usability Testing: How to Plan, Design, and Conduct Effective Tests.* Hoboken: John Wiley & Sons, 2008.

- Sauro, Jeff, and James R. Lewis. *Quantifying the User Experience: Practical Statistics for User Research.* Cambridge, MA: Morgan Kaufmann, 2016.
- Salmon, Merrilee, John Earman, Clark Glymour, James G. Lenno, Peter Machamer, J.E. McGuire, John D. Norton, Wesley C. Salmon, and Kenneth F. Schaffner. *Introduction to the Philosophy of Science.* Upper Saddle River, NJ: Prentice-Hall, 1992.

For a general introduction to user experience research methods, outside of experimentation at scale, a few good resources are:

- Kuniavsky, Mike, Elizabeth Goodman, and Andrea Moed. *Observing the User Experience: A Practitioner's Guide to User Research.* 2nd ed. Elsevier, 2012.
- Portigal, Steve. *Interviewing Users: How to Uncover Compelling Insights.* Brooklyn, NY: Rosenfeld Media, 2013.
- Sharon, Tomer. *Validating Product Ideas: Through Lean User Research.* Brooklyn, NY: Rosenfeld Media, 2016.

A text that is popular with students and professionals, this introduces a lot of the philosophy behind as well as the interdisciplinary skills needed for interaction design, human–computer interaction, information design, web design and ubiquitous computing:

- Preece, Jenny, Helen Sharp, and Yvonne Rogers. *Interaction Design: Beyond Human-Computer Interaction.* 4th ed. Hoboken: John Wiley & Sons, 2015.

For an introduction to qualitative methods that complement our approach in this book, a good text is this one:

- Patton, Michael Quinn. *Qualitative Research & Evaluation Methods. Integrating Theory and Practice.* 4th ed. Thousand Oaks, CA: SAGE Publications, 2014.

For a humorous, accessible discussion of *p*-values and statistics:

- Vickers, Andrew J. *What is a* p*-value anyway? 34 Stories to Help You Actually Understand Statistics.* New York: Pearson, 2009.

For more on design thinking, here are some excellent resources:

- Brown, Tim. "Design Thinking." *Harvard Business Review*, June 2008.
- Kelley, Tom, and Jonathan Littman. *The Ten Faces of Innovation: IDEO's Strategies for Defeating the Devil's Advocate and Driving Creativity Throughout Your Organization.* New York: Currency/Doubleday, 2005.
- Lawson, Bryan. *How Designers Think.* Oxford UK: Architectural Press/Elsevier, 2006.
- Patnaik, Dev. "Forget Design Thinking and Try Hybrid Thinking," *Fast Company*, August 25, 2009.
- Rowe, G. Peter. *Design Thinking.* Cambridge, MA: The MIT Press, 1987.

For more cautionary tales in research:

- Hargittai, Eszter, and Christian Sandvi, eds. *Digital Research Confidential: The Secrets of Studying Behavior Online.* Cambridge, MA: The MIT Press, 2015.

Online Articles, Papers, and Blogs

There are a number of online resources in the form of blogs, articles, checklists, and Q&A sites which can be a great source of additional information:

- The User Testing blog (*https://www.usertesting.com/blog/*)
- The Interaction Design Foundation (*https://www.interaction-design.org/*)
- The Nielson Norman Group (*https://www.nngroup.com/*)
- The Design Council (*http://www.designcouncil.org.uk*): The double diamond diagram was developed through in-house research at the Design Council in 2005 as a simple graphical way of describing the design process.

Here are some great articles we've found about A/B testing:

- "A/B Testing: a checklist," by Lisa Qian (*http://oreil.ly/2n8lwm7*)
- "How do you build and maintain an A/B testing roadmap?" answer from Ronny Kohavi on Quora (*http://bit.ly/2jwWaA7*)
- "Design Like You're Right, Test Like You're Wrong," by Colin McFarland (*http://bit.ly/2lxUYyd*)
- "Four Reasons to use the One Metric that Matters," by Benjamin Yoskovitz and Alistair Croll (*http://oreil.ly/2lWdgW4*)
- "A/B Testing - Concept != Execution," by Erin Weigel (*http://bit.ly/2mySSxQ*)
- "Overlapping Experiment Infrastructure: More, Better, Faster," by Diane Tang, Ashish Agarwal, Deirdre O'Brien, Mikey Meyer (*http://bit.ly/2mySVK2*)
- "Online Controlled Experiments at Large Scale," by Ron Kohavi, Alex Deng, Brian Frasca, Toby Walker, Ya Xu, Nils Pohlmann (*http://bit.ly/2mvoILz*)
- A/B Testing @ Internet Scale by Ya Xu (*http://bit.ly/2mfXqbv*)
- "Implications of use of multiple controls in an A/B test," by Lucille Lu (*http://bit.ly/2myQZBs*)
- "Why most A/B tests give you bullshit results," by Justin Megahan (*http://bit.ly/2mg4iWd*)
- "Experiments at Airbnb," by Jan Overgoor (*http://bit.ly/1f0kvIE*)
- "Common Pitfalls in Experimentation," by Colin McFarland (*http://bit.ly/2lQ7Jzr*)
- "A/B Testing and the Benefits of an Experimentation Culture," by Wyatt Jenkins (*http://bit.ly/2mZoDgY*)
- "Power, minimal detectable effect and bucket imbalance in A/B Tests," by Twitter Engineering (*http://bit.ly/2mvt0Cu*)
- "We need to fail forward if we want to succeed," by Mary Porter (*http://bit.ly/2ly4i5n*)
- "The Morality Of A/B Testing," by Josh Constine (*http://tcrn.ch/2mvtQPX*)

- "Consumer Subject Review Boards—A Thought Experiment," by Ryan Calo (*http://stanford.io/2md7DEb*)
- "Experimentation Jargon Buster," by Rik Higham (*http://bit.ly/2n8G3ag*)
- "The Difference Between "Significant" and "Not Significant" is not Itself Statistically Significant" by Andrew Gelman and Hal Stern (*http://bit.ly/2mpIDYL*)

Courses

Coursera courses (*https://www.coursera.org/*) may be helpful for thinking more deeply about the issues in these chapters. As the content is largely focused on our own experiences. Good examples could include:

- Basic Statistics (*https://www.coursera.org/learn/basic-statistics/*)
- Inferential Statistics (*http://bit.ly/2nrDQeb*)
- Improving your statistical inferences (*https://www.coursera.org/learn/statistical-inferences/*)
- User Research and Design (*http://bit.ly/2nJcNqR*)
- Another take on experiment design (*https://www.coursera.org/learn/designexperiments/*)

Tools

There are a number of tools available for companies to implement A/B testing on their own. The following is a short list to help you get started:

- Adobe Target (*https://www.adobe.io/apis/marketingcloud/target.html*)
- Google Optimize (*https://www.google.com/analytics/optimize/*)
- Hypothesis Kit from Rik Higham (*http://www.experimentation-hub.com/hypothesis-kit.html*)
- Optimizely (*https://www.optimizely.com/*)
- *p*-value calculator from Rik Higham *http://www.experimentation-hub.com/p-value.html*)
- VWO (Visual Website Optimizer) (*https://vwo.com/*)

Professional Groups, Meetups, and Societies

If you would like to meet others who are involved in user research, various professional societies and social groups exist, including the following:

- The Association for Computing Machinery (ACM)'s Special Interest Group on Human Computer Interaction
- IxDA: Interaction Design Association
- The User Experience Professionals Association (UXPA)

[*Index*]

C

D

E

F

G

H

N

O

P

Q

R

V

W

About the Authors

Rochelle King is Global VP of Design and User Experience at Spotify where she is responsible for the teams that oversee user research and craft the product experience at Spotify. Prior to Spotify, Rochelle was VP of User Experience and Product Services at Netflix, where she managed the Design, Enhanced Content, Content Marketing, and Localization teams at Netflix. Collectively, these groups were responsible for the UI, layout, metadata (editorial and visual assets), and presentation of the Netflix service internationally across all platforms. Rochelle has over 14 years of experience working on consumer-facing products. You can find her on Twitter *@rochelleking*.

Dr. Elizabeth Churchill is a Director of User Experience at Google. Her work focuses on the connected ecosystems of the Social Web and Internet of Things. For two decades, Elizabeth has been a research leader at well-known corporate R&D organizations including Fuji Xerox's research lab in Silicon Valley (FXPAL), the Palo Alto Research Center (PARC), eBay Research Labs in San Jose, and Yahoo! in Santa Clara, California.

Elizabeth has contributed groundbreaking research in a number of areas, publishing over 100 peer-reviewed articles, coediting 5 books in HCI-related fields, contributing as a regular columnist for the Association of Computing Machinery's (ACM) *Interactions* magazine since 2008, and publishing an academic textbook, *Foundations for Designing User-Centered Systems*. She has also launched successful products, and has more than 50 patents granted or pending.

Caitlin Tan is a User Researcher at Spotify, and a recent graduate from MIT.

Colophon

The animal on the cover of *Designing with Data* is a red-tailed comet (*Sappho sparganurus*). The species name *sparganurus* stems from Greek words meaning "decorated tail"; the genus name refers to Sappho, the ancient Greek poet. This hummingbird is found primarily in woodland areas throughout Bolivia, Argentina, Chile, and Peru, where it is known in Spanish as *picaflor cometa*.

The red-tailed comet is famous for its dazzling green and golden-red plumage, including the iridescent reddish tail for which it is named. The tail is forked and slightly longer than the length of its body. Males typically reach 19–20 centimeters in length, while females are smaller (around 12–14 centimeters) and possess shorter tails. They also tend to be more muted in color. All red-tailed comets have long, extensible tongues that they use to feed on nectar.

Many of the animals on O'Reilly covers are endangered; all of them are important to the world. To learn more about how you can help, go to *animals.oreilly.com*.

The cover image is by Karen Montgomery, based on a black and white image from *Wood's Animate Creation*. The cover fonts are URW Typewriter and Guardian Sans. The text font is Scala Regular; and the heading font is Gotham Narrow Medium.

O'Reilly Media, Inc.介绍

O'Reilly Media通过图书、杂志、在线服务、调查研究和会议等方式传播创新知识。自1978年开始，O'Reilly一直都是前沿发展的见证者和推动者。超级极客们正在开创着未来，而我们关注真正重要的技术趋势——通过放大那些"细微的信号"来刺激社会对新科技的应用。作为技术社区中活跃的参与者，O'Reilly的发展充满了对创新的倡导、创造和发扬光大。

O'Reilly为软件开发人员带来革命性的"动物书"；创建第一个商业网站（GNN）；组织了影响深远的开放源代码峰会，以至于开源软件运动以此命名；创立了Make杂志，从而成为DIY革命的主要先锋；一如既往地通过多种形式缔结信息与人的纽带。O'Reilly的会议和峰会集聚了众多超级极客和高瞻远瞩的商业领袖，共同描绘出开创新产业的革命性思想。作为技术人士获取信息的选择，O'Reilly现在还将先锋专家的知识传递给普通的计算机用户。无论是书籍出版、在线服务还是面授课程，每一项O'Reilly的产品都反映了公司不可动摇的理念——信息是激发创新的力量。

业界评论

"O'Reilly Radar博客有口皆碑。"

——Wired

"O'Reilly凭借一系列（真希望当初我也想到了）非凡想法建立了数百万美元的业务。"

——Business 2.0

"O'Reilly Conference是聚集关键思想领袖的绝对典范。"

——CRN

"一本O'Reilly的书就代表一个有用、有前途、需要学习的主题。"

——Irish Times

"Tim是位特立独行的商人，他不光放眼于最长远、最广阔的视野，并且切实地按照Yogi Berra的建议去做了：'如果你在路上遇到岔路口，走小路（岔路）。'回顾过去，Tim似乎每一次都选择了小路，而且有几次都是一闪即逝的机会，尽管大路也不错。"

——Linux Journal

出版说明

随着计算机技术的成熟和广泛应用，人类正在步入一个技术迅猛发展的新时期。计算机技术的发展给人们的工业生产、商业活动和日常生活都带来了巨大的影响。然而，计算机领域的技术更新速度之快也是众所周知的，为了帮助国内技术人员在第一时间了解国外最新的技术，东南大学出版社和美国O'Reilly Meida，Inc.达成协议，将陆续引进该公司的代表前沿技术或者在某专项领域享有盛名的著作，以影印版或者简体中文版的形式呈献给读者。其中，影印版书籍力求与国外图书"同步"出版，并且"原汁原味"展现给读者。

我们真诚地希望，所引进的书籍能对国内相关行业的技术人员、科研机构的研究人员和高校师生的学生和工作有所帮助，对国内计算机技术的发展有所促进。也衷心期望读者提出宝贵的意见和建议。

最新出版的影印版图书，包括：

- 《学习 OpenCV 3(影印版)》
- 《数据科学:R 语言实现(影印版)》
- 《数据驱动设计(影印版)》
- 《设计数据密集型应用(影印版)》
- 《Scikit-Learn 与 TensorFlow 机器学习实用指南(影印版)》
- 《Perl 语言入门 第 7 版(影印版)》
- 《Python 漫游指南(影印版)》
- 《算法技术手册 第 2 版(影印版)》
- 《RxJava 反应式编程(影印版)》
- 《设计人见人爱的产品(影印版)》
- 《你好，创业公司(影印版)》
- 《可持续性设计(影印版)》
- 《数据映射经验谈(影印版)》
- 《基础设施即代码(影印版)》
- 《Cassandra 权威指南 第 2 版(影印版)》
- 《网站运维工程(影印版)》